3 200483

C000172142

THE VAGABOND PATH

By the same Author

★

ALLEGRA
(Hogarth Press)

LEOPARDI
(Hamish Hamilton)

WAR IN VAL D'ORCIA
(Jonathan Cape)

THE LAST ATTACHMENT
(John Murray)

MERCHANT OF PRATO
(Jonathan Cape)

A MEASURE OF LOVE
(Jonathan Cape)

THE WORLD OF SAN BERNARDINO
(Jonathan Cape)

IMAGES AND SHADOWS
(John Murray)

THE VAGABOND PATH

An Anthology compiled by

IRIS ORIGO

"C'est une espineuse entreprise, et plus qu'il ne semble, de suivre une allure si vagabonde que celle de nostre espirit; de pénétrer les profondeurs opaques de ses replis internes; de choisir et arrester tant de menus airs de ses agitations . . ."

MONTAIGNE

1972

CHATTO & WINDUS

LONDON

Published by
Chatto & Windus Ltd
42 William IV Street
London WC2N 4DF
*
Clarke, Irwin & Co Ltd
Toronto

ISBN 0 7011 1877 6

Printed in Great Britain by
T. H. Brickell & Son Ltd
Gillingham, Dorset

To
Elsa and Aileen

CONTENTS

PREFACE

WHY one more anthology? To each compiler, it seems that his own is a little different from those made by other people – and indeed, unless it is, there is no excuse for it. The standard representative anthologies, and those of translations from the classics or from modern foreign languages, fulfil an obvious and desirable purpose: they may attract some readers to further exploration. But in addition there are many personal selections: the fruit of one person's reading and taste over a long period, transcribed from his commonplace books. I am thinking, for instance, of Maurice Baring's *Das Gepäck*, which went with him on all his travels, and of the one compiled by Ronald Storrs, who could quote longer passages from Shakespeare and Dante by heart on long journeys, than anyone I have ever met. In addition, there have been a great many anthologists who have built their books around a single, sometimes rather forced, theme: Books of Sorrow, of Praise, of Comfort, of Prayer, of Joy, of Sleep and so forth – or have put together reading matter for bed-time or waking, for wet weekends or "The Open Road". These are the compilations which Robert Graves and Laura Riding attacked some thirty years ago in the provocative and witty pamphlet, *Against Anthologies*, claiming

(1) that they are merely commercial enterprises;
(2) that they give an entirely false impression of the poets represented, since they necessarily only reproduce a few samples of their work, and often the same ones over and over again, "like sheep at a gap";
(3) that repetition and juxtaposition flatten and distort these poems;
(4) that, if the anthologist has a strong personality, this intervenes between the reader and the original poem "and thus prevents a direct introduction to the poem by *the poet himself*, who alone has the right to give it". (They give as an instance Walter de la Mare's *Come Hither*, saying that "the poems included are so honestly Mr. de la Mare's favourite poems that they seem a mere extension of the De la Mare atmosphere backwards through English poetry");
(5) that they are often just plain silly.

There is something to be said for all these remarks, especially 4 and 5, but I think that these critics go too far when they assert that, by imposing their own taste upon their readers, the anthologists "have deprived the reading public of self respect". This, surely, is nonsense. The reader of an anthology is no more obliged to swallow its contents whole than to admire *every* poem in a book by a single author; he will take from it what he likes himself.

However, even these critics admit that "the private anthology which grows direct out of serious reading", may have some value. "It resembles, at its best, a creation." This, I think, is true, and whether it is an interesting creation or not will of course depend entirely on what the anthologist's own mind is like. I do not myself think it matters if his choice (to borrow a phrase from Naomi Royde-Smith) is "wilful and prejudiced" – qualities which, in this connection, I consider virtues rather than defects – but I do think that the compiler should not fall over backwards in his efforts to avoid the obvious, so that his collection gives the impression of poems or sayings set together *merely* because they are unfamiliar.

An anthologist's voice is like that of an actor in a Greek play. His stylised mask conceals his features; yet it is in his power to give the words he repeats their full resonance, perhaps even to enhance their beauty. And, oddly enough – perhaps because he feels protected behind his mask – the anthologist may sometimes produce a work more personal, more self-revealing, than most autobiographies or novels. This has happened, I think, to the book which I still consider one of the best anthologies: Maurice Baring's *Have you anything to declare?* The novels which, during his lifetime, brought Baring success and fame, now lie on the upstairs passage-shelves of country houses dedicated to fiction for the wakeful guest, but his anthology is as undated as when it first appeared. About a third of his book is given up to passages from the classics or from Dante, but these are almost always followed by translations and comments of his own, or by variations on a similar theme in another language – French or German, Italian or Russian – so that one receives a great impression of the richness and variety of the stream of European poetry, and – in the words of Father Ronald Knox – of Baring's "almost gluttonous delight in the deft manipulation" of his translations.

Perhaps one of the reasons why Baring's anthology appeals to me so much is that the kind of pleasure he took in making it is very similar to the way in which I, too, was first taught to feel the beauty of the written word. I had the good fortune, at the age of twelve, to start Greek and Latin with an enlightened and genial Italian professor, Solone Monti, who taught me, rather like Benjamin Constant's tutor, as if we were making up a new language together. "Listen", he would say, "there is a

Greek word which it is very difficult to translate into a modern European language. It is πρώσωποy (Sappho uses it of Aphrodite, with the adjective "immortal"). Now what shall we do with it? "Face" or "look" won't do, and still less the French *figure* or *regard* – and *viso* is as bad as "face". Dante would have said *volto* – can you think of a similar English word?"

"Countenance?" I shyly suggested, "Her immortal countenance?"

"Yes, good girl", and he beamed at me through his thick spectacles. "I often think that Greek goes into English better than into any other living language."

But then he read me Sappho's lines about "the hyacinth which the shepherds tread underfoot upon the mountains", and, this time, an Italian translation by his own friend, Manara Valgimigli, who had been Pascoli's pupil with him:

Come sui monti un fiore di giacinto:
lo pestano coi piedi i pastori,
e a terra
il fiore purpureo giace.

"You see?" he said, "economy, conciseness – they can be achieved in Italian, too. And yet there also must be 'a dying fall . . .'."

So for four years we wandered through fields of amaranth, and if now, sixty-five years later, I have left behind me almost all the Greek he taught me, I have remained with a vivid sense that, though some things can be said with more precision and ease in one language than in another, the only limits to our delight are those set up by ourselves.

It was while I was working with Monti that I began to keep the commonplace books which are the foundation of this anthology and which I have gone on keeping, at intervals, ever since. Yet when I began to sift the fruit of all these years of reading, it was the problem of translation that I found most difficult to solve, since I have often been unable to discover satisfactory translations of the foreign poems I liked best, and have been even more dissatisfied with my own. (Where no translator's name is given, it means that I have tried myself, though seldom, to my mind, successfully.) I have been particularly conscious of my deficiencies in the translations from Italian, since it is the foreign language that I happen to know best, and – as Dr. J. M. Cohen has pointed out – "the more intimate the translator's knowledge of the original tongue, the more conscious he must be of what he has failed to bring over".

Two great poets, who were also great translators, Dryden and Leopardi, have expressed remarkably similar views about the craft of translation. "I have endeavoured," wrote Dryden, "to make Virgil speak such English as he would himself have spoken, if he had been born in England, and in the present age." And Leopardi: "The perfection of a translation consists in this, that the author translated should not seem something Greek rendered into Italian or something French into German, but should become, in Italian or German, precisely as the writer was, in Greek or French."

The difficulty of achieving these aims is not purely a linguistic one. It is due to the swift and constant changes (not only in diction, but in taste and mental climate) of what is, to each successive generation of translators, "the present age", – so that a nineteenth-century translation of a fourteenth-century poem, for instance (I am thinking of D. G. Rossetti's translations of *La Vita Nuova*) merely sets up a new barrier between the original and ourselves. As C. Day Lewis has said: "The translator must seem to speak for himself, and in a sense for his own time, no less than did the original. That is why great works ought to be translated afresh for each period of our culture." Dryden's translation of the *Aeneid*, for instance, and Vincenzo Monti's, are separated not only by the English and Italian languages, but by the different climates of the 18th and 19th century. And what is left of Virgil?

Personally, I still think that the best translations are those written by a contemporary or near-contemporary of the original author (provided, of course, that he was also a good poet). But how few, how rare these are! Today many readers prefer to read foreign poems in plain prose translations, as literal as possible, believing that this will prevent the erection of the double barrier of which I have spoken. Certainly such a book as the recently-published *Penguin Book of Greek Verse*, translated by Constantine Tryphanos, is an instance of how successful, at its best, this method can be – and besides, the attempt to produce a literal prose translation must necessarily induce a quality as valuable in a translator as in a biographer: humility. But there are some kinds of poetry where, all the same, a great deal is lost on the way. The elaborate verse-forms and formal phraseology of some of the great French and Italian poets of the 14th and 15th centuries – Petrarch and Tasso, for instance, or Du Bellay and Ronsard – can hardly be rendered in even the most accurate prose: and indeed, I have preferred to omit almost all the greatest lyrics of these poets. Leopardi, too, is almost untranslateable – partly because of his misleading economy and simplicity, his preference for "the lesser word" – a word only found after a long and fastidious process of selection and rejection, and one which, in translation, often seems merely flat. Perhaps one should use for him a method similar to that which Arthur Waley used for his incomparable translations from the Chinese and which Dr. J. M. Cohen has called the "re-creative", as opposed to "the imitative" form of translation – but it is possible that, to an Italian reader, the result might seem a beautiful poem, indeed, but not Leopardi. However, it is certainly true, as Arthur Waley has remarked, that one of the habits a translator should cultivate is "the habit of hearing voices talk" – if only to avoid the language which he aptly calls "translators' pidgin".

The general principle followed in this book has been to give French poetry in the original only (without a translation), but French prose only in translation. Latin, Italian, German, and Spanish verse (with the exception of some very long Latin passages) are given in both the original and the translation, and prose in these languages, in the English translation only. Greek, whether ancient or modern, Chinese, whether ancient or modern, and Russian are given only in translation, owing to the compiler's ignorance.

Would the reader like to know some of the poems I have felt obliged to leave out, because of the difficulty of finding adequate translations?:

Giraut de Bornelh's enchanting Provençal poem, *L'Alba*.

The whole of Dante's *La Vita Nuova*.

All but two sonnets by Petrarch (and unfortunately the Earl of Surrey did not translate any of the ones I most wished to include).

Several delightful minor Italian lyrics of the 14th or 15th centuries of which the vitality and gaiety, in translation, died away.

Rilke's "*Herr, es ist Zeit*" (though *Das Karoussel*, *Der Knabe*, *Kindheit*, and parts of *Die Erste Elegie* are all included in J. B. Leishmann's admirable translations).

Apart from the problems of translation, the passages from my commonplace books which I have ended by retaining are probably not quite the same as I would have chosen twenty or even ten years ago. After so much reading, what now appeals to me most – in addition to some passages concerned with natural beauty or human affections – is concerned with the human spirit, and the "vagabond path" it pursues. To follow its meanderings is, as Montaigne remarked, "a thorny enterprise" (*une espineuse entreprise*) and one about which no two people will entirely agree. The only unity one can hope for, is that which comes from being faithful to one's own taste, accepting one's blind spots and especially, perhaps, avoiding the snare of including contemporary work, merely because it is up to date.

"There are people", said Sainte-Beuve, "whose watch stops at a certain hour and who remain permanently at that age." This only wholly applies to the incurably immature, but it is true, to some extent, of almost everyone. For most of us there is a moment – which does not necessarily come to everyone at the same age – at which our taste is set, and what we read or see after that time will probably, consciously or unconsciously, hark back to the standards formed then. This book does not set up to be a collection of the "best" poetry, such as was attempted by George Moore in *Pure Poetry* and (more recently and with a wider range) by Huntington Cairns in *The Limits of Art*. Big fish and little fish have swum into my net – and occasionally, perhaps, a sea anemone or little shell which the critic may not welcome, but which at some time pleased me. In short, this is simply a selection made by a woman of seventy out of the miscellaneous reading of over fifty years: it contains some work of permanent value to any generation, and some which may only appeal to people born within the first ten or twenty years of this century. Some passages have been omitted on grounds of over-familiarity – but not everything that is well known, for why should not the reader, too, occasionally enjoy the pleasure of recognition? – and a few lush or romantic passages in early commonplace books have been left out, merely because what is dry seasons better than what is sweet. "*Le style*", Jacques Chardonne has rightly remarked, "*qui a resonné avec trop de charme s'éteint. Le temps conserve de préférence ce qui est un peu sec.*" Finally I must admit (and why, in view of my age, should I not?) that I have devoted more space to nostalgia than to passion, and have left the door wider open to "news from a foreign country" than I would have done twenty years ago, since that land now seems less foreign and less far.

The order of the various sections was guided by an attempt to follow the general trend of the spirit's "vagabond path" – though the progress is not always chronological: I have, for instance, preferred to place the visionary world of 'Far' before the clear light of early morning. But for no two people does the path wind in quite the same direction at the same time; and so perhaps an anthology can only be wholly satisfactory to its compiler.

Within each section, I have not followed a chronological order, except when it came naturally, but have rather tried to bring together similar or contrasting variations upon the same theme. Some passages placed under one heading, too, might really just as well be under another, and perhaps that does not matter very much, since this is a book to be dipped into, rather than read; indeed I would prefer the various sections to slide into one another, for who shall say where the demarcation lies between love and friendship, or between memory and grief? So I should like the reader of these pages to wander back and forth, as our vagabond spirit wanders: from love to joy and grief, from delight to despair, from childhood to old age, from the artist's deliberate acceptance of the laws of the Muses to the untrammelled pleasures of everyday life – swept forward on the stream of poetry.

I hesitated whether to include any prose passages at all, but finally decided to do so, since most of them are directly concerned either with the cultivation of one of the arts (particularly poetry) or with the greatest art of all: that of living.

In *Hope against Hope*, the tragic story of the life of the great Russian poet Osip Mandelstam recorded by his wife Nadezhda Yakovlevna, there is a passage in which – after describing their six years of exile in Siberia, their subsequent homelessness, poverty, inability to obtain work and unceasing apprehension of future disaster, and finally her husband's second arrest and death – Nadezhda Mandelstam proclaims her conviction "that we shall soon witness a complete resurgence of humane values. The values we thought had been abolished," she says, "are being restored, and they must be taken account of, *even by people who could do quite well without them.** This has come as a surprise both to those who never gave them up themselves and to those who tried to bury them once and for all. Somehow or other they lived on underground, taking refuge in all those hushed homes with their dimmed lights. Now they are on the move . . ." She adds that her husband, too, used to ask himself (he died in Siberia in 1937 or '38) "what it was that made someone a member of the intelligentsia." Finally, he decided that what really mattered was a person's feeling about poetry. "Poetry", she comments, "does indeed have a very great place in this country. It arouses people and shapes their minds. No wonder the birth of the new intelligentsia is accompanied by a craving for poetry never seen before – it is the golden treasury in which our values are preserved . . . The keepers of the flame hid in darkened corners, but the flame did not go out. It is there for all to see."

I take pleasure in quoting, after these words, some prophetic remarks written by Sir William Temple some three hundred years earlier:

"I know very well that many, who pretend to be Wise by the forms of being Grave, are apt to despise both Poetry and Musick as Toys and Trifles too light for the Use or Entertainment of serious men. But

*My italics.

whoever find themselves wholly insensible to their Charms would, I think, do well to keep their own Counsel, for fear of reproaching their own Temper, and bringing the Goodness of their Natures, if not of their Understandings, into Question . . . While this World lasts I doubt not but the Pleasure and Request of these two Entertainments will do so too; and happy those that content themselves with these or any other so easy and so innocent, and do not trouble the World or other Men, because they cannot be quiet themselves."

FAR

"Wohin der Weg?"
"Kein Weg! Ins Unbetretene"

GOETHE: *Faust*

FAR

Introductory Note

WHERE is "Far"? And where the road?

For some people, it is the path that leads back to childhood: the road taken by Traherne, Blake, Wordsworth, Rilke, Alain-Fournier. "There was a time when meadow grove and stream . . ." "It is a country," wrote Forrest Reid, "whose image was stamped upon our soul before we opened our eyes on earth, and all our life is little more than a trying to get back there, our art than a mapping of its forests and its streams."

For others, it is the road that seeks the unfamiliar, the exotic, "by a silent shore, by a far distant sea": the road to Babylon, to the Gardens of the Hesperides, to the lost Atlantis, to Kubla Khan. For others yet, it is the search for the dwelling of "that maid from St. Juliot", of "le pays qui te ressemble", of Leopardi's "woman who cannot be found", about whom he wrote: "The author does not know whether this lady of his – and in calling her so, he shows that he loves no one but her – was ever born or ever will be; he only knows that she does not live on earth, and that we are not her contemporaries. He searches for her in the ideas of Plato, in the moon, the planets of the solar system, the constellations of the stars." She is Dante's Beatrice, Petrarch's Laura. "I have heard", wrote Leopardi, in his *Dialogue between Torquato Tasso and his Familiar Spirit*, "about a man, who, when the woman he loved appeared before him in a pleasant dream, avoided seeing her again or being with her all the next day, knowing that she would never be able to equal the image left him during his sleep . . . So . . . we must excuse the superstitious men who, before going to bed, would pray and make libations to Mercury, the bearer of dreams, so that he might bring them happy ones, and indeed would keep a carved image of that god at the foot of their bedsteads. Thus, since they could never find happiness in their waking hours, they sought it in their sleep, and I believe that in some way they partially succeeded, and that Mercury, more than the other gods, granted them their prayers."

These were the hopes, too, of De Quincey, Sir Thomas Browne, John Aubrey, Gérard de Nerval, Coleridge – all seeking the world of dreams and apparitions beyond the gates of ivory or horn. For such men, this subliminal world is often more vivid, more real than their daily life, "the slumber of the body seems to be but the waking of the soul".

The quotations here, are of course, only a very small sample of those that have been written about this world, so distant and so near. I cannot even claim to consistency in my omissions, since though I regretfully felt it was not possible to print again either "Kubla Khan" or "Christabel", I could not bear to give up Blake's "Land of Dreams", which is nearly equally familiar. But then readers will have the pleasure of criticising my omissions, and adding their own choices. "Escapism?" Of course. But is not poetry one of the more harmless forms of escape?

'THROUGH PARADISE IN A DREAM'

If a man could pass through Paradise in a dream, and have a flower presented to him as a pledge that his soul had really been there, and if he found that flower in his hand when he awoke – Aye and what then?

Samuel Taylor Coleridge: *Anima Poetae*

'BEFORE A DREAM'

. . . there is little encouragement to dream of Paradise itself. Nor will the sweetest delight of Gardens afford much comfort in sleep; wherein the dulnesse of that sense shakes hands with delectable odours; and though in the Bed of *Cleopatra*, can hardly with any delight raise up the ghost of a Rose.

Sir Thomas Browne

SOMNIA

Dreams, dreams that mock us with their flitting shadows,
They come not from the temples of the gods,
They send them not, the powers of the air.
Each man makes his own dreams. The body lies
Quiet in sleep, what time the mind set free
Follows in darkness what it sought by day.
He who makes kingdoms quake for fear and sends
Unhappy cities ruining in fire,
Sees hurtling blows and broken fighting ranks
And death of kings and sodden battle fields.
The lawyer sees the judge, the crowded court,
The miser hides his coin, digs buried treasure,
The hunter shakes the forests with his hounds,
The sailor rescues from the sea his ship,
Or drowning, clings to it. Mistress to lover
Writes a love-letter: the adulteress
Yields in her sleep, and in his sleep the hound
Is hot upon the traces of the hare.
The wounds of the unhappy in the night
Do but prolong their pain.

Petronius Arbiter. Transl. Helen Waddell
in *Medieval Latin Lyrics*

'SOMEWHAT LESS CHANGEABLE'

If we dreamed the same thing every night, it would affect us as much as the objects we see every day. And if an artisan was sure of dreaming for twelve hours every night that he was king, I believe he would be almost as happy as a king who dreamed for twelve hours every night that he was an artisan . . .

For life is a dream, but somewhat less changeable.

PASCAL: *Penseés*. Transl. by A. J. Krailsheimer

'THE WAKING OF THE SOUL'

There is surely a nearer apprehension of any thing that delights us in our dreams, than in our waked senses; without this I were unhappy; for my awaked judgment discontents me, ever whispering unto me, that I am from my friend; but my friendly dreams in night requite me, and make me think I am within his arms. I thank God for my happy dreams, as I do for my good rest, for there is a satisfaction in them unto reasonable desires, and such as can be content with a fit of happiness. And surely it is not a melancholy conceit to think we are all asleep in this World, and that the conceits of this life are as mere dreams to those of the next, as the Phantasms of the night, to the conceits of the day. There is an equal delusion in both, and the one doth but seem to be the emblem or picture of the other; we are somewhat more than our selves in our sleeps, and the slumber of the body seems to be but the waking of the soul . . .

SIR THOMAS BROWNE

TO DREAM

To dream is a second life. I have never been able to pierce without a shudder those ivory gates or those of horn, which separate us from the invisible world. The first moments of sleep are the image of death. A cloudly numbness seizes hold of our thoughts, and we cannot determine the precise instant in which our *self*, in another form, continues the work of existence. It is a dim underworld which gradually becomes a little less dark and in which appear, in the shadows and night, the gravely motionless figures who inhabit the world of limbo. Then the picture takes shape, a fresh light illuminates it and makes those strange apparitions move: the world of spirits is open to us.

GÉRARD DE NERVAL: *Aurelia*

The maidens came
When I was in my mother's bower.
I had all that I would.
  The bailey beareth the bell away.
  The lily, the rose, the rose I lay.
The silver is white, red is the gold;
The robes they lay in fold;
  The bailey beareth the bell away,
  The lily, the rose, the rose I lay.
And through the glass windows shines the sun,
How should I love and I so young?
  The bailey beareth the bell away;
  The lily, the rose, the rose I lay.

ANON. (early 16th cent.)

THE LAND OF DREAMS

Awake, awake, my little Boy!
Thou wast thy Mother's only joy;
Why dost thou weep in thy gentle sleep?
Awake! thy Father does thee keep.

"O, what land is the Land of Dreams?
What are its Mountains, and what are its Streams?
O Father, I saw my Mother there,
Among the Lillies by waters fair.

"Among the Lambs, clothed in white,
She walked with her Thomas in sweet delight.
I wept for joy, like a dove I mourn;
O! when shall I again return?"

Dear Child, I also by pleasant Streams
Have wandere'd all night in the Land of Dreams;
But tho' calm and warm the waters wide,
I could not get to the other side.

"Father, O Father! what do we here
In this Land of unbelief and fear?
The Land of Dreams is better far,
Above the light of the Morning Star."

WILLIAM BLAKE

KILMENY

. . . .

"Kilmeny, Kilmeny, where have you been?"

Kilmeny looked up with a lovely grace,
But nae smile was seen on Kilmeny's face;
As still was her look, and as still was her ee
As the stillness that lay on the emerant lea,
Or the mist that sleeps on a waveless sea.
For Kilmeny had been she knew not where,
And Kilmeny had seen what she could not declare;
Kilmeny had been where the cock never crew,
Where the rain never fell, and the wind never blew;
But it seemed as the harp of the sky had rung,
And the airs of heaven played round her tongue,
When she spake of the lovely forms she had seen,
And a land where sin had never been;
A land of love, and a land of light,
Withouten sun, or moon, or night;
Where the river swa'd a living stream,
And the light a pure celestial beam:
The land of vision it would seem,
A still, an everlasting dream

. . . .

JAMES HOGG

'TWO APPARITIONS'

Anno 1670, not far from Cyrencester, was an Apparition. Being demanded, whether a good spirit or bad? returned no answer, but disappeared with a curious Perfume and a most melodious Twang. Mr. W. Lillie believes it was a Fairie.

Another time, as he [Thomas Traherne] was in bed, he saw a basket come sailing in the air, along by the valance of his bed; I think he said there was fruit in the basket; it was a Phantom.

JOHN AUBREY: *Miscellanies*

AN APPARITION OF MILTON

What would you give to have such a dream about Milton, as I had about a week since? I dreamed that, being in a house in the city, and with much company, looking towards the lower end of the room from the upper end of it, I descried a figure, which I immediately knew to be Milton's. He was very gravely, but very neatly attired in the fashion of his day, and had a countenance which filled me with those feelings that an affectionate child has for a beloved father.... My first thought was wonder, where he could have been concealed so many years; my second, a transport of joy to find him still alive; my third, another transport to find myself in his company; and my fourth, a resolution to accost him. I did so, and he received me with a complacence, in which I saw equal sweetness and dignity. I spoke of his Paradise Lost, as every man must, who is worthy to speak of it at all ... He answered me by a smile, and a gentle inclination of his head. He then grasped my hand affectionately, and with a smile that charmed me, said, "Well, you for your part will do well also". At last recollecting his great age (for I understood him to be two hundred years old), I feared that I might fatigue him by much talking; I took my leave, and he took his, with an air of the most perfect good breeding. His person, his features, his manner, were all so perfectly characteristic, that I am persuaded an apparition of him could not represent him more completely.

WILLIAM COWPER: *Letter to William Hayley* 1793

'THE DANCING LADIES'

Often I used to see, after painting upon the blank darkness a sort of rehearsal whilst waking, a crowd of ladies, and perhaps a festival and dances. And I heard it said or I said to myself, "These are English ladies from the unhappy times of Charles I. These are the wives and daughters of those who met in peace, and sat at the same tables, and were allied by marriage, or by blood; and yet, after a certain day in August 1642, never smiled upon each other again nor met but in the field of battle; and at Marston Moor, at Newbury, or at Naseby, cut asunder all this of love by the cruel sabre, and washed away in blood the memory of ancient friendship". The ladies danced, and looked as lovely as at the court of George IV.

THOMAS DE QUINCEY

THE DANCERS OF HUAI-NAN

I saw them dancing at Huai-nan and made this poem of praise:

The instruments of music are made ready,
Strong wine is in our cups;
Flute-songs flutter to a din of magic drums.
Sound scuds and scatters, surges free as a flood...
And now when the drinkers were all drunken,
And the sun had fallen to the west,
Up rose the fair ones to the dance,
Well painted and apparelled,
In veils of soft gossamer
All wound and meshed;
And ribbons they unravelled,
And scarfs to bind about their heads.
The wielder of the little stick
Whispers them to their places, and the steady drums
Draw them through the mazes of the dance.
They have raised their long sleeves, they have covered their eyes;
Slowly their shrill voices
Swell the steady song.
And the song said:

> *As a frightened bird whose love*
> *Has wandered away from the nest,*
> *I flutter my desolate wings.*
> *For the wind blows back to my home,*
> *And I long for my father's house.*

Subtly from slender hips they swing,
Swaying, slanting delicately up and down.
And like the crimson lotus flower
Glows their beauty, shedding flames afar.
They lift languid glances,
Peep distrustfully, till of a sudden
Ablaze with liquid light
Their soft eyes kindle. So dance to dance
Endlessly they weave, break off and dance again.
Now flutter their skirts like a great bird in flight,
Now toss their long white sleeves like whirling snow.
So the hours go by, till at last
The powder has blown from their cheeks, the black from their brows,

Flustered now are the fair faces, pins of pearl
Torn away, tangled the black tresses.
With combs they catch and gather in
The straying locks, put on the gossamer gown
That trailing winds about them, and in unison
Of body, song and dress, obedient
Each shadows each, as they glide softly to and fro.

CHANG HÊNG, 78–139. Transl. by Arthur Waley

MEETING IN THE ROAD

In a narrow road where there was not room to pass
My carriage met the carriage of a young man.
And while his axle was touching my axle
In the narrow road I asked him where he lived.
"The place where I live is easy enough to find,
Easy to find and difficult to forget.
The gates of my house are built of yellow gold,
The hall of my house is paved with white jade,
On the hall table flagons of wine are set,
I have summoned to serve me dancers of Han-tan.[1]
In the midst of the courtyard grows a cassia-tree –
And candles on its branches flaring away in the night."

Transl. by ARTHUR WALEY

[1] Capital of the kingdom of Chao, where the people were famous for their beauty. The date of this poem is not given, but it is included in a group of poems of the first century A.D.

L'INVITATION AU VOYAGE

Mon enfant, ma soeur,
Songe à la douceur
D'aller là-bas vivre ensemble!
Aimer à loisir
Aimer et mourir
Au pays qui te ressemble!
Les soleils mouillés
De ces ciels brouillés
Pour mon esprit ont les charmes
Si mystérieux
De tes traîtres yeux,
Brillant à travers leurs larmes.

Là, tout n'est qu'ordre et beauté,
Luxe, calme et volupté.

Des meubles luisants,
Polis par les ans,
Décoreraient notre chambre;
Les plus rares fleurs
Mêlant leurs odeurs
Aux vagues senteurs de l'ambre.
Les riches plafonds,
Les miroirs profonds,
La splendeur orientale,
Tout y parlerait
A l'âme en secret
Sa douce langue natale.

Là, tout n'est qu'ordre et beauté,
Luxe, calme et volupté.

Vois sur ces canaux
Dormir ces vaisseaux
Dont l'humeur est vagabonde;
C'est pour assouvir
Ton moindre désir
Qu'ils viennent du bout du monde.
Les soleils couchants
Revêtent les champs,
Les canaux, la ville entière,

D'hyacinthe et d'or;
Le monde s'endort
Dans une chaude lumière.

Là, tout n'est qu'ordre et beauté,
Luxe, calme et volupté.

CHARLES BAUDELAIRE

A DREAM OR NO

Why go to Saint-Juliot? What's Juliot to me?
Some strange necromancy
But charmed me to fancy
That much of my life claims the spot as its key.

Yes. I have dreams of that place in the West,
And a maiden abiding
Thereat as in hiding;
Fair-eyed and white-shouldered, broad-browed and brown-tressed.

And of how, coastward bound on a night long ago,
There lonely I found her,
The sea-birds around her,
And other than nigh things uncaring to know.

So sweet her life there (in my thought has it seemed)
That quickly she drew me
To take her unto me,
And lodge her long years with me. Such have I dreamed.

But nought of that maid from Saint-Juliot I see;
Can she ever have been here,
And shed her life's sheen here,
The woman I thought a long housemate with me?

Does there even a place like Saint-Juliot exist?
Or a Vallency Valley,
With stream and leafed alley,
Or Beeny, or Bos with its flounce flinging mist?

THOMAS HARDY

THE UNKNOWN BIRD

Three lovely notes he whistled, too soft to be heard
If others sang; but others never sang
In the great beechwood all that May and June.
No one saw him; I alone could hear him
Though many listened. Was it but four years
Ago? or five? He never came again.

Oftenest when I heard him I was alone,
Nor could I ever make another hear.
La-la-la-! He called, seeming far-off –
As if a cock crowed past the edge of the world,
As if the bird or I were in a dream.
Yet that he travelled through the trees and sometimes
Neared me, was plain, though somehow distant still
He sounded. All the proof is – I told men
What I had heard.

I never knew a voice,
Man, beast, or bird, better than this. I told
The naturalists; but neither had they heard
Anything like the notes that did so haunt me,
I had them clear by heart and have them still.
Four years, or five, have made no difference. Then
As now that La-la-la! was bodiless sweet:
Sad more than joyful it was, if I must say
That it was one or other, but if sad
'Twas sad only with joy too, too far off
For me to taste it. But I cannot tell
If truly never anything but fair
The days were when he sang, as now they seem.
This surely I know, that I who listened then,
Happy sometimes, sometimes suffering
A heavy body and a heavy heart,
Now straightway, if I think of it, become
Light as that bird wandering beyond my shore.

EDWARD THOMAS

FRAMMENTO

Alceta Odi, Melisso: io vo' contarti un sogno
Di questa notte, che mi torna a mente
In riveder la luna. Io me ne stava
Alla finestra che risponde al prato,
Guardando in alto: ed ecco all'improvviso
Distaccasi la luna; e mi parea
Che quanto nel cader s'approssimava,
Tanto crescesse al guardo; infin che venne
A dar di colpo in mezzo al prato; ed era
Grande quanto una secchia, e di scintille
Vomitava una nebbia, che stridea
Sì forte come quando un carbon vivo
Nell'acqua immergi e spegni. Anzi a quel modo
La luna, come ho detto, in mezzo al prato
Si spegnava annerando a poco a poco,
E ne fumavan l'erbe intorno intorno.
Allor mirando in ciel, vidi rimaso
Come un barlume, o un'orma, anzi una nicchia
Ond' ella fosse svelta; in cotal guisa,
Ch'io n'agghiacciava; e ancor non m'assicuro.

Melisso E ben hai che temer, che agevol cosa
Fora cader la luna in sul tuo campo.

Alceta Chi sa? non veggiam noi spesso di state
Cader le stelle?

Melisso Egli ci ha tante stelle,
Che picciol danno è cader l'una o l'altra
Di loro, e mille rimaner. Ma sola
Ha questa luna in ciel, che di nessuno
Cader fu vista mai se non in sogno.

GIACOMO LEOPARDI

A FRAGMENT

Alcetas Hear me, Melissus; I will tell you a dream
I had last night, which comes to mind again,
Now that I see the moon. I stood at the window
Which looks out on the field, and turned my eyes
Up to the sky; and then, all of a sudden,
The moon was loosened; and it seemed to me
That coming nearer and nearer as it fell down,
The bigger it appeared, until it tumbled
In the middle of the field, with a crash, and was
As big as a bucket is; and it spewed forth
A cloud of sparks, which spluttered, just as loud
As when you put a live coal under water
Till is goes out. For it was in that way
The moon, I'm telling you, in the middle of the field,
Went out, and little by little it all turned black.
And round about the grass went up in smoke.
And then, looking up at the sky, I saw was left
A kind of glimmer, or mark, or rather a socket,
From which it had been torn, and at that sight
I froze with terror; and don't feel easy yet.

Melissus And well you might, indeed; for sure enough,
The moon *might* tumble down into your field.

Alcetas Who knows? For don't we often see in summer
Stars falling?

Melissus But then, there are so many stars:
And little harm if one or other of them
Do fall – there's thousands left. But there is only
This one moon in the sky, and nobody
Has ever seen it fall, except in dreams.

Transl. by JOHN HEATH-STUBBS

‘UNA CASA PENSILE IN ARIA’

Una casa pensile in aria sospesa con funi a una stella.

LEOPARDI: *Zibaldone* I

A house floating in the air held by ropes to a star.

DER KNABE

Ich möchte einer werden so wie die,
die durch die Nacht mit wilden Pferden fahren,
mit Fackeln, die gleich aufgegangnen Haaren
in ihres Jagens grossem Winde wehn.
Vorn möcht ich stehen wie in einem Kahne,
gross und wie eine Fahne aufgerollt.
Dunkel, aber mit einem Helm von Gold,
der unruhig glänzt. Und hinter mir gereiht
zehn Männer aus derselben Dunkelheit
mit Helmen, die, wie meiner, unstät sind,
bald klar wie Glas, bald dunkel, alt und blind.
Und einer steht bei mir und bläst uns Raum
mit der Trompete, welche blitzt und schreit,
und bläst uns eine schwarze Einsamkeit,
durch die wir rasen wie ein rascher Traum:
die Häuser fallen hinter uns ins Knie,
die Gassen biegen sich uns schief entgegen,
die Plätze weichen aus: wir fassen sie,
und unsre Rosse rauschen wie ein Regen.

RAINER MARIA RILKE

THE BOY

I'd like, above all, to be one of those
who drive with wild black horses through the night,
torches like hair uplifted in affright
when the great wind of their wild hunting blows.
I'd like to stand in front as in a boat,
tall, like a long floating flag unrolled.
And dark, but with a helmet made of gold,
restlessly flashing. And behind to ride
ten other looming figures side by side,
with helmets matching mine for changefulness,
now clear as glass, now old and lustreless.
And one to stand by me and blow us space
with the brass trumpet that can blaze and blare,
blowing a black solitude through which we tear
like dreams that speed too fast to leave a trace.
Houses behind us fall upon their knees,
alleys cringe crookedly before our train,
squares break in flight: we summon and we seize:
we ride, and our great horses rush like rain.

Transl. by J. B. Leishman

MIRAGE

I saw a man on a horse
Riding against the sun:
"Hullo, Don Cossack," I cried –
He shouted, "Hullo, my son."

The Caspian sea shimmered
The Kazak tents shone,
For a moment in England,
then the horseman was gone.

Richard Church

THE TOY HORSE

See him, the gentle Bible beast,
With lacquered hoofs and curling mane,
His wondering journey from the East
Half done, between the rock and plain,

His little kingdom at his feet
Through which the silver rivulets flow,
For while his hoofs in silence beat
Beside him Eden and Canaan go.

The great leaves turn and then are still.
Page after page through deepening day
He steps, and from each morning hill
Beholds his stationary way.

His lifted foot commands the West,
And, lingering, halts the turning sun;
Endless departure, endless rest,
End and beginning here are one.

Dumb wooden idol, you have led
Millions on your calm pilgrimage
Between the living and the dead,
And shine yet in your golden age.

EDWIN MUIR

EL NIÑO MUDO

El niño busca su voz.
(La tenia el rey de los grillos.)
En una gota de agua
buscaba su voz el niño.

No la quiero para hablar;
Me haré con ella un anillo
que llevarà mi silencio
en su dedo pequeñito.

En una gota de agua
buscaba su voz el niño.

(La voz cautiva, a lo lejos,
Se ponía un traje de grillo.)

GARCÍA LORCA

THE DUMB CHILD

The child is searching for his voice.
(The king of the crickets had it.) In a drop
of water the child was searching for his voice.

I do not want it to speak with; I shall make
with it a ring that my silence will wear on
its little finger.
In a drop of water the child was searching for
his voice. (The captive voice, in the distance,
was putting on the garb of a cricket.)

From the prose translation by J. L. GILI

SENLIN: A BIOGRAPHY

By a silent shore, by a far distant sea,
White unicorns come gravely down to the water.
In the lilac dusk they come, they are white and stately

. . . .

One by one they come and drink their fill;
And daisies burn like stars on the darkened hill

. . . .

White amid the eternal black,
One by one in the moonlight there,
Neighing far off on the haunted air,
The unicorns come down to the sea.

CONRAD AIKEN

BOATS OF CANE

A traveller once told
How to an inland water slanting come
Slim boats of cane from rivers of Cathay,
With trembling mast so slight,
It seemed God made them with a hand of air
To sail upon His light;
And there
Soft they unload a jar of jade and gold
In the cold dawn when birds are dumb,
And then away,
And speak no word and seek no pay,
Away they steal
And leave no ripple at the keel.

So the tale is writ;
And now, remembering you, I think of it.

GEOFFREY SCOTT

THE MOUNTAINS

The days have closed behind my back
  Since I came into these hills.
Now memory is a single field
  One peasant tills and tills.

So far away, if I should turn
  I know I could not find
That place again. These mountains make
  The backward gaze half-blind.

Yet sharp my sight till it can catch
  The ranges rising clear
Far in futurity's high-walled land;
  But I am rooted here.

And do not know where lies my way,
  Backward or forward. If I could
I'd leap time's bound or turn and hide
  From time in my ancestral wood.

Double delusion! Here I'm held
  By the mystery of the rock,
Must watch in a perpetual dream
  The horizon's gates unlock and lock,

See on the harvest fields of time
  The mountains heaped like sheaves,
And the valleys opening out
  Like a volume's turning leaves,

Dreaming of a peak whose height
  Will show me every hill,
A single mountain on whose side
  Life blooms for ever and is still.

EDWIN MUIR

EARLY IN THE MORNING

EARLY IN THE MORNING

Introductory Note

THE quotations chosen for this section reflect only one aspect of a child's vision: wonder. In this vision, the line of demarcation between imagination and reality hardly exists – and the same continues to be true of some of the greatest poets. Blake, Keats and Leopardi, for instance, all believed that the soil from which poetry springs is a return to the primitive forms of man's imagination, to the Golden Age. "The nature of my Works", said Blake, "is visionary or imaginative; it is an Endeavour to restore what the Ancients called the Golden Age . . . This world of Imagination is the World of Eternity." To Keats, the imagination was "the Rudder of Poetry". "The Imagination may be compared to Adam's dream – he awoke and found it truth." As for Leopardi – "If I knew," he wrote, "how to depict and awaken in others what I saw and felt in my childhood, I would consider myself a divine poet . . . What a fine time that was, when everything came to life in the human fancy and behaved in a human fashion . . . when we were sure that beautiful Hamadryads and Fauns and Sylvans and Pan lived in the woods, and Naiads in the springs. And, clasping a tree to your breast you almost felt it tremble in your hand and believed it to be a human being, like Cypress." He maintained, indeed, that "the greater part of the vague images and sensations that come to us, even after childhood is over . . . are nothing but a memory of that time – a recollection, a repetition, an echo or a reflection of that ancient image."

It was to this gift that the great Italian modern poet and critic, Giuseppe Ungaretti, referred when he wrote that "a work of art is convincing when, enriched with our own memories, it moves our imagination so completely as to give back to us the gaze of innocence. Memory and innocence are the two inseparable poles of Leopardi's poetry." It is this innocent gaze which illuminates the best work of Traherne, Blake, Dylan Thomas: and sometimes, of Wordsworth Coleridge, Hardy, Rilke. But with the last two, the "shades of the prison-house" have already begun to fall. "Nothing gold can stay."

WONDER

How like an Angel came I down!
How Bright are all Things here!
When first among his Works I did appear
O how their GLORY me did Crown?
The World resembled his *Eternitie*,
In which my Soul did Walk;
And evry Thing that I did see,
Did with me talk.

The Skies in their Magnificence,
The Lively, Lovely Air;
Oh how Divine, how Soft, how Sweet, how fair!
The Stars did entertain my Sence,
And all the Works of GOD so Bright and pure,
So Rich and Great did seem,
As if they ever must endure,
In my Esteem.

A Native Health and Innocence
Within my Bones did grow,
And while my GOD did all his Glories shew,
I felt a Vigour in my Sence
That was all SPIRIT. I within did flow
With Seas of Life, like Wine;
I nothing in the World did know,
But 'twas Divine.

Harsh ragged Objects were conceald,
Oppressions Tears and Cries,
Sins, Griefs, Complaints, Dissentions, Weeping Eys,
Were hid: and only Things reveald,
Which Heav'nly Spirits, and the Angels prize.
The State of Innocence
And Bliss, not Trades and Poverties,
Did fill my Sence.

The Streets were pavd with Golden Stones,
The Boys and Girles were mine,
Oh how did all their Lovly faces shine!
The Sons of Men were Holy Ones.
In Joy, and Beauty, then appear'd to me,
And evry Thing which here I found,
While like an Angel I did See,
Adornd the Ground.

Rich Diamond and Pearl and Gold
In evry Place was seen;
Rare Splendours, Yellow, Blew, White and Green,
Mine Eys did evry where behold.
Great Wonders clothd with Glory did appear,
Amazement was my Bliss.
That and my Wealth was evry where:
No Joy to this!

Cursd and Devisd Proprieties,
With Envy, Avarice
And Fraud, those Feinds that Spoyl even Paradice,
Fled from the Splendor of mine Eys.
And so did Hedges, Ditches, Limits, Bounds,
I dreamd not ought of those,
But wanderd over all mens Grounds,
And found Repose.

Proprieties themselvs were mine,
And Hedges Ornaments;
Walls, Boxes, Coffers, and their rich Contents
Did not Divide my Joys, but all combine.
Clothes, Ribbans, Jewels, Laces, I esteemd
My Joys by others worn;
For me they all to wear them seemd
When I was born.

THOMAS TRAHERNE

FERN HILL

Now as I was young and easy under the apple boughs
About the lilting house and happy as the grass was green,
    The night above the dingle starry,
        Time let me hail and climb
    Golden in the heydays of his eyes,
And honoured among wagons I was prince of the apple towns
And once below a time I lordly had the trees and leaves
        Trail with daisies and barley
    Down the rivers of the windfall light.

And as I was green and carefree, famous among the barns
About the happy yard and singing as the farm was home,
    In the sun that is young once only,
        Time let me play and be
    Golden in the mercy of his means,
And green and golden I was huntsman and herdsman, the calves
Sang to my horn, the foxes on the hills barked clear and cold,
        And the sabbath rang slowly
    In the pebbles of the holy streams.

All the sun long it was running, it was lovely, the hay
Fields high as the house, the tunes from the chimneys, it was air
    And playing, lovely and watery
        And fire green as grass.
    And nightly under the simple stars
As I rode to sleep the owls were bearing the farm away,
All the moon long I heard, blessed among stables, the nightjars
    Flying with the ricks, and the horses
        Flashing into the dark.

And then to awake, and the farm, like a wanderer white
With the dew, come back, the cock on his shoulder: it was all
    Shining, it was Adam and maiden,
        The sky gathered again
    And the sun grew round that very day.
So it must have been after the birth of the simple light
In the first, spinning place, the spellbound horses walking warm
    Out of the whinnying green stable
        On to the fields of praise.

And honoured among foxes and pheasants by the gay house
Under the new made clouds and happy as the heart was long,
In the sun born over and over,
I ran my heedless ways,
My wishes raced through the house high hay
And nothing I cared, at my sky blue trades, that time allows
In all his tuneful turning so few and such morning songs
Before the children green and golden
Follow him out of grace.

Nothing I cared, in the lamb white days, that time would take me
Up to the swallow thronged loft by the shadow of my hand,
In the moon that is always rising,
Nor that riding to sleep
I should hear him fly with the high fields
And wake to the farm forever fled from the childless land.
Oh as I was young and easy in the mercy of his means,
Time held me green and dying
Though I sang in my chains like the sea.

DYLAN THOMAS

HERE WE COME A-PIPING

Here we come a-piping,
In Springtime and in May;
Green fruit a-ripening,
And Winter fled away.
The Queen she sits upon the strand
Fair as lily, white as wand;
Seven billows on the sea,
Horses riding fast and free,
And bells beyond the sand.

Nursery Rhyme: arranged by WALTER DE LA MARE

Rosy apple, lemon, or pear,
Bunch of roses she shall wear;
Gold and silver by her side,
I know who will be the bride.
Take her by her lily-white hand,
  Lead her to the altar;
Give her kisses, – one, two, three, –
  Mother's runaway daughter.

From *Traditional Games* collected by LADY GOMME

THE LITTLE NUT TREE

With Variations

I

I had a little nut tree,
    Nothing would it bear,
But a silver nutmeg
    And a golden pear.
The King of Spain's daughter
    Came to visit me,
And all was because of
    My little nut tree.
I skipped over water,
    I danced over sea,
And all the birds in the air
    Could not catch me.

ANON.

II

The King of China's daughter,
So beautiful to see,
With her face like yellow water, left
Her nutmeg tree.
Her little rope for skipping
She kissed and gave it me –

Made of painted notes of singing birds,
Among the fields of tea.
I skipped across the nutmeg grove –
I skipped across the sea;
But neither sun nor moon, my dear,
Has yet caught me.

ANON.

'Tis the witching hour of night
Orbed is the moon and bright,
And the stars they glisten, glisten,
Seeming with bright eyes to listen –
For what listen they?
For a song and for a charm
See they glisten in alarm,
And the moon is waxing warm
To hear what I shall say.
Moon! keep wide thy golden ears –
Hearken stars! and hearken spheres!
Hearken, thou eternal sky!
I sing an infant's lullaby,
A pretty lullaby.
Listen, listen, listen, listen,
Glisten, glisten, glisten, glisten,
And hear my lullaby!
Though the rushes that will make
Its cradle still are in the lake –
Though the linen that will be
Its swathe, is on the cotton tree –
Though the wollen that will keep
It warm, is on the silly sheep –
Listen starlight, listen, listen,
Glisten, glisten, glisten, glisten
And hear my lullaby! . . .[1]

JOHN KEATS

[1]John Keats in a letter to his brother George, in which he wrote: "If I had a prayer to make for any great good . . . it should be that one of your Children should be the first American Poet." Oct. 1818.

'MON PETIT FILS'

Mon petit fils qui n'as encore rien vu
A ce matin, ton père te salue . . .

Jan, petit Jan, viens voir ce tant beau monde,
Ce ciel d'azur, ces estoiles luisantes,
Ce soleil d'or, cette grant terre ronde.
Cette ample mer, ces rivières bruyantes,
Ces beaux oyseaux qui chantent à plaisir
Ces poissons frais et ces bestes paissantes;
Viens voir le tout à souhait et désir.

Petit enfant! peux-tu le bienvenu
Etre sur terre, où tu n'apportes rien,
Mais où tu viens comme un petit ver nu?
Tu n'as de drap, ni linge que soit tien,
Or ny argent, n'aucun bien terrein.
A père et mère apportes seulement
Peyne et soucy et voilà tout ton bien.
Pauvre enfant, tu viens bien povrement.

De ton honneur ne veuil plus être chiche,
Petit enfant de grand bien puissant,
Tu viens au monde aussi grand, aussi riche
Que le roy, et aussi florissant.
Ton héritage est le ciel splendissant;
Tes serviteurs sont les anges sans vice;
Ton trésorier, c'est le Dieu Tout-puissant:
Grâce divine est ta mère nourrice.

ANON

ON LEAPING OVER THE MOON

I saw new Worlds beneath the Water ly,
New Peeple; yea, another Sky
And Sun, which seen by Day
Might things more clear display.
Just such another
Of late my Brother
Did in his Travel see, and saw by Night,
A much more strange and wondrous Sight:
Nor could the World exhibit such another,
So Great a Sight, but in a Brother . . .

As much as others thought themselves to ly
Beneath the Moon, so much more high
Himself he thought to fly
Above the starry Sky,
As *that* he spy'd
Below the Tide
Thus did he yield me in the shady Night
A wondrous and instructive Light,
Which taught me that under our Feet there is,
As o'r our Heads, a Place of Bliss.

To the same purpos; he, not long before,
Brought home from Nurse, going to the door
To do som little thing
He must not do within,
With Wonder cries,
As in the Skies
He saw the Moon, *O yonder is the Moon*
Newly com after me to Town,
That shin'd at Lugwardin but yesternight,
Where I enjoyed the self-same Light.

. . . .

THOMAS TRAHERNE

NURSES SONG

When the voices of children are heard on the green,
And laughing is heard on the hill,
  My heart is at rest within my breast
And everything else is still.

"Then come home, my children, the sun is gone down
And the dews of night arise;
Come, come, leave off play, and let us away
Till the morning appears in the skies."

"No, no, let us play, for it is yet day
And we cannot go to sleep;
Besides, in the sky the little birds fly,
And the hills are all cover'd with sheep."

"Well, well, go and play till the light fades away,
And then go home to bed."
  The little ones leaped and shouted and laugh'd
And all the hills echoed.

William Blake

'A HOME FOR GODS, NOT MEN'

When thunder and winds, sun and stars, animals and plants, and even the walls of the house, all seemed friends or enemies – none indifferent and none meaningless; when every object that we saw seemed in a certain way to beckon and almost to wish to speak to us: when, never alone, we would speak to pictures and walls and trees and flowers and clouds, as if they had done us good or harm . . . when wonder, so dear to us that we have often wished to believe, in order to be able to wonder, possessed us all the time; when the colours of things and light and the stars and fire and the flight of insects, the song of birds, the transparency of water, all was new and unfamiliar; when no incident seemed commonplace, nor did we know the cause of anything, but made it up for ourselves; when tears were daily events, and all the passions still vivid and unruled and never forcibly suppressed. How easily at that time one's imagination took fire, how it enlarged small things and adorned bare ones and lit up darkness; what living images, what happy dreams, what indescribable inventions, what stuff for poetry; what richness, vigour, strength, emotion and delight! I remember hearing in fancy in my childhood strains sweeter than can be heard in our real world. I remember looking up at shepherds and their flocks painted on the ceiling of my room and imagining a pastoral life so lovely that were it to come true, this would not be our earth, but paradise, a home for gods, not men.

LEOPARDI: An Italian's essay about romantic poetry

DAS KARUSSELL

Jardin du Luxembourg

Mit einem Dach und seinem Schatten dreht
sich eine kleine Weile der Bestand
von bunten Pferden, alle aus dem Land,
das lange zögert, eh es untergeht,
Zwar manche sind an Wagen angespannt,
doch alle haben Mut in ihren Mienen;
ein böser roter Löwe geht mit ihnen
und dann und wann ein weisser Elefant.

Sogar ein Hirsch ist da, ganz wie im Wald,
nur dass er einen Sattel trägt und drüber
ein kleines blaues Mädchen aufgeschnallt.

Und auf dem Löwen reitet weiss ein Junge
und hält sich mit der kleinen heissen Hand,
dieweil der Löwe Zähne zeigt und Zunge.

Und dann und wann ein weisser Elefant.

Und auf den Pferden kommen sie vorüber,
auch Mädchen, helle, diesem Pferdesprunge
fast schon entwachsen; mitten in dem Schwunge
schauen sie auf, irgendwohin, herüber-

Und dann und wann ein Weisser Elefant.

Und das geht hin und eilt sich, dass es endet,
Und Kreist und dreht sich nuz und hat Kein Ziel.
Ein Rot, ein Grün, ein Grau vorbeigesendet,
ein kleines kaum begonnenes Profil-.
Und manchesmal ein Lächeln, hergewendet,
ein seliges, das blendet und verschwendet
an dieses atemlose blinde Spiel . . .

Rainer Maria Rilke

THE MERRY-GO-ROUND

Jardin du Luxembourg

With roof and shadow for a while careers
the stud of horses, variously bright,
all from that land that hesitates for quite
a length of time before it disappears.
Several indeed pull carriages, with tight-
held rein, but all have boldness in their bearing;
with them a wicked scarlet lion's faring
and now and then an elephant all white.

Just as in woods, a stag comes into view,
save that it has a saddle and tied fast
thereon a little maiden all in blue.

And on the lion a little boy is going,
whose small hot hands hold on with all his might,
while raging lion's tongue and teeth are showing.

And now and then an elephant all white.

And on the horses they come riding past,
girls too, bright-skirted, whom the horse-jumps here
scarce now preoccupy: in full career
elsewhither, hitherwards, a glance they cast –

And now and then an elephant all white.

And this keeps passing by until it's ended,
and hastens aimlessly until it's done.
A red, a green, a grey is apprehended,
a little profile, scarcely yet begun. –
And now and then a smile, for us intended,
blissfully happy, dazzlingly expended
upon this breathless, blindly followed fun . . .

Transl. by J. B. Leishman

A POET'S CHILD

Hartley fell down and hurt himself – I caught him up crying and screaming and ran out doors with him. The Moon caught his eye – he ceased crying immediately – and his eyes and the tears in them, how they glittered in the Moonlight!

THE SEEMS

A little boy, lying in bed one night in the year 1802, was feeling unhappy. He called for a candle – the *seems*, he said, were troubling him. "What do you mean, my love?" "The Seems, the seems. What seems to be and is not, men and faces and I do not know what – ugly and sometimes pretty and those turn ugly, and they seem when my eyes are open, and worse when they are shut – and the candle cures the *seems*."

SAMUEL TAYLOR COLERIDGE

A CHILD AT BEDTIME

The room opened full of gold, his father stooped through the door and closed it quietly; came quietly to the crib. His face was kind.

"Wuzza matter?" he asked, teasing gently, his voice at his deepest.

"Daddy", the child said thinly. He sucked the phlegm from his nose and swallowed it . . .

"Why, what's wrong?" his father exclaimed; and now his voice was entirely kind. He lifted the child's head a little more, knelt and looked carefully into his eyes; the child felt the strength of the other hand, covering his chest, patting gently. He endeavoured to make a little more of his sobbing than came out, but the moment had departed.

"Bad dreams?"

He shook his head, no.

"Then what's the trouble?"

He looked at his father.

"Feared a-fraid of the dark?"

He nodded; he felt tears on his eyes.

"Noooooooo," his father said, pronouncing it like do. "You're a big boy now. Big boys don't get skeered of a little dark. Big boys don't cry. Where's the dark that skeered you? Is it over here?" With his head he indicated the darkest corner. The child nodded. He strode over, struck a match on the seat of his pants.

Nothing there.

"Nothing there that oughtn't to be . . . Under here?" he indicated the bureau. The child nodded, and began to suck at his lower lip. He struck another match, and held it under the bureau, then under the washstand.

Nothing there. There either . . .

"Boogee man, all gone, scared away, huh?"

He nodded.

"Now go on to sleep then, son," his father said. He saw that the child very badly did not want him to go away, and realized suddenly that he might have lied about being scared, and he was touched, and put his hand on his son's forehead. "You just don't want to be lonesome," he said tenderly; "just like little ole Jackie. You just don't want to be left alone." The child lay still.

"Tell you what I'll do," his father said, "I'll sing you one song, and then you be a good boy and go on to sleep. Will you do that?" The child pressed his forehead upward against the strong warm hand and nodded. . . .

The child still stared up at him; because there was so little light or perhaps because he was so sleepy, his eyes seemed very dark, although the father knew they were nearly as light as his own. He took his hand away and blew the moisture dry on the child's forehead, smoothed his hair away, and put his hand back:

What in the world you doin Google Eyes? he sang, very slowly, while he and the child looked at each other.

What in the world you doin, Google Eyes?
What in the world you doin Google Eyes?
What in the world you doin Google Eyes?

His eyes slowly closed, sprang open, almost in alarm, closed again.

Where did you get them great big Google Eyes?
Where did you get them great big Google Eyes?
You're the best there is and I need you in my biz,
Where in the world did you get them Google Eyes?

He waited. He took his hand away. The child's eyes opened and he felt as if he had been caught at something. He touched the forehead again, more lightly. "Go to sleep, honey," he said. "Go on to sleep now." The child continued to look up at him and a tune came unexpectedly into his head, and lifting his voice almost to tenor he sang, almost inaudibly:

Oh, I hear them train car wheels arumblin,
Ann, they're mighty near at hand,
I hear that train come arumblin,
Come arumblin through the land.

Git on board, little children,
Git on board, little children,
Git on board, little children,
There's room for many and more.

To the child it looked as if his father were gazing off into a great distance and, looking up into these eyes which looked so far away, he too looked far away:

Oh, I look a way down yonder,
Ann, uh what dyou reckon I see,
A band of shinin angels,
A comin after me,
Git on board, little children,
Git on board, little children,
Git on board, little children,
There's room for many and more.

He did not look down but looked straight on into the wall in silence for a good while, and sang:

Oh, every time the sun goes down
There's a dollar saved for Betsy Brown,
Sugar Babe.

He looked down. He was almost certain now that the child was asleep. So much more quietly that he could scarcely hear himself, and that the sound stole upon the child's near sleep like a band of shining angels, he went on:

There's good old sayin, as you all know,
That you can't track a rabbit when there ain't no snow
Sugar Babe.

Here again he waited, his hand listening against the child for he was so fond of the last verse that he always hated to have to come to it and end it; but it came into his mind and became so desirable to sing that he could resist it no longer:

Oh, 'tain't agoin' to rain on, 'tain't agoin' to snow:

He felt a strange coldness on his spine and saw the glistening as a great cedar moved and tears came into his eyes:

But the sun's agoin' to shine, an' the wind's agoin' to blow
Sugar Babe. . . .

JAMES AGEE: From *A Death in the Family*

Pour l'enfant amoureux de cartes et d'estampes,
L'univers est égal à son vaste appetit.
Ah, que le monde est grand à la clarté des lampes!
Aux yeux du souvenir que le monde est petit!

CHARLES BAUDELAIRE

PRIÈRE D'UN PETIT ENFANT NÈGRE

Seigneur, je suis très fatigué.
Je suis né fatigué.
Et j'ai beaucoup marché depuis le chant du coq
Et le morne est bien haut qui mène à leur école.
Seigneur, je ne veux plus aller à leur école,
Faites, je vous en prie, que je n'y aille plus.
Je veux suivre mon père dans les ravines fraîches
Quand la nuit flotte encore dans le mystère des bois
Où glissent les esprits que l'aube vient chasser.
Je veux aller pieds nus par les rouges sentiers
Que cuisent les flammes de midi,
Je veux dormir ma sieste au pied des lourds manguiers,
Je veux me rèveiller
Lorsque là-bas mugit la sirène des blancs
Et que l'Usine
Sur l'océan des cannes
Comme un bateau ancré
Vomit dans la campagne son équipage nègre . . .
Seigneur, je ne veux plus aller à leur école,
Faites, je vous prie, que je n'y aille plus.
Ils racontent qu'il faut qu'un petit nègre y aille
Pour qu'il devienne pareil
Aux messieurs de la ville
Aux messieurs comme il faut.
Mais moi je ne veux pas
Devenir, comme ils disent,
Un monsieur de la ville,
Un monsieur comme il faut.
Je préfère flâner le long des sucreries
Où sont les sacs repus
Que gonfle un sucre brun autant que ma peau brune.
Je préfère vers l'heure où la lune amoureuse
Parle bas à l'oreille des cocotiers penchés

Ecouter ce que dit dans la nuit
La voix cassée d'un vieux qui raconte en fumant
Les histoires de Zamba et de compère Lapin
Et bien d'autres choses encore
Qui ne sont pas dans les livres.
Les nègres, vous le savez, n'ont que trop travaillé.
Pourquoi faut-il de plus apprendre dans des livres
Qui nous parlent de choses que ne sont point d'ici?
Et puis elle est vraiment trop triste leur école,
Triste comme
Ces messieurs de la ville,
Ces messieurs comme il faut
Qui ne savent plus danser le soir au clair de lune
Qui ne savent plus marcher sur la chair de leurs pieds
Qui ne savent plus conter les contes aux veillées.
Seigneur, je ne veux plus aller à leur école.

GUY TIROLIEN

KINDHEIT

Da rinnt der Schule lange Angst und Zeit
mit Warten hin, mit lauter dumpfen Dingen.
O Einsamkeit, o schweres Zeitverbringen . . .
Und dann hinaus: die Strassen sprühn und klingen
und auf den Plätzen die Fontänen springen,
und in den Gärten wird die Welt so weit. –
Und durch das alles gehn im kleinen Kleid,
ganz anders als die andern gehn und gingen–:
O wunderliche Zeit, o Zeitverbringen,
o Einsamkeit.

Und in das alles fern hinauszuschauen:
Männer und Frauen; Männer, Männer, Frauen
und Kinder, welche anders sind und bunt;
und da ein Haus und dann und wann ein Hund
und Schrecken lautlos wechselnd mit Vertrauen–:
O Trauer ohne Sinn, o Traum, o Grauen,
o Tiefe ohne Grund.

Und so zu spielen: Ball und Ring und Reifen
in einem Garten, welcher sanft verblasst,
und manchmal die Erwachsenen zu streifen,
blind und verwildert in des Haschens Hast,
aber am Abend still, mit kleinen steifen
Schritten nachhaus zu gehn, fest angefasst–:
O immer mehr entweichendes Begreifen,
o Angst, o Last.

Und stundenlang am grossen grauen Teiche
mit einem kleinen Segelschiff zu knien;
es zu vergessen, weil noch andre, gleiche
und schönere Segel durch die Ringe ziehn,
und denken müssen an das kleine bleiche
Gesicht, das sinkend aus dem Teiche schien–:
O Kindheit, o entgleitende Vergleiche.
Wohin? Wohin?

RAINER MARIA RILKE

CHILDHOOD

The school's long stream of time and tediousness
winds slowly on, through torpor, through dismay,
O loneliness, O time that creeps away . . .
Then out at last: the streets ring loud and gay,
and in the big white squares the fountains play,
and in the parks the world seems measureless: –
And to pass through it all in children's dress,
with others, but quite otherwise than they: –
O wondrous time, O time that fleets away,
O loneliness!

And out into it all to gaze and gaze:
men, women, women, men in blacks and greys,
and children, brightly dressed, but differently;
and here a house, and there a dog, maybe,
and fear and trust changing in subtle ways: –
O grief uncaused, O dream, O dark amaze,
O still-unsounded seas!

And then with bat and ball and hoop to playing
in parks where the bright colours softly fade,
brushing against the grown-ups without staying
when ball or hoop their alien walks invade;
but when the twilight comes, with little swaying
footsteps going home with unrejected aid: –
O thoughts that fade into the darkness, straying
alone, afraid!

And hours on end by the grey pond-side kneeling
with little sailing-boats and elbows bare;
forgetting it, because one like it's stealing
below the ripples, but with sails more fair;
and, having still to spare, to share some feeling
with the small sinking face caught sight of there: –
Childhood! Winged likenesses half-guessed at, wheeling,
oh, where, oh, where?

Transl. by J. B. Leishman

L'ENFANT ET LA RIVIERE

De sa rive l'enfance
Nous regarde couler:
"Quelle est cette rivière
Où mes pieds sont mouillés
Ces barques agrandies
Ces reflets devoilés,
Cette confusion
Où je me reconnais,
Quelle est cette façon
D'être et d'avoir été?"
Et moi qui ne peux pas répondre
Je me fais songe pour passer aux pieds d'une ombre.

JULES SUPERVIELLE

MIDNIGHT ON THE GREAT WESTERN

In the third-class seat sat the journeying boy,
And the roof-lamp's oily flame
Played down on his listless form and face,
Bewrapt past knowing to what he was going,
Or whence he came.

In the band of his hat the journeying boy
Had a ticket stuck; and a string
Around his neck bore the key of his box,
That twinkled gleams of the lamp's sad beams
Like a living thing.

What past can be yours, O journeying boy
Towards a world unknown,
Who calmly, as if incurious quite
On all at stake, can undertake
This plunge alone?

Knows your soul a sphere, O journeying boy,
Our rude realms far above,
Whence with spacious vision you mark and mete
This region of sin that you find you in,
But are not of?

THOMAS HARDY

RETROSPECTION

We wove a web in childhood,
A web of sunny air;
We dug a spring in infancy
Of water pure and fair;

We sowed in youth a mustard seed,
We cut an almond rod;
We are now grown up to riper age –
Are they withered in the sod? . . .

The mustard-seed in distant land
Bends down a mighty tree,
The dry unbudding almond-wand
Has touched eternity . . .

CHARLOTTE BRONTË

NOTHING GOLD CAN STAY

Nature's first green is gold,
Her hardest hue to hold.
Her earliest leaf's a flower;
But only so an hour.
Then leaf subsides to leaf.
So Eden sank to grief,
So dawn goes down to day.
Nothing gold can stay.

ROBERT FROST

LOVE SOUGHT OR LOST

Love's feeling is more soft and sensible
Than are the tender horns of cockled snails.

SHAKESPEARE: *Love's Labours Lost*

LOVE SOUGHT OR LOST

Introductory Note

GREAT self-restraint has been required in compiling this section, since so large a proportion of the world's great poems are also love-poems. The title is meant to convey that the poems selected deal rather with the pursuit or the loss of love than with its fulfilment, with desire or nostalgia rather than passion; but such definitions cannot be clear-cut, and some poems of fulfilment seem to have stolen in, too.

I can give no good reason for some of my choices. If I were to say that I have tried to avoid what is too familiar, readers might well point out that I should have omitted the first poem of all, while others will certainly regret the absence of some of their own favourites – but to criticize and complain is surely part of the fun of reading an anthology. I can only say that I have applied the same criterion here as in the rest of this book – including only what I have found moving myself, – since it is only thus that I can hope to produce some semblance of unity out of such varied material. This has caused me to include one or two poems which cannot strictly be called great poetry, but which, at some particular moment, awoke an echo.

I at first decided to include no love-letters, chiefly because I felt that the most moving that have been ever written, those of Keats, could not be quoted once again – and then I went back on my decision, and put in two "unlettered" letters – those on page 66 – for which, I think, Keats himself would have found a place.

The moon hath sunk, and the Pleiads,
And midnight is gone,
And the hour is passing, passing,
And I lie alone.

SAPPHO. Transl. Walter Headlam

By day mine eyes, by night my soul desires thee,
Weary, I lie alone.
Once in a dream it seemed thou wert beside me;
O far beyond all dreams, if thou wouldst come!

MS of BEAUVAIS. Transl. by Helen Waddell

'CRAS AMET QUI NUNQUAM AMAVIT'

. . . iam loquaces ore rauco stagna cycni perstrepunt:
adsonat Terei puella subter umbram populi,
ut potes motus amoris ore dici musicos,
at neges queri sororem de marito barbaro.

cras amet qui nunquam amavit quique amavit cras amet.

illa cantat, nos tacemus: quando ver venit meum?
quando fiam uti chelidon ut tacere desinam?
perdidi musam tacendo, nec me Apollo respicit:
sic Amyclas, cum tacerent, perdidit silentium.

cras amet qui nunquam amavit quique amavit cras amet.

Last two verses of the *Pervigilium Veneris*

Now the tall swans with hoarse cries thrash the lake:
The girl of Tereus pours from the poplar ring
Musical change – sad sister who bewails
Her act of darkness with the barbarous king!

Tomorrow may loveless, may lover tomorrow make love.

She sings, we are silent. When will my spring come?
Shall I find my voice when I shall be as the swallow?
Silence destroyed the Amyclae: they were dumb.
Silent, I lost the Muse. Return, Apollo!

Tomorrow let loveless, let lover tomorrow make love.

Transl. by ALLEN TATE

The inclusion of these stanzas of the *Pervigilium Veneris*, a poem of which I have never before found a satisfactory rendering, is partly due to my having met with Allen Tate's translation. In a note he says that by some scholars this poem is supposed to have been written as early as the reign of Hadrian (117–138 A.D.) but he himself inclines to agree with J. W. Mackail that it is of the fourth century. He also observes that it is in the last two stanzas (those quoted here) that "a first-rate lyrical imagination suddenly appears". *Terei puella* is more than a classical allusion; she is a real bird singing in a real poplar tree, answering the dissonance of the swans as they strike the lake".[1]

PLUCKING THE RUSHES

(A boy and girl are sent to gather rushes for thatching)

Green rushes with red shoots,
Long leaves bending to the wind –
You and I in the same boat
Plucking rushes at the Five Lakes.
We started at dawn from the orchid-island;
We rested under the elms till noon.
You and I plucking rushes
Had not plucked a handful when night came!

ANON. (4th or 5th cent.). Transl by Arthur Waley

[1]Allen Tate, Introductory Note to *The Vigil of Venus* in *The Swimmers and other Selected Poems*, 1970.

DUM ESTAS INCHOATUR

Dum estas inchoatur
ameno tempore,
Phebusque dominatur
depulso frigore,

Unius in amore
puelle vulneror
multimodo dolore,
per quem et atteror.

Ut mei misereatur,
ut me recipiat,
et declinetur ad me,
et ita desinat!

MS. of BENEDICTBEUERN (13th cent.)

While summer on is stealing
  And come the gracious prime,
And Phoebus high in heaven,
  And fled the rime,

For love of one young maiden,
  My heart hath ta'en its wound,
And manifold the grief that I
  In love have found.

Ah, would she but have pity,
  And take me to her grace,
And stooping lean down o'er me,
  And so would rest!

Transl. by HELEN WADDELL
in *Medieval Latin Lyrics*

IN UN BOSCHETTO

In un boschetto trovai pasturella,
  più che la stella bella al mi' parere.
Capegli avea biondetti e ricciutelli,
  e gli occhi pien d'amor, cera rosata:
  con sua verghetta pasturava agnelli,
  e, scalza, di rugiada era bagnata:
  cantava come fosse innamorata,
  era adornata di tutto piacere.
D'amor la salutai immantenente,
  e domandai s'avesse compagnia:
  ed ella mi rispose dolcemente
  che sola sola per lo bosco gía
  e disse: – Sappi quando l'augel pia
  allor disia'lme' cuor drudo avere. –
Poi che mi disse di sua condizione,
  e per lo bosco augelli audío cantare,
  fra me stesso dicea: – Or'è stagione
  di questa pasturella gio' pigliare. –
  Merzè le chiesi solo che di basciare
  e d'abbracciare – le fosse'n volere.
Per man mi prese d'amorosa voglia
  e disse che donata m'avea 'l core:
  menommi sott'una freschetta foglia
  là dov'i' vidi fior d'ogni colore;
  e tanto vi sentia gioia e dolzore
  che dio d'amore parvemi vedere.

GUIDO CAVALCANTI

Within a wood I found a shepherdess, who seemed to me more lovely than a star. Her curls were fair, her eyes full of love, her complexion rosy. With a little staff she was herding her lambs, and her bare feet were wet with dew.

At once I greeted her lovingly, and asked her if she had any company, and she gently replied that she was walking alone, alone in the woods, and said: "You must know that when I hear the birds chirping, then my hearts longs for a lover."

Since she had told me this about her state, and I heard birds singing in the wood, I told myself, "This is the time to take delight in this shepherdess." I begged her first only for a kiss and an embrace, if that was to her mind.

She took me by the hand with fond desire and said that she had given me her heart: she led me beneath some fresh green leaves where I saw flowers of every colour, and then I felt so great a joy and pain, I thought that I had seen the god of Love.

MADRIGALE

Ore, fermate il volo
nel lucido oriente,
mentre se'n vola il ciel rapidamente:
e, carolando intorno
a l'alba mattutina
ch'esce da la marina,
l'umana vita ritardate e'l giorno.
E voi, Aure veloci,
portate i miei sospiri
là dove Laura spiri,
e riportate a me sue chiare voci,
Sì ch'io l'ascolti io solo
sol voi presenti e'l signor nostro Amore,
Aure soavi ed Ore.

TORQUATO TASSO

Hours, hold back your flight
Here in the shining East,
while rapidly the heavens fly away,
and, carolling around
the early dawn
that rises from the sea,
delay the birth of human life and day.
And you, swift Airs,
carry my sighs
wherever Laura lies
and bring her clear words back unto my ear,
That I, and I alone, her voice may hear,
With only you and Love, our Lord, close by –
O gentle Airs and Hours.

No translation of this madrigal – one of the loveliest ever written – can render the exquisite assonance of the words "Ore" and "Aure", and their echo in the name "Laura". In these lines all the artificial virtuosity of this metrical form, all its associations with the elaborate and formal *ars amatoria* of the Renaissance courts, are purified by Tasso's gravity into a perfect lyric. "It is", says Francesco Flora, "like an air for a dance, in the midst of a tragedy".

COMPLAINT OF THE ABSENCE OF HER LOVER BEING UPON THE SEA

O happy dames that may embrace
The fruit of your delight;
Help to bewail the woful case,
And eke the heavy plight,
Of me, that wonted to rejoice
The fortune of my pleasant choice:
Good ladies! help to fill my mourning voice.

In ship freight with remembrance
Of thoughts and pleasures past,
He sails that hath in governance
My life while it will last;

With scalding sighs, for lack of gale,
Furthering his hope, that is his sail,
Toward me, the sweet port of his avail.

Alas! how oft in dreams I see
Those eyes that were my food;
Which sometime so delighted me,
That yet they do me good:
Wherewith I wake with his return,
Whose absent flame did make me burn:
But when I find the lack, Lord! how I mourn.

When other lovers in arms across,
Rejoice their chief delight;
Drowned in tears, to mourn my loss,
I stand the bitter night
In my window, where I may see
Before the winds how the clouds flee:
Lo! what mariner love hath made of me.

And in green waves when the salt flood
Doth rise by rage of wind;
A thousand fancies in that mood
Assail my restless mind.
Alas! now drencheth[1] my sweet foe,
That with the spoil of my heart did go,
And left me; but, alas! why did he so?

And when the seas wax calm again,
To chase from me annoy,
My doubtful hope doth cause me plain;
So dread cuts off my joy.
Thus is my wealth mingled with woe:
And of each thought a doubt doth grow;
Now he comes! will he come? alas! no, no!

EARL OF SURREY

[1]Is drowned

A LAMENT

Departe, departe, departe –
Allace! I must departe
From hir that hes my hart,
  With hairt full soir;
Aganis my will in deid
And can find no remeid:
I wait the pains of deid –
Can do no moir . . .

Adew, my ain sueit thing,
My joy and comforting,
My mirth and sollesing
  Of erdly gloir:
Fair weill, my lady bricht,
And my remembrance rycht;
Fair weill and haif gud nycht:
I say no moir.

ALEXANDER SCOTT

A FAREWELL

Oft have I mused, but now at length I find
Why those that die, men say they do depart:
Depart ! a word so gentle to my mind,
Weakly did seem to paint death's ugly dart.

But now the stars with their strange course do bind
Me one to leave, with whom I leave my heart.
I hear a cry of spirits faint and blind,
That parting thus, my chiefest part I part.

. . . .

SIR PHILIP SIDNEY

SONG

Sweetest love, I do not goe,
For wearinesse of thee,
Nor in hope the world can show
A fitter Love for mee;
But since that I
Must dye at last, 'tis best,
To use my selfe in jest
Thus by fain'd deaths to dye;

Yesternight the Sunne went hence,
And yet is here to day,
He hath no desire nor sense,
Nor halfe so short a way:
Then feare not mee,
But beleeve that I shall make
Speedier journeyes, since I take
More wings and spurres than hee.

O how feeble is mans power,
That if good fortune fall,
Cannot adde another houre,
Nor a lost houre recall!
But come bad chance,
And wee joyne to'it our strength,
And wee teach it art and length,
It selfe o'r us to'advance.

When thou sigh'st, thou sigh'st not winde,
But sigh'st my soule away,
When thou weep'st, unkindly kinde,
My lifes blood doth decay.
It cannot bee
That thou lov'st mee, as thou say'st,
If in thine my life thou waste,
That art the best of mee.

Let not thy divining heart
Forethinke me any ill,
Destiny may take thy part,
And may thy feares fulfill;

But thinke that wee
Are but turn'd aside to sleepe;
They who one another keepe
Alive, ne'r parted bee.

JOHN DONNE

'THE LOWEST TREES HAVE TOPS'

The lowest trees haue topps, the ante her gall,
The flie her spleene, the little sparke his heat:
The slender hears cast shadows, though but small,
And bees haue stinges, although they be not great;
Seas haue their source, and soe haue shallow springes:
And Loue is Loue, in beggers and in Kinges.

Wher waters smothest ronne, ther deepest are the foords,
The diall stirrs, yet none perceiues it moove;
The firmest fayth is fownd in fewest woordes,
The turtles doe not singe, and yet thye loue;
True heartes haue ears and eyes, no tongues to speake:
They heare and see, and sigh, and then they breake.

EDWARD DYER

Love is abroad as naked as my nail
And little birds do flicker from their nests.

NICHOLAS BRETON

LOVE'S SECRET

Never seek to tell thy love,
Love that never told can be;
For the gentle wind does move
Silently, invisibly.

I told my love, I told my love,
I told her all my heart,
Trembling, cold, in ghastly fears.
Ah! she doth depart!

Soon as she was gone from me,
A traveller came by,
Silently, invisibly:
O, was no deny.

WILLIAM BLAKE

A SILVIA

Silvia, rimenbri ancora
Quel tempo della tua vita mortale,
Quando beltà splendea
Negli occhi tuoi ridenti e fuggitivi,
E tu, lieta e pensosa, il limitare
Di gioventù salivi?

Sonavan le quiete
stanze, e le vie dintorno,
Al tuo perpetuo canto,
Allor che all'opre femminili intenta
Sedevi, assai contenta
Di quel vago avvenir che in mente avevi.
Era il maggio odoroso: e tu solevi
Così menare il giorno.

Io gli studi leggiadri
Talor lasciando e le sudate carte,
Ove il tempo mio primo
E di me spendea la miglior parte,
D'in su i veroni del paterno ostello
Porgea gli orecchi al suon della tua voce,
Ed alla man veloce
Che percorrea la faticosa tela.
Mirava il ciel sereno
Le vie dorate e gli orti,
E quindi il mar da lungi, e quindi il monte.
Lingua mortal non dice
Quel ch'io sentiva in seno . . .

GIACOMO LEOPARDI

TO SYLVIA

Sylvia, do you remember yet
The season of your mortal lifetime here,
When beauty shone indeed
In the elusive laughter of your eyes,
And full of joy and wonder you approached
The threshold of your years?

The quiet chambers rang,
And all the ways around,
With your continual song;
When you were sitting at your woman's work,
Intent, happy enough
With what bright future occupied your mind.
It was the fragrant Maytime; even so
You used to pass the day.

I, at my easy task,
Sometimes laying aside the well-thumbed page
Which had consumed away
My better parts and my first youthful age,
Upon the balcony of my father's house,
Pricked up my ears at music of your voice
And at your hand which sped
About your labours as you wove your web.
I gazed on the clear skies,
Gardens, and golden ways,
And there the far-off sea, and here the mountains.
No mortal tongue can say
What were my feelings then.
. . . .

Transl. JOHN HEATH-STUBBS

I have quoted only the first three stanzas of Leopardi's *A Silvia,* since this exquisite lyric seems to me to tail away in the final stanzas. It was written in 1828, in memory of a young girl, Teresa Fattorini, whom, nearly ten years before, the poet used to see from the window of his library at Recanati, sitting at her loom and singing. She died of consumption, after much suffering, and in his "Recollections of Childhood and Youth" Leopardi noted:

"The life of man then seemed to me like the time when, as a child, I was taken to visit a friend's house, and began to play at a table with the other boys, and then my parents got up and called me and my heart was wrung, but I had to go, leaving my occupations half begun and the chairs upset and the children weeping."[1]

[1]Leopardi *Poesie e Prose* a cura di Francesco Flora, Vol. I

DESEO

Sólo tu corazón caliente
y nada más.

Mi pará so un campo
sin ruiseñor
ni liras,
con un río discreto
y una fuentecilla.

Sin la espuela del viento
sobre la fronda,
in la estrella que quiere
ser hoja.

Una enorme luz
que fuera
luciérnaga
de otra,
en un campo de miradas rotas.

Un reposo claro
y allí nuestros besos,
lunares sonoros
del eco,
se abrirían muy lejos.

Y tu corazón caliente,
nada más.

GARCÍA LORCA

Only your warm heart, and no more.
My paradise a field without nightingale or lyre, with a discreet river and a small fountain.
Without the spur of the wind over the foliage, without the star wanting to be a leaf.
A great light which would be glow-worm of another, in a field of broken glances.
A serene rest, where our kisses, resonant specks of the echo, would open far away.
And your warm heart, no more.

Transl. by J. M. Gili

TWO LOVE-LETTERS

Dear Marey, dear Marey, I hant got no partcler news to tell ye at present but my sister that marryd have got such a nice littel babey, and I wish how as that we had got such a little dear too. Dearest Mary, I shall not be happy until then. Dearest Mary pure and holy meek and loly lovely Rose of Sharon. Sometimes I do begin to despare as I am afraid our knot will never be tied, but my Master have promised I how as that when I git ye he will put ye in the Dairy yard to feed the Piggs and give ye atin pense a week. . . . I be coming over tomorrow to buy the ring and you must come to the stashun to meet me and bring a pese of string with you the size of your fingar. . . . Father is going to give us a bedstead and Granny a 5 lb note to buy such as washing stand fire irons mousetrap and Sope, and we must wayte till we can to buy carpeting and glass, crockery-ware and chiny. . . . And Father is going to get us a Rooseter for our Weding Brakefast. Dearest Mary pure and holey meek and loly lovely Rose of Sharon. So no more at present from your future husband William Taylor.

Dear Alf, I seen you last night in my dream. O my dear I cried waking up. What a silly girl you been and got! The pain is bad this morning but I laugh at the sollum looks of the sisters and the sawbones. I can see they think I am booked but they dont know what has befallen between you and me. How could I die and leave my dear. I spill my medecine this morning thinking of my dear. Hoping this finds you well no more now yours truly Liz.

The first of these letters, from a country boy to his girl, was picked up on the beach at Sidmouth in 1887 by William de Morgan. The other was written about thirty years ago by a girl in a hospital ward in London, on the day before her death.

BRIDIN VESEY
(after the Irish)

I would marry Bridin Vesey
Without a shoe or petticoat,
A comb, a cloak or dowry
Or even one clean shift;
And I would make novena
Or imitate the hermits
Who spend their lives in fasting
All for a Christmas gift.
O cheek like dogwood fruiting,
O cuckoo of the mountain,
I would send darkness packing
If you would rise and go
Against the ban of clergy
And the sour lips of your parents
And take me to an altar stone
In spite of all Mayo.

That was the sullen morning
They told the cruel story,
How scorning word or token
You rose and went away.
'Twas then my hands remembered,
My ears still heard you calling,
I smelt the gorse and heather
Where you first learned to pray.
What could they know, who named you,
Of jug and bed and table,
Hours slipping through our fingers,
Time banished from the room?
Or what of all the secrets
We knew among the rushes
Under the Reek when cuckoos
Brightened against the moon?

You are my first and last song,
The harp that lilts my fingers,
Your lips like frozen honey,
Eyes like the mountain pool,
Shaped like the Reek your breast is,
Whiter than milk from Nephin,
And he who never saw you
Has lived and died a fool.
Oh, gone across the mearing
Dividing hope from sadness
What happy townland holds you?
In what country do you reign?
In spite of all the grinning lads
At corner and in haybarn
I'll search all Ireland over
And bring you home again.

DONAGH MACDONAGH

It is late, last night the dog was speaking of you. The snipe was speaking of you in her deep marsh. It is you are the lonely bird throughout the woods and that you may be without a mate until you find me.

You promised me and you said a lie to me that you would be before me when the sheep are flocked. I gave a whistle and three hundred cries to you, and I found nothing there but a bleating lamb.

You promised me a thing that was hard for you, a ship of gold under a silver mast, twelve towns and a market in all of them and a fine white court by the side of the sea.

You promised me a thing that is not possible; that you would give me gloves of the skin of a fish; that you would give me shoes of the skin of a bird, a suit of the dearest silk in Ireland.

My mother said to me, not to be talking to you, today or tomorrow or Sunday. It was a bad time she took for telling me that, it was shutting the door after the house was robbed.

You have taken the East from me, you have taken the West from me, you have taken what is before me and what is behind me; you have taken the moon, you have taken the sun from me, and my fear is great, you have taken God from me.

ANON. (recorded by W. B. Yeats)

RIVER ROSES

By the Isar, in the twilight
We were wandering and singing,
By the Isar, in the evening
We climbed the huntsman's ladder and sat swinging
In the fir-tree overlooking the marshes,
While river met with river, and the ringing
Of their pale-green glacier water filled the evening.

By the Isar, in the twilight
We found the dark wild roses
Hanging red at the river; and simmering
Frogs were singing, and over the river closes
Was savour of ice and of roses; and glimmering
Fear was abroad. We whispered: "No one knows us.
Let it be as the snake disposes
Here in this simmering marsh."

(Earlier Version)

. . . and over the river closes
Was scent of roses, and glimmering
In the twilight, our kisses across the roses
Met, and her face, and my face, were roses.

D. H. Lawrence

SHE TELLS HER LOVE WHILE HALF ASLEEP

She tells her love while half asleep;
  In the dark hours,
  With half words whispered low:
As Earth stirs in her winter sleep
  And puts out grass and flowers
    Despite the snow,
    Despite the falling snow.

Robert Graves

THE DOOR

When she came suddenly in
It seemed the door could never close again,
Nor even did she close it – she, she –
The room lay open to a visiting sea
That no door could restrain.

Yet when at last she smiled, tilting her head
To take her leave of me,
Where she had smiled, instead
There was a dark door closing endlessly,
The waves receded.

ROBERT GRAVES

the first of all my dreams was of
a lover and his only love,
strolling slowly(mind in mind)
through some green mysterious land

until my second dream begins—
the sky is wild with leaves;which dance
and dancing swoop(and swooping whirl
over a frightened boy and girl)

but that mere fury soon became
silence:in huger always whom
two tiny selves sleep(doll by doll)
motionless under magical

foreverfully falling snow.
And then this dreamer wept:and so
she quickly dreamed a dream of spring
—how you and i are blossoming

E. E. CUMMINGS

lady will you come with me into
the extremely little house of
my mind. Clocks strike. The

moon's round,through the window

as you see and really i have no
servants. We could almost live

at the top of these stairs,there's a free
room. We almost could go(you
and i)into a together whitely big
there is but if so or so

slowly i opened the window a
most tinyness,the moon(with white wig
and polished buttons)would take you away

—and all the clocks would run down the next day.

E. E. CUMMINGS

ON NE PEUT ME CONNAÎTRE

On ne peut me connaître
Mieux que tu me connais

Tes yeux dans lesquels nous dormons
Tous les deux
Ont fait à mes lumières d'homme
Un sort meilleur qu'aux nuits du monde.

Tes yeux dans lesquels je voyage
Ont donné aux gestes des routes –
Un sense détaché de la terre.

Dans tes yeux ceux qui nous révèlent
Notre solitude infinie
Ne sont plus ce qu'ils croyaient être

On ne peut te connaître
Mieux que je te connais.

PAUL ÉLUARD

IN THE MORNING YOU ALWAYS COME BACK

Lo spiraglio dell'alba
respira con la tua bocca
in fondo alle vie vuote.
Luce grigia i tuoi occhi,
dolci gocce dell'alba
sulle colline scure.
Il tuo passo e il tuo fiato
come il vento dell'alba
sommergono le case.
La città abbrividisce,
odorano le pietre –
sei la vita, il risveglio.

Stella sperduta
nella luce dell'alba
cigolío della brezza,
tepore, respiro –
è finita la notte.

Sei la luce e il mattino.

IN THE MORNING YOU ALWAYS COME BACK

The glimmer of dawn
breathes with your mouth
at the end of the empty streets.
Your eyes are grey lights,
sweet drops of dawn
on the dark hills.
Your passing and your breath
like the wind of dawn
overwhelm the houses.
The city is trembling,
the stones give forth their odour –
you are life, awakening.

Lost star in the light of dawn,
twittering of the breeze,
warmth and breath –
the night is over.

You are the light and the morning.

'VERRÀ LA MORTE E AVRÀ I TUOI OCCHI'

Verrà la morte e avrà i tuoi occhi –
questa morte che ci accompagna
dal mattino alla sera, insonne,
sorda, come un vecchio rimorso
o un vizio assurdo. I tuoi occhi
saranno una vana parola,
un grido taciuto, un silenzio.
Cosí li vedi ogni mattina
quando su te sola ti pieghi
nello specchio. O cara speranza,
quel giorno sapremo anche noi
che sei la vita e sei il nulla.

Per tutti la morte ha uno sguardo.
Verrà la morte e avrà i tuoi occhi.
Sarà come smettere un vizio,
come vedere nello specchio
riemergere un viso morto,
come ascoltare un labbro chiuso.
Scenderemo nel gorgo muti.

DEATH WILL COME AND WILL HAVE YOUR EYES

Death will come and will have your eyes –
this death that is our companion
from morning until night, sleepless,
deaf, like an old remorse
or a ridiculous vice. Your eyes
will be a word spoken in vain,
a cry held back, a silence.
Thus do you see them each morning
as you lean alone towards yourself
in your looking-glass. Dear hope,
that day we too shall know
that you are life and you are nothingness.

For each man Death has a look he knows.
Death will come and will have your eyes.
It will be like giving up a vice,
like seeing in a glass
a dead face reappearing,
like listening to closed lips.
Dumb we shall descend into the abyss.

PASSERÒ PER PIAZZA DI SPAGNA

Sarà un cielo chiaro
S'apriranno le strade
sul colle di pini e di pietra.
Il tumulto dello strade
non muterà quell'aria ferma.
I fiori spruzzati
di colori alle fontane
occhieggeranno come donne
divertite. Le scale
le terrazze le rondini
canteranno nel sole.
S'aprirà quella strada,
le pietre canteranno,
il cuore batterà sussultando
come l'acqua nelle fontane –
sarà questa la voce
che salirà le tue scale.
Le finestre sapranno
l'odore della pietra e dell'aria
mattutina. S'aprirà una porta.
Il tumulto delle strade
sarà il tumulto del cuore
nella luce smarrita.

Sarai tu – ferma e chiara.

I WILL GO THROUGH PIAZZA DI SPAGNA

It will be a clear sky.
The roads will unfold
towards the hill of pine-trees and of stone.
The turmoil of the streets
will not touch that still air.
The flowers sprayed with colours
will give a sidelong glance
at the fountains, like laughing women.
The steps, the terraces, the swallows
will sing in the sun.
That road will unfold,
the stones will sing,
the heart will beat, throbbing
like the water in the fountains –
that will be the voice
rising up your steps.
The windows will savour
the odour of the stones and of the air.
the morning air. A door will open.
The turmoil of the street
will become the heart's turmoil
in the lost light.

It will be you – steady and clear.

These verses belong to a sequence of ten poems, eight in Italian and two in English, entitled *Verrà la morte e avrà i tuoi occhi* (Death will come and will have your eyes) in the volume, "Poesie del disamore". They were written between March 11th and April 11th 1950 for the American actress Constance Dowling, and were found, after Pavese's suicide, in a folder in his desk.

Only three of the poems have been quoted here.

MEMORY

One had a lovely face,
And two or three had charm,
But charm and face were in vain
Because the mountain grass
Cannot but keep the form
Where the mountain hare has lain.

W. B. Yeats

Roma, a letto, dormicchiando, nella
notte tra il 27 e il 28 giugno 1966

UNO

S'incomincia per cantare
E si canta per finire

DUE

E' nato per cantare
Chi dall'amore muore

E' nato per amare
Chi dal cantare muore.

TRE

Chi è nato per cantare
Anche morendo canta.

QUATTRO

Chi nasce per amare
D'amore morirà.

CINQUE

Nascendo non sai nulla,
Vivendo impari poco,
Ma forse nel morire ti parrà
Che l'unica dottrina
Sia quella che si affina
Se in amore si segrega.

SEI

Potremmo seguitare

GIUSEPPE UNGARETTI: *Vita di un uomo*

In Rome, dozing in bed, on the night
between June 27th and 28th 1966

ONE

One begins by singing
And sings when the end comes.

TWO

The man is born to sing
Who dies of love.
The man is born to love
Who dies of singing.

THREE

The man who is born to sing
Will still sing as he dies.

FOUR

The man who is born to love
Will die of loving.

FIVE

You know nothing at your birth,
You learn a little while you live,
But perhaps as you die you will feel
That the only wisdom
Is the one which becomes finer
When shut away in love.

SIX

We could go on.

FOR THEM TO COME

One candle is enough.   Its dim light
is more appropriate,   it will be kindlier
when Shadows come,   the Shadows of Love.

One candle is enough.   Tonight the room
must not have too much light.   Immersed entirely in revery
and in suggestion,   and in the low light –
Thus deep in revery   I will dream a vision so

that Shadows may come,   the Shadows of love.

C. P. CAVAFY. Transl. by Rae Dalven

SONG

Sunset ends the day,
The years shift their place,
Under the sun's sway
Times from times fall;
Mind fighting mind
The secret cords unwind
No power can replace:
Love gathers all.

The living and the dead
Centuries separate,
Man from himself is led
Through mazes past recall,
Distraction can disguise
The wastrel and the wise
Till neither knows his state:
Love gathers all.

Father at odds with son
Breeds ageless enmity,
Friendships undone
Build up a topless wall;

Achilles and Hector slain
Fight, fight and fight again
In measureless memory:
Love gathers all.

The quarrel from the start,
Long past and never past,
The war of mind and heart,
The great war and the small
That tumbles the hovel down
And topples town on town
Come to one place at last:
Love gathers all.

EDWIN MUIR

HOME

Home is the place where, when you have to go there,
They have to take you in.
I should have called it
Something you somehow haven't to deserve.

ROBERT FROST

HOME

Introductory Note

WHAT do we mean by "home"? Plainly, a great many different things. Ideally. of course, the word should conjure up warmth, familiarity, security, a safe harbour for the traveller, a return to "the heart's affections". These are, however, not the only images that the word evokes. To many young people, in all periods of history, home has seemed, at one time or another, an uneasy prison; and for many parents, it has also held associations of responsibility, frustration or anxiety – and often, too (for themselves or for their children) of hopes unfulfilled. Since, however, an anthology is fortunately not a compendium but a selection, the passages included here are chiefly ones that show home at its pleasantest. I have started with home-coming, and – if it had been possible to include music – would have placed here the wonderful last lines and bars of Mahler's *Der Abschied* (after Wang-Sei) – "Ich wandle nach der Heimat, meiner Stätte . . ." But too much is lost without the music and in translation.

After home-coming, home itself. I have chosen the rural peace of two cottages – very different from each other, yet each as restful to contemplate as an interior by Vermeer – the thatched cottage of 'Tao Chen in the the 1st century A.D. and, in eighteenth century England, the house of John Clare's old couple, "secluded there, from all the world considers joy or care". And for the gentle pleasures of daily life at home – all the more diligently fostered, perhaps, because of the knowledge of how thin the ice was that lay between the peace they brought and an abyss of despondency and despair, – two letters describing Cowper's life at Olney.

Marriage has been the aspect of "home" which, in selection, has presented the greatest difficulties: in spite of Tolstoy's aphorism, both happy and unhappy families have been so in so many different ways that it was difficult to choose. Here again, it seemed natural to begin with Odysseus' lines about marriage to Nausicaa, and on the whole I have confined myself to the happier aspects of married life, if only because the inclusion of descriptions of unhappy, or even happy but *difficult* marriages, would have made this section much too long – since apparently married friction often renders its victims extremely articulate. (The *Journals* of both Tolstoy and his wife, the *Letters* of Dickens and of Thackeray, and both the *Letters* and the *Journals* of Jane Carlyle, are among the first that come to mind.) However, I have included two protests by unwilling brides (one from China and one from Renaissance Italy), and I have also quoted two passages that appeal to me (one from Congreve and one from Yeats) about the safeguards of married formality. And finally I have quoted three letters of farewell between husband and wife which I have found deeply moving: one from China, one from Greece, and one – to me the most poignant – from an English miner's wife, whose husband was killed in the mining disaster at Whitehaven in 1914.

There is comparatively little here about children – not only because one aspect of childhood has already appeared in "Early in the Morning", but because their life at home and their relationship with their parents is and has always been – in its deviations between theory and practice – so complex and confused a story as to deserve a whole book to itself. It is the fashion now to claim that the gulf between children and their parents has never been so great as it is now, but I do not think that the facts bear this out. Both Bacon's and Lord Halifax's remarks on pp. 103 and 106 seem to me to be equally applicable to any period – but widely varying periods and settings, too, have produced the spontaneous, loving letters by young children to their parents which I have also quoted. And there is an equally universal applicability not only to children, but to all human affections, in Po Chüi's poem with which this section ends: "Why did I think that I alone should escape?"

THE HOME-COMING OF ODYSSEUS

Odysseus and Euryclea

The old woman brought a basin and half filled it with cold water, then poured in hot water and got ready to wash his feet. But Odysseus quickly moved away from the fireplace and turned his back to the light, for he had just remembered something; he was afraid she might touch the scar of an old wound, and everything might come out.

This was a wound made by the tusk of a wild boar . . .

The boar was aroused by the trampling of men and dogs; out he came from the bushes and faced them, his back bristling and his eyes flashing fire. There he stood close to them, and Odysseus in front of the rest ran at him, pointing his spear to deal him a blow; but the boar charged sideways and struck him first. . . .

All this passed through the mind of Odysseus, as the old nurse touched him with the palm of her hand and felt the scar. She knew him! and dropped the leg, which fell in the basin with a clang, so that all the water was spilt. Joy and sorrow together filled her heart, the tears rose in her eyes, her voice choked, but she touched his chin and said, "Surely tha'rt my baby! And I never knew thee till I had felt my master all over!"

Odysseus and Laertes

So he found his father alone in the vineyard digging about one of the plants. He had on him a dirty old shirt full of patches, with patched leather gaiters to save his shins from scratches, and leather gauntlets against the brambles. On his head he wore a goatskin hat, in the carelessness of his sorrow.

When Odysseus saw him at last, worn with age and full of sorrow, he stood still under a spreading pear-tree and the tears came into his eyes. What should he do? . . .

Laertes answered: "If you are really Odysseus my son come home again, give me a clear sign to prove that you speak the truth."

Odysseus said: "That wound first of all – look, here it is for you to see! You remember how the boar gashed me with his tusk as I ran on him? . . . Yes and let me tell you the trees you gave me in this jolly orchard, when I was a little boy and went round the garden with you and begged for each! We walked among these very trees, you told me their names every one! Thirteen pear trees you gave me and ten apples, forty figs; rows of vines you promised, fifty of them bearing at different times through the vintage, with grapes of all sorts, whenever Zeus made them heavy in the season of the year!"

The old man's knees crickled under him, and his heart melted, as he heard the signs recounted which he knew so well; he laid his arms about his son's neck, and Odysseus held him fainting.

From *The Odyssey*, Books XIX and XXIV.
Transl. by W. H. D. Rouse

Heureux qui, comme Ulysse, a fait un beau voyage,
Ou comme cestuy là qui conquit la toison,
Et puis est retourné, plein d'usage et raison,
Vivre entre ses parents le reste de son aage!

Quand revoiray-je, hélas, de mon petit village
Fumer la cheminée: et en quelle saison
Revoiray-je le clos de ma pauvre maison,
Qui m'est une province, et beaucoup d'avantage?

Plus me plaist le séjour qu'ont basty mes ayeux
Que des palais Romains le front audacieux:
Plus que le marbre dur me plaist l'ardoise fine,

Plus mon Loyre Gaulois, que le Tybre Latin,
Plus mon petit Lyré, que le Mont Palatin,
Et plus que l'air marin la douceur Angevine.

Joachim du Bellay

. . . This is the thing familiar, known;
The safety that the wanderer finds,
Out of the world, one thing his own,
A pause, a lull in journeying, return
After the querying and astonishment;
Reward that only rovers earn
Who have strayed, departed from the peace,
Whether in soul or body widely flown,
Gone after Arabian Nights, the Golden Fleece,
And come back empty-handed, as they went . . .

Vita Sackville-West: *The Land*

THE RETURN OF THE EXILE

"Old friend, what are you looking for?
After those many years abroad you come
With images you tended
Under foreign skies
Far away from your own land."

"I look for my old garden;
The trees come only to my waist,
The hills seem low as terraces;
Yet when I was a child
I played there on the grass
Underneath great shadows
And used to run across the slopes
For hours and hours, breathless."

"My old friend, rest a little.
You will soon get used to it.
Together we will climb
The hill paths that you know;
Together we will sit and rest
Underneath the plane trees' dome;
Little by little they'll come back to you,
Your garden and your slopes."

"I look for my old house,
The house with the tall windows
Darkened by the ivy,
And for that ancient column
The landmark of the sailor.
How can I get into this hutch?
The roof's below my shoulders
And however far I look
I see men on their knees;
You'd say that they were praying."

"My old friend, can't you hear me?
You will soon get used to it.
Here is your house in front of you,
And at this door will soon come knocking
Your friends and your relations
To give you a fine welcome."

"Why is your voice so far away?
Raise your head a little higher
That I may grasp the words you say,
For as you speak you seem to grow
Shorter still and shorter
As though you were sinking down into the ground."

"My old friend, just think a little.
You will soon get used to it;
Your homesickness has built for you
A non-existent land with laws
Outside the earth and man."

"Now I hear nothing, – not a sound.
My last friend too has sunk and gone.
How strange it is, this levelling
All around from time to time:
They pass and mow here
Thousands of scythe-bearing chariots."

GEORGE SEFERIS. Transl. by Rex Warner

A SOLDIER AT THE FRONT

When at last I come home, I shall go down our lane,
Go all down our lane, quietly and slowly
Shall see again the stile, and all the windows, all,
If someone speaks to me, I shall be dumb.

But then I shall see, but then I shall see,
A rare thing. I shall dry up with longing
Until I see it again, until I see it again.
And say to it, my house, my hearth, my nest.

Ah, how I shall crumple down upon that doorstep,
That will be a defeat! Come, let's encounter it!
When that marvellous woman comes to meet me,
I shall fall down in the grass, the deep green grass.

There in the deep grass, when I come home,
I shall sit with my wife, keep my eyes on her for three days.
At night, sleep beside her. And in the morning
Her hands upon the sheets will be marvellous, marvellous.

I'll tell her everything. And be clean. And then get up
And water the window-boxes. And find under the leaves
Green, blessed life. I shall be like a peasant or shepherd.

Transl. from the Czech poem by FRANA SRAMEK

READING THE BOOK OF HILLS AND SEAS

In the month of June the grass grows high
And round my cottage thick-leaved branches sway.
There is not a bird but delights in the place where it rests;
And I too – love my thatched cottage.
I have done my ploughing;
I have sown my seed.
Again I have time to sit and read my books.
In the narrow lane there are no deep ruts;
Often my friends' carriages turn back.
In high spirits I pour out my spring wine
And pluck the lettuce growing in my garden.
A gentle rain comes stealing up from the east
And a sweet wind bears it company.
My thoughts float idly over the story of the king of Chou,
My eyes wander over the pictures of Hills and Seas.
At a single glance I survey the whole Universe.
He will never be happy, whom such pleasures fail to please!

T'AO CH'IEN (A.D. 372–427). Transl. by Arthur Waley

THE OLD COTTAGERS

The little cottage stood alone, the pride
Of solitude surrounded every side.
Bean fields in blossom almost reached the wall;
A garden with its hawthorn hedge was all
The space between. – Green light did pass
Through one small window, where a looking-glass
Placed in the parlour, richly there revealed
A spacious landscape and a blooming field.
The pasture cows that herded on the moor
Printed their footsteps to the very door,
Where little summer flowers with seasons blow
And scarcely gave the eldern leave to grow.
The cuckoo that one listens far away
Sung in the orchard trees for half the day;
And where the robin lives, the village guest,
In the old weedy hedge the leafy nest
Of the coy nightingale was yearly found,
Safe from all eyes as in the loneliest ground;
And little chats that in bean stalks will lie
A nest of cobwebs there will build, and fly
Upon the kidney bean that twines and towers
Up little poles in wreaths of scarlet flowers.

There a lone couple lived, secluded there
From all the world considers joy or care,
Lived to themselves, a long lone journey trod,
And through their Bible talked aloud to God;
While one small close and cow their wants maintained,
But little needing, and but little gained.
Their neighbour's name was peace, with her they went;
With tottering age, and dignified content,
Through a rich length of years and quiet days,
And filled the neighbouring village with their praise.

JOHN CLARE

'DAILY LIFE AT OLNEY'

My dear, I will not let you come until the end of May or beginning of June, because before that time my greenhouse will not be ready to receive us, and it is the only pleasant room belonging to us. When the plants go out, we go in. I line it with mats and spread the floor with maps; and there you shall sit with a bed of mignonette at your side, and a hedge of honeysuckles, roses, and jasmine; and I will make you a boquet of myrtle every day. Sooner than the time I mention the country will not be in complete beauty. And I will tell you what you shall find at your first entrance. Imprimis, as soon as you have entered the vestibule, if you cast a look on either side of you, you shall see on the right hand a box of my making. It is the box in which have been lodged all my hares, and in which lodges Puss at present; but he, poor fellow, is worn out with age, and promises to die before you can see him. On the right hand stands a cupboard, the work of the same Author. It was once a dove-cage, but I transformed it....

I have made in the orchard the best winter-walk in all the parish sheltered from the east and from the north-east, and open to the sun, except at his rising, all the day. Then we will have Homer and Don Quixote; and then we will have saunter and chat and one laugh more before we die....

William Cowper to Lady Hesketh,
February 9, 1786 and June 27, 1788.

I feel here no restraint, and none is wished to be inspired . . . We rise at whatever hour we choose; breakfast at half after nine, take about an hour to satisfy the *sentiment* not the *appetite*, for talk, for we talk – good heavens! how we talk! and enjoy ourselves most wonderfully. Then we separate – Mr. Cowper to Homer, Mr. Rose to transcribing what is translated, Lady Hesketh to work and to books alternately. Mrs. Unwin, who in everything but her face is like a kind angel come from heaven to guard the health of our poet, is busy in domestic concerns. At one, our labours finished, the poet and I walk for two hours. Then drink most plentiful draughts of instruction which flow from his lips, instruction so sweet and goodness so exquisite that one *loves* it for its flavour. At three we return and dress, and the succeeding hour brings dinner upon the table, and collects again the smiling countenances of the family to partake of the neat and elegant meal. Conversation continues until tea-time, when an entertaining volume engrosses our thoughts till the last meal is announced. Conversation again; and then rest before twelve to enable us to rise again to the same round of innocent virtuous pleasure."

Letter from SAMUEL ROSE to his sister

IN THE VALLEY OF THE ELWY

I remember a house where all were good
  To me, God knows, deserving no such thing:
  Comforting smell breathed at very entering,
Fetched fresh, as I suppose, off some sweet wood.
That cordial air made those kind people a hood
  All over, as a bevy of eggs the mothering wing
  Will, or mild nights the new morsels of spring:
Why, it seemed of course; seemed of right it should. . . .

GERARD MANLEY HOPKINS

How few of his friends' houses would a man choose to be at when he is sick.

BOSWELL: *Life of Dr. Johnson*

COMFORT

As I mused by the hearthside,
  Puss said to me:
"There burns the Fire, man,
  And here sit we.

"Four Walls around us
  Against the cold air;
And the latchet drawn close
  To the draughty Stair.

"A Roof o'er our heads
  Star-proof, moon immune,
And a wind in the chimney
  To wail us a tune.

"What Felicity!" miaowed he,
  "Where none may intrude;
Just Man and Beast – met
  In this Solitude!

"Dear God, what security,
  Comfort and bliss!
And to think, too, what ages
  Have brought us to this!

"You in your sheep's-wool coat,
  Buttons of bone,
And me in my fur-about
  On the warm hearthstone."

WALTER DE LA MARE

WINTER NIGHT

Snow swept over the earth,
Swept it from end to end.
The candle on the table burned,
The candle burned.

Like swarms of summer midges
Drawn to the flame
The snowflakes
Flocked to the window.

The driven snow drew circles and arrows
On the window pane
The candle on the table burned,
The candle burned.

On the bright ceiling
Fell the shadows
Of crossed hands, crossed feet,
Crossed fate.

Two shoes fell to the floor
With a thud.
From the night-light
Wax tears dropped on a frock.

And everything was lost
In the white-haired, white, snowy darkness.
The candle on the table burned,
The candle burned.

A draught from the corner
Puffed at the candle's flame,
And like an angel, the heat of temptation
Raised two wings in the form of a cross.

The snow swept all through February
And now and again
The candle on the table burned,
The candle burned.

BORIS PASTERNAK. Transl. by Max Hayward
and Manya Harari

THE HOUSE WHERE I WAS BORN

An elegant, shabby white-washed house
With a slate roof. Two rows
Of tall sash windows. Below the porch, at the foot of
The steps, my father, posed
In his pony trap and round clerical hat.
This is all the photograph shows.

No one is alive to tell me
In which of those rooms I was born,
Or what my mother could see, looking out one April
Morning, her agony done,
Or if there were pigeons to answer my cooings
From that tree to the left of the lawn.

Elegant house, how well you speak
For the one who fathered me there,
With your sanguine face, your moody provincial charm,
And that Anglo-Irish air
Of living beyond one's means to keep up
An era beyond repair.

Reticent house in the far Queen's County,
How much you leave unsaid.
Not a ghost of a hint appears at your placid windows
That she, so youthfully wed,
Who bore me, would move elsewhere very soon,
And in four years be dead.

I know that we left you before my seedling
Memory could root and twine
Within you. Perhaps that is why so often I gaze
At your picture, and try to divine
Through it the buried treasure, the lost life –
Reclaim what was yours, and mine.

I put up the curtains for them again
And light a fire in their grate;
I bring the young father and mother to lean above me,
Ignorant, loving, complete;
I ask the questions I never could ask them
Until it was too late.

C. Day Lewis

ODYSSEUS TO NAUSICAA

For nothing is better and more precious than when two of one heart and mind keep house together, husband and wife . . . but they know it best themselves.

From *The Odyssey*, Book VI. Transl. by W. H. D. Rouse

Uxor, vivamus ut viximus, et teneamus
nomina, quae primo sumpsimus in thalamo;
nec feret ulla dies, ut commutemur in aevo,
quin tibi sim juvenis tuque puella mihi . . .

Ausonius

Love, let us live as we have lived, and keep
The names we whispered in our wedding-bed;
Nor let old age e'er lead us to forget
That I am still your boy and you my girl.

ACME ET SEPTIMIUS

Whilst on *Septimius*' panting Brest,
(Meaning nothing less than Rest)
Acme lean'd her loving head,
Thus the pleas'd *Septimius* said.

My dearest *Acme*, if I be
Once alive, and love not thee
With a Passion far above
All that e're was called Love,
In a *Lybian* desert may
I become some Lions prey,
Let him, *Acme*, let him tear
My Brest, when *Acme* is not there.

The God of Love who stood to hear him,
(The God of Love was always near him)
Pleas'd and tickl'd with the sound,
Sneez'd aloud, and all around
The little Loves that waited by,
Bow'd and blest the Augurie.

Acme enflam'd with what he said,
Rear'd her gently-bending head,
And her purple mouth with joy
Stretching to the delicious Boy
Twice (and twice could scarce suffice)
She kist his drunken, rowling eyes.

My little Life, my All (said she)
So may we ever servants be
To this best God, and ne'r retain
Our hated Liberty again,
So may thy passion last for me,
As I a passion have for thee,
Greater and fiercer much than can
Be conceiv'd by Thee a Man.
Into my Marrow is it gone,
Fixt and setled in the Bone,
It reigns not only in my Heart,
But runs, like Life, through ev'ry part.
She spoke; the God of Love aloud,
Sneez'd again, and all the crowd
Of little Loves that waited by,
Bow'd and blest the Augurie.
This good Omen thus from Heaven
Like a happy signal given,
Their Loves and Lives (all four) embrace,
And hand in hand run all the race.
To poor *Septimius* (who did now
Nothing else but *Acme* grow)
Acme's bosome was alone,
The whole worlds Imperial Throne,
And to faithful *Acme's* mind
Septimius was all Human kind.
If the Gods would please to be
But advis'd for once by me,
I'de advise 'em when they spie,
Any illustrious Piety,
To reward Her, if it be she;
To reward Him, if it be He;
With such a Husband, such a Wife,
With *Acme's* and *Septimius'* Life.

ABRAHAM COWLEY, after Catullus

THE UNWILLING BRIDE

I wish to leave the world, and to serve God
  And so to bid farewell to vanity,
  Because I see the strength and power increase
  Of madness, villainy and falsity;
And see the death of wit and courtesy
  And of fine taste, and every other good:
  Therefore I crave no husband and no lord
  Nor will I choose to live within the world.
Remembering how men adorn themselves
  With what is ill, I do despise each one,
  And turn with my whole self to God alone.
But by my father I am much dismayed
  Who from Christ's service seeks to draw me home,
  Nor do I know whose bride I must become.

The accomplished damsel

Lasciar vorrei lo mondo, e Dio servire
  e dipartirmi d'ogni vanitate,
  però che veggo crescere e salire
  mattezza, villania e falsitate,
et ancor senno e cortesia morire
  e lo fin pregio, e tutta la bontate
  ond'io marito non vorría nè sire
  nè stare al mondo per mia volontate.
Membrandomi che ogn'uom di mal s'adorna,
  di ciaschedun son forte disdegnosa,
  e verso Dio la mia persona torna.
Lo padre mio mi fa forte pensosa,
  che di servire a Cristo mi distorna:
  non saccio a cui mì vuol dare per isposa.

La compiuta donzella (13th century)

LAMENT OF HSI-CHÜN

My people have married me
In a far corner of Earth;
Sent me away to a strange land,
To the king of Wu-sun.
A tent is my house,
Of felt are my walls;
Raw flesh my food
With mare's milk to drink.
Always thinking of my own country,
My heart sad within.
Would I were a yellow stork
And could fly to my old home!

Transl. by ARTHUR WALEY

LA SPOSA

Dice una balia: – A voi son tutte cose.
Voi giacerete soletta in quel letto;
noi tutte quante di qua dormiremo. –
Mostrano a lei la guardaroba allato,
dov'elle dicon che stanno a guardare.
Lavano il viso e le mani alla donna
d'acqua rosata mischiata in viuole,
ché in quel paese così é l'usanza;
concian sua testa e avvolgon le trecce;
stannole intorno, aiùtolla spogliare:
chi la discalza, beata colei!
E i suoi calzari non son miga di cuoio.
Guàrdolla in viso sed ella ha paura;
quella le prega di lor rimanere;
diconle di dormir di fuor del letto
a piè di lei in sui drappi ch'i' ho detto;
fànnone vista, e la donna sorride.
Méttolla a letto, sègnolla prima,

volgon le coltra: è la faccia scoverta.
Tutte le viste di pietre e di drappi
perdono a quella beltate amorosa
ch'esce degli occhi che d'attorno volge.
Luce il visaggio; ismarriscono le balie.
Chiude la donna li suoi occhi e dorme.

FRANCESCO DA BARBERINO

A nurse said: "All these things are yours. You will sleep alone in that bed, and we shall all sleep over there" – and they show her the wardrobe room next door, where they say they will remain on guard. They wash her face and hands with rose-water mixed with violets, for thus is the custom there; they dress her hair and wind its tresses; they stand about her, help her to undress; blessed is the one who takes off her shoes – the shoes she wears are not of leather (i.e. of silk or satin). They look in her face to see if she is afraid, they tell her they will sleep outside the bed at her feet, on the stuffs I have described: they pretend to do so, and the girl smiles. They put her to bed, blessing her first, turn back the blankets; her face is left uncovered. All the splendour of precious stones and silks fades before the loving beauty of her eyes as she looks around her. Her face is glowing; the nurses are dazzled. The girl closes her eyes and sleeps.

This fragment comes from a famous Tuscan book of precepts for women's comportment, *Del Reggimento e Costume di Donna.* The preceding verse had described the beauties of the bridal chamber, – which included silk sheets, coverlets embroidered in pearls, song birds in a glass cage, several puppies, and balsam in crystal vases. Convention required, in order to shield a bride's modesty, a pretence that the women who put her to bed on her bridal night would remain to protect her – but in the following verse "all the women betray her" and go to call her husband.

A PRAYER FOR MY DAUGHTER

. . . .

In courtesy I'd have her chiefly learned;
Hearts are not had as a gift but hearts are earned
By those that are not entirely beautiful;
Yet many, that have played the fool
For beauty's very self, has charm made wise,
And many a poor man that has roved,
Loved and thought himself beloved.
From a glad kindness cannot take his eyes.

May she become a flourishing hidden tree
That all her thoughts may like the linnet be,
And have no business but dispensing round
Their magnanimities of sound,
Nor but in merriment begin a chase,
Nor but in merriment a quarrel.
O may she live like some green laurel
Rooted in one dear perpetual place. . . .

And may her bride-groom bring her to a house
Where all's accustomed, ceremonious;
For arrogance and hatred are the wares
Peddled in the thoroughfares.
How but in custom and in ceremony
Are innocence and beauty born?
Ceremony's a name for the rich horn,
And custom for the spreading laurel tree.

W. B. YEATS

'MIRABELL AND MILLAMANT'

Millamant Good Mirabell, don't let us be familiar or fond, nor kiss before Folks, like my Lady Fadler and Sir Francis: Nor go to Hide Park together the first Sunday in a new Chariot, to provoke Eyes and Whispers. And then never be seen there again, as we were proud of one another the first Week, and asham'd of one another ever after. Let us never Visit together, nor go to a Play together, but let us be very strange and well-bred: let us be as strange as if we had been marry'd a great while, and as well-bred as if we were not marry'd at all.

WILLIAM CONGREVE: *The Way of the World*

TO HIS WIFE

Since my hair was plaited and we became man and wife
The love between us was never broken by doubt.
So let us be merry this night together,
Feasting and playing while the good time lasts.
I suddenly remember the distance that I must travel;
I spring from bed and look out to see the time.
The stars and planets are all grown dim in the sky;
Long, long is the road; I cannot stay.
I am going on service, away to the battle-ground,
And I do not know when I shall come back.
I hold your hand with only a deep sigh;
Afterwards, tears – in the days when we are parted.
With all your might enjoy the spring flowers,
But do not forget the time of our love and pride.
Know that if I live, I will come back again,
And if I die, we will go on thinking of each other.

GENERAL SU WU* (*c.* 100 B.C.). Transl. by Arthur Waley

*General Su Wu was taken prisoner by the Huns and was not relased for nineteen years.

A WIFE'S GRAVE

These words, Phocaea, were Theano's last
When into the night where no man reaps she passed:
"Woe's me, Apellichus! How wide, how wide,
Husband, the gulf whereo'er your ship must ride!
But Death stands close to me. Ah, would that I
Might put my hand in your hand as I die!"

DAMAGETUS. Transl. by R. A. Furness

THE MINER'S WIFE

"... God took my man but I could never forget him he was the best man that ever lived at least I thought that, maybe it was just that I got the right kind of man. We had been married for 25 years and they were hard years at that, many a thing we both done without for the sake of the children. We had 11 and if I had him back I would live the same life over again. Just when we were beginning to stand on our feet I lost him I can't get over it when I think of him how happy he was that morning going to work and telling me he would hurry home, but I have been waiting a long time now. At night when I am sitting and I hear clogs coming down the street I just sit and wait hoping they are coming to my door, then they go right on and my heart is broke."

Letter from a miner's wife, whose husband was killed in the mining disaster at Whitehaven in 1914.

The Joyes of Parents are Secret; and so are their Griefes, and Feares: They cannot utter the one; Nor they will not utter the other. Children sweeten Labours; but they make Misfortunes more bitter; They increase the Cares of Life; but they mitigate the Remembrance of Death.

FRANCIS BACON

TO HIS SWEETEST CHILDREN

I have given you, forsooth, kisses in plenty and but few stripes.
If ever I have flogged you 'twas but with a peacock's tail.

SIR THOMAS MORE

SOME CHILDREN'S LETTERS

I

"A Schoolboy's Letter"

Theon to his father Theon, greeting. It was a fine thing not to take me with you to town! If you won't take me with you to Alexandria, I won't write to you or speak to you or say good-bye to you. If you go to Alexandria, I won't ever take your hand nor greet you again. That is what will happen if you won't take me. Mother said to Archelaus: "It quite upsets him to be left behind." It was good of you to send me a present the day you sailed. Send me a lyre, now, I beg you. If you don't, I won't eat, I won't drink. That's that.

OXYRHYNCUS PAPYRI, CXIX (2nd or 3rd century A.D.)
Transl. from the Greek by F. A. Wright

II

"The Pony"

Magnificent Father, Lucrezia and I are trying who can write best. She writes to grandmother Lucrezia, I, my father, to you. The one who obtains what he asks for will win. Till now Lucrezia has had all she wished for. I, who have always written in Latin in order to give a more literary tone to my letters, have not yet had that pony you promised me; so that I am laughed at by all. See to it therefore, Your Magnificence, that she should not always be the winner.

26th May, 1479

Magnificent Father mine, – That pony does not come, and I am afraid that it will remain so long with you that Andrea will cause it to change from a beast to a man, instead of curing its hoof. – We are all well and studying. Giovanni is beginning to spell. By this letter you can judge where I am in writing; as for Greek I keep myself rather in exercise by the help of Martino than make any progress. Giuliano laughs and thinks of nothing else; Lucrezia sews, sings, and reads; Maddalena knocks her head against the wall, but without doing herself any harm; Luisa begins to say a few little words; Contessina fills the house with her noise . . . Nothing is wanting to us save your presence.

Magnificent Father mine, – I fear that some misfortune has happened to that pony, for had it been well I know you would have sent it to me as you promised. I beg of you therefore as a grace that you will take this fear from me; for I think of it night and day, and until the pony comes I shall have no peace. In case that one cannot come be pleased to send me another. For, as I have already written to you, I am here on foot, and sometimes it is necessary for me to go in the company of my friends. See to this therefore, Your Magnificence.

Magnifico Patri meo, – I cannot tell you, Magnificent Father, how glad I am to have the pony, and how his arrival incites me to work. If I desire to praise him, *Ante diem clauset componet vesper Olympo*. He is so handsome and so perfect that the trumpet of Maronius would hardly suffice to sing his praises. You may think how I love him; particularly when his joyous neighs resound and rejoice all the neighbourhood. I owe you and I send you many thanks for such a fine gift and I shall try and repay you by becoming what you wish. I promise you that I shall try with all my heart.

Four letters from Piero de' Medici to his father
Lorenzo the Magnificent

III

"*The busybody*"

"You want to know what I do. I am a busybody, and do any silly thing; I drew eyes and noses until about a fortnight ago. I have drawn a little boy since, a man's face and a little boy's face. Next Monday I shall begin to read Ovid's Metamorphoses and Eutropius. I want to learn how to measure the stars. I shall not, I suppose, paint the worse for knowing everything else."

Letter from William Hazlitt at ten years old to his brother

Leonardo da Vinci would have been of the same opinion.

IV

"Maman!"

We are very dull here since you left . . . Come home soon! We don't know what to say or do without you; we are quite lost. We are always thinking of you. *Maman, maman*! Your dutiful son Victor.

From VICTOR HUGO to his mother, during a brief absence.

V

"Splendid in all your ways"

You are so very nice, you know. I never meant to annoi you, because I love you so much, you know, or to vex you in any way. I am sure everyone you meet must think you very nice, and splendid in all your ways. Mother, I don't want to go with the others away next summer. I am very sorry I weren't nice to Madam. I will always be nice to her in futcher. Your loving Monnie.

MONICA MEYNELL to her mother.

Love is presently out of Breath, when it has to go Uphill, from Children to the Parents.

LORD HALIFAX (1633–1695): *Advice to a Daughter*

This advice was drawn up for Lord Halifax's daughter Elizabeth, the mother of the famous Earl of Chesterfield. With regard to religion; he said to his daughter "that he believed as much as he could, and imagined that God would forgive him if, unlike an ostrich, he could not digest iron".

TWO POEMS ABOUT CHILDREN

The Silver Spoon

To distant service my heart is well accustomed;
When I left home, it wasn't that which was difficult
But because I had to leave Kuei at home –
For this it was that tears filled my eyes.
Little boys ought to be daintily fed:
Mrs. Tsou, please see to this!
That's why I've packed and sent a silver spoon;[1]
You will think of me and eat up your food nicely!

Children

My nephew, who is six years old, is called 'Tortoise';
My daughter of three – little 'Summer Dress'.
One is beginning to learn to joke and talk;
The other can already recite poems and songs.
At morning they play clinging about my feet;
At night they sleep pillowed against my dress.
Why, children, did you reach the world so late,
Coming to me just when my years are spent?
Young things draw our feelings to them;
Old people easily give their hearts.
The sweetest vintage at last turns sour;
The full moon in the end begins to wane.
And so with men the bonds of love and affection
Soon may change to a load of sorrow and care.
But all the world is bound by love's ties;
Why did I think that I alone should escape?

PO CHÜ-I (9th cent.). Transl. by Arthur Waley

[1]While on the road to his new province, Hang-Chow, the poet sends a silver spoon to his nephew, A-Kuei, whom he had been obliged to leave behind with his nurse, Mrs. Tsou.

FRIENDSHIP

"Luy seul jouyssoit de ma vraye image, et l'emporta."

MONTAIGNE

FRIENDSHIP

Introductory Note

HERE the choice has been easier: the Chinese and the French are the best. Indeed the difficulty of not including too many Chinese poems has been so great that I have cheated a little and have placed some of them in the section entitled "*Les Souvenirs*".

There is a special interest, however – and, at least to me, a quality profoundly moving – in what must be the oldest existant account of a friendship, the Sumerian epic *Gilgamesh*. This epic, written on clay tablets discovered in Nineveh in the nineteenth century by two Englishmen, Austen Layard and George Smith, and the Turkish archaeologist, Hormuzd Rassam, is at least fifteen hundred years older than the Homeric epics, and was possibly known to early Biblical authors. Its theme is the universal one of friendship and heartbreak at its loss. In its own words:

"It is an old story
But one that can still be told
About a man who loved
And lost a friend to death
And learned he lacked the power
To bring him back to life.
It is the story of Gilgamesh
And his friend Enkidu."

Gilgamesh (I am quoting from the notes to the fine rendering of this epic by Herbert Mason) was "the fifth king of Uruk after the great flood. He is two-thirds god, one-third man." Enkidu is the friend of Gilgamesh, "figure of natural man, patron saint of animals". In the passage quoted here, he has been wounded to death by Humbaba, "guardian of the cedar forest; nature divinity". Just before the passage quoted in the text, when both he and Gilgamesh know that he is dying, Enkidu foresees what his friend's solitude will be:

... You'll be alone and wander
Looking for that life that's gone or some
Eternal life you have to find.
He drew closer to his friend's face.
My pain is that my eyes and ears
No longer see and hear the same
As yours do. Your eyes have changed.

FRIENDSHIP

You are crying. You never cried before.
It's not like you.
Why am I to die,
You to wander on alone?
Is that the way it is with friends?

Gilgamesh sat hushed as his friend's eyes stilled.
In his silence he reached out
To touch the friend whom he had lost.

To the French passages about friendship – perhaps the most famous in literature on that theme – there is nothing to add except two other short passages by Montaigne. The first, which is quoted as a heading to this section, has not been included in Montaigne's essays since the publication in 1920 of the *exemplaire de Bordeaux* – Montaigne's own copy of his essays into which, until the end of his life, he continued to add marginalia, to change phrases and to erase sentences. The reason is that this phrase, which first appeared in the last edition published in Montaigne's lifetime (1588) was crossed out in the Bordeaux *exemplaire*. There is, however, some reason to believe that it was *not* crossed out by Montaigne himself, but by Mademoiselle de Gournay, who appears to have tampered with the essays to give the impression that she, and not Etienne de la Boëtie, had been Montaigne's closest friend.[1]

Finally, there are a few poignant lines written by Montaigne, many years after the death of de la Boëtie, in the margin of his essays.

"Three and four times happy is the man who can entrust his pitiful old age to the eye of a friend . . . O my friend! Am I the better for having tested it [friendship] or am I worse off? Surely I am the better? Mourning him consoles and honours me."

In the end, it is this belief – that to grieve and to remember is in itself both "a consolation and an honour" – that makes human loss endurable.

[1] I am indebted for this information to Professor Walter Kaiser, who also quotes the marginal passage quoted above (which was not translated by Florio, since it, too, was crossed out by a later hand) in the introduction to his *Selected Essays of Montaigne*, p. xxxix.

GILGAMESH AND ENKIDU

Gilgamesh wept bitterly for his friend.
He felt himself now singled out for loss
Apart from everyone else. The word *Enkidu*
Roamed through every thought
Like a hungry animal through empty lairs
In search of food. The only nourishment
He knew was grief, endless in its hidden source
Yet never ending hunger.

All that is left to one who grieves
Is convalescence. No change of heart or spiritual
Conversion, for the heart has changed
And the soul has been converted
To a thing that sees
How much it costs to lose a friend it loved.
It has grown past conversion to a world
Few enter without tasting loss
In which one spends a long time waiting
For something to move one to proceed.
It is that inner atmosphere that has
An unfamiliar gravity or none at all
Where words are flung out in the air but stay
Motionless without an answer,
Hovering about one's lips
Or arguing back to haunt
The memory with what one failed to say,
Until one learns acceptance of the silence
Amidst the new debris
Or turns again to grief
As the only source of privacy,
Alone with someone loved

. . . .

Gazing into the valley
He felt overcome with pain
As a man
Who has been in prison
Feels his chains
At his release from fear.
He spoke Enkidu's name aloud
As if explaining to the valley
Why he was there, wishing his friend

Could see the same horizon,
Share the same delights: My friend Enkidu
Died. We hunted together. We killed Humbaba
And the Bull of Heaven. We were always
At each other's side, encouraging when one
Was discouraged or afraid or didn't
Understand. He was this close to me.
He held his hands together to describe
The closeness. It seemed for a moment
He could almost touch his friend,
Could speak to him as if he were there:
Enkidu. Enkidu. But suddenly the silence
Was deeper than before
In a place where they had never been
Together.
He sat down on the ground and wept:
Enkidu. Enkidu.

As when we can recall so vividly
We almost touch
Or think of all the gestures that we failed
To make.

After several minutes he stood up
Explaining only to himself why he
Had come – To find the secret of eternal life
To bring Enkidu back to life –
Recognizing now the valley was deaf
To loss known only to himself.

From *Gilgamesh*. Transl. by HERBERT MASON

AN OATH OF FRIENDSHIP

(1)

In the country of Yüeh when a man made friends with another they set up an altar of earth and sacrificed upon it a dog and a cock, reciting this oath as they did so:

If you were riding in a coach
And I were wearing a "li",[1]
And one day we met in the road,
You would get down and bow.
If you were carrying a "tēng"[2]
And I were riding on a horse,
And one day we met in the road
I would get down for you.

Transl. by ARTHUR WALEY

This poem is undated, but has been placed by the translator with other poems of the first century A.D.

ON A DEAD FRIEND

This little stone, good Sabinus, is the record of our great friendship; ever will I require thee; and thou, if it is permitted among the dead, drink not of the water of Lethe for me.

ANON. Transl. from the Greek by J. W. MACKAIL

Non ego perfidum
dixi sacramentum: ibimus, ibimus,
utcumque praecedes, supremus
carpere iter comites parati.

HORACE

No idle oath
Has Horace sworn: whene'er you go,
We both will travel, travel both
The last dark journey down below.

Transl. by JOHN CONINTON

[1]A peasant's hat made of straw.
[2]An umbrella under which a cheap-jack sells his wares.

TO AUSONIUS

Ego te per omne quod datum mortalibus
et destinatum saeculum est,
claudente donec continebor corpore,
discernar orbe quolibet,
nec ore longe, nec remotum lumine,
tenebo fibris insitum,
videbo corde, mente complectar pia,
ubique praesentem mihi.
et cum solutus corporali carcere,
terraque provolavero,
quo me locarit axe communis Pater
illic quoque animo te geram.
neque finis idem, qui meo me corpore,
et amore laxabit tuo.
mens quippe, lapsis quae superstes artubus
de stirpe durat caeliti.
Sensus necesse est simul et affectus suos
retineat ut vitam suam;
et ut mori sic oblivisci non capit,
perenne vivax et memor.

I, through all chances that are given to mortals,
And through all fates that be,
So long as this close prison shall contain me,
Yea, though a world shall sunder me and thee,

Thee shall I hold, in every fibre woven,
Not with dumb lips, nor with averted face
Shall I behold thee, in my mind embrace thee,
Instant and present, thou, in every place.

Yea, when the prison of this flesh is broken,
And from the earth I shall have gone my way,
Wheresoe'er in the wide universe I stay me,
There shall I bear thee, as I do today.

Think not the end, that from my body frees me,
Breaks and unshackles from my love to thee;
Triumphs the soul above its house in ruin,
Deathless, begot of immortality.

Still must she keep her senses and affections,
Hold them as dear as life itself to be,
Could she choose death, then might she choose forgetting:
Living, remembering, to eternity.

PAULINUS OF NOLA: *Carmina*, XI.
Transl. by Helen Waddell in *Medieval Latin Lyrics.*

I have quoted in full this poem by Paulinus, for the sake of the moving story attached to it, which is told both by Boissier in *La fin du paganisme* and by Helen Waddell, in a note to her selection of *Medieval Latin Lyrics.* Ausonius (353–431 A.D.), to whom the poem was addressed, was nominally a Christian, but both by temperament and inheritance was deeply imbued with the pagan tradition and the values of ancient Rome. Born in Aquitaine, he became the tutor of the Emperor's son, Gratian, and was rewarded with the office of Consul, only returning in middle age to his country estate near Bordeaux. Here he became the tutor of a remarkable young man, Pontius Meropius Paulinus, who later on became St. Paulinus of Nola. For some years the old upholder of pagan civilization – while his world was crumbling about him and the barbarians were at the gate – strove to instil his own ideals into his pupil and basked in his success (for Paulinus became more brilliant and more successful than his master). Then one day Paulinus – who had already been converted to Christianity and had married a Spanish woman – left for Spain, and for over three years he sent no news. When, at last, he replied to his old master's appeals, it was plain that, perhaps partly owing to the sudden death of his only child – he had become a dedicated Christian; a man who had rejected "what may be seen, to reach what may not be seen". Ausonius had lost him for good. But still Ausonius persisted – addressing his next letter "To Paulinus, when he had answered many things, but had not said that he would come". Perhaps this sentence reached its mark, for Paulinus replied with the poem quoted here – a lyrical testimony to friendship, addressed to a man of seventy. But he did not say "that he would come". Soon after, Ausonius died, and in the same year Paulinus – formerly governor of a Roman Province and a Consul before he was thirty – became the humble parish priest of the shrine of St. Felix at Nola, "to guard his temple and to sweep its threshold". "*Voilà le rêve,*" Boissier comments, "*de ce sénateur et ce consulaire!*"

THREE POEMS BY PO CHÜ-I

I

To Yüan Chēn

Since I left my home to seek official state
Seven years I have lived in Ch'ang-an.
What have I gained? Only you, Yüan;
So hard it is to bind friendships fast.
We have roamed on horseback under the flowering trees;
We have walked in the snow and warmed our hearts with wine.
  We have met and parted at the Western Gate
And neither of us bothered to put on Cap or Belt.
We did not go up together for Examination;
We were not serving in the same Department of State.
The bond that joined us lay deeper than outward things;
The rivers of our souls spring from the same well!

II

To Li Chien

Worldly matters again draw my body;
Worldly things again seduce my heart.
Whenever for long I part from Li Chien
Grandually my thoughts grow narrow and covetous.
I remember how once I used to visit you;
I stopped my horse and tapped at the garden-gate.
Often when I came you were still lying in bed;
Your little children were sent to let me in.
And you, laughing, ran to the front-door
With coat-tails flying and cap all awry.
On the swept terrace, green patterns of moss;
On the dusted bench the shade of the creepers was cool.
To gaze at the hills we sat in the eastern lodge;
To wait for the noon we walked to the southern moor.
At your quiet gate only birds spoke;
In your distant street few drums were heard.
Opposite each other all day we talked,
And never once spoke of profit or fame.

Since we parted hands, how long has passed?
Thrice and again the full sun has shone.
For when we parted the last flowers were falling,
And to-day I hear new cicadas sing.
The scented year suddenly draws to its close,
Yet the sorrow of parting is still unsubdued.

III

On Board Ship, Reading Yüan Chēn's Poems

I take your poems in my hand and read them beside the candle;
The poems are finished: the candle is low, dawn not yet come.
My eyes smart; I put out the lamp and go on sitting in the dark,
Listening to waves that, driven by the wind, strike the prow of the ship.

Po Chü-I (772–846). Transl. by Arthur Waley

The translator's introduction to Po Chü-I's poems (in *170 Chinese Poems*) says that he had three friends "with whom he maintained a lifelong intimacy", the first and closest being Yüan Chēn, who was only twenty-two when they first met, and from whom he was separated for some years after Yüan Chēn was banished for provoking a high official. Two other poems to Yüan Chēn are in the section "Les Souvenirs", since Yüan Chēn died some thirteen years before Po Chü-I.

ELEGY ON THE DEATH OF SIR PHILIP SIDNEY

Silence augmenteth grief, writing encreaseth rage,
Staled are my thoughts, which loved and lost the wonder of our age:
Yet quickened now with fire, though dead with frost ere now,
Enraged I write I know not what; dead, quick, I know not how.

Hard-hearted minds relent and rigour's tears abound,
And envy strangely rues his end, in whom no fault she found
Knowledge her light hath lost; valour hath slain her knight.
Sidney is dead; dead is my friend; dead is the world's delight.

Farewell to you, my hopes, my wonted waking dreams,
Farewell, sometimes enjoyed joy; eclipsed are thy beams.
Farewell, self-pleasing thoughts, which quietness brings forth
And farewell, friendship's sacred league, uniting minds of worth.

And farewell, merry heart, the gift of guiltless minds,
And all sports which for lives restore variety assigns;
Let all that sweet is void; in me no mirth may dwell.
Philip, the cause of all this woe, my life's content, farewell! . . .

FULKE GREVILLE, LORD BROOKE

The same writer composed the following Epitaph for himself on his Monument in Warwick:

Fulke Greville, Servant to Queen Elizabeth,
Counsellor to King James, and Friend to
Sir Philip Sidney.

Those we ordinarily call friends and amities are but acquaintances and familiarities, tied together by some occasion or commodities, whereby our minds are entertained. In the amity I speak of, they intermix and confound themselves one in the other, with so universal a commixture that they wear out and can no longer find the seam that hath conjoined them together. If a man urge me to tell wherefore I loved him, I feel it cannot be expressed but by answering: "Because it was he, because it was myself . . ."

Our minds have jumped so unitedly together, they have with so fervent an affection considered of each other, and with like affection so discovered and sounded even to the very bottom of each other's heart and entrails, that I did not only know his as well as mine own, but I would verily rather have trusted him, concerning any matter of mine than myself . . .

It is a great and strange wonder for a man to double himself; and those that talk of tripling know not nor cannot reach unto the height of it. Nothing is extreme that hath his like. And he who shall presuppose that of two I love the one as well as the other and they inter-love one another, and love me as much as I love them, he multiplieth in brotherhood a thing most singular and a lonely one, and than which one alone is also the rarest to be found in the world . . .

Ancient Menander accounted him happy that had but met the shadow of a true friend: verily he had reason to say so, especially if he had tasted of any. For truly, if I compare all the rest of my forepassed life, which although I have, by the mere mercy of God, passed at rest and ease and, except to losing so dear a friend, free from all grievous affliction, with an ever-quietness of mind, as one that have taken my natural and original commodities in good payment without searching any others – if, as I say, I compare it all unto the four years I so happily enjoyed the sweet company and dear, dear society of that worthy man, it is nought but a vapor, nought but a dark and irksome (night).

Since the time I lost him . . . I do but languish, I do but sorrow . . . And even those pleasures all things present me with, instead of yielding me comfort, do but redouble the grief of his loss . . . All things were with us at half; methinks I have stolen his part from him.

MONTAIGNE: *Of Friendship*. Transl. by John Florio

To be with those one loves, that is enough: to dream, to talk to them or not to talk, to think about them, to think about the most trivial things, but in their company – it is all one.

LA BRUYÈRE

It is a silent contract between two feeling and virtuous persons. I say *feeling*, for a monk or a hermit may not be unkind and yet can live without becoming acquainted with friendship. I say *virtuous*, for evil men only have accomplices, lovers of pleasure have only boon-companions, men with an eye to money have partners, political men gather together litigants, most idle men have mistresses, and princes have their courtiers: only virtuous men have friends.

VOLTAIRE

'DR. JOHNSON ON FRIENDSHIP'

A man, Sir, should keep his frendships *in constant repair.*

DR. JOHNSON

Boswell: I mentioned that Mr. Wilkes had attacked Garrick to me, as a man who had no friend.

Johnson: I believe he is right, Sir. οι φιλοι ου φιλος. He had friends but no friend . . .

Boswell: Garrick did not need a friend, as he got from everybody all he wanted. What is a friend? One who supports you and comforts you, while others do not. Friendship, you know Sir, is the cordial drop, 'to make the nauseous draught of life go down': but if the draught be not nauseous, if it be all sweet, there is no occasion for that drop.

Johnson: Many men would not be content to live so. I hope I should not. They would wish to have an intimate friend, with whom they might compare minds, and cherish private virtues."

BOSWELL: *Life of Dr. Johnson*

FRIENDSHIP WITH A BROTHER

Sometimes I fancy an immense separation, and sometimes, as at present, a direct communication of Spirit with you. That will be one of the grandeurs of immortality – There will be no space and consequently the only commerce between spirits will be by their intelligence of each other – when they will completely understand each other – while we in the world merely comprehend each other in different degrees – the higher the degree of good so higher is our Love and friendship . . . The reason why I do not feel at the present moment so far from you is that I remember your Ways and Manners and actions; I know your manner of thinking, your manner of feeling; I know what shape your joy or your sorrow would take; I know the manner of your walking, standing, sauntering, sitting down, laughing, punning, and every action so truly that you seem near to me. You will remember me in the same manner – and the more when I tell you that I shall read a passage of Shakespeare every Sunday at ten o'clock – you read one at the same time and we shall be as near each other as blind bodies can be in the same room."[1]

The following letter was written about nine months later – only a year before the writer's death.

From the time you left me, our friends say I have altered completely – am not the same person – perhaps in this letter I am, for in a letter one takes up one's existence from the time we last met; I dare say you have altered also – every man does – our bodies every seven years are completely fresh-materiald – seven years ago it was not this hand that clench'd itself against Hammond. We are like the relict garments of a Saint; the same and not the same for the careful Monks patch it and patch it: till there's not a thread of the original garment left, and still they show it for St. Anthony's shirt. This is the reason why men who have been bosom friends, on being separated for any number of years, afterwards meet coldly, neither of them knowing why. The fact is they are both altered – Men who live together have a silent moulding and influencing power over each other. They interassimilate. 'Tis an uneasy thought that in seven years the same hands cannot greet each other again.[2]

. . . .

JOHN KEATS: *Letters to his brother George*,
[1]Dec. 1818–Jan. 1819; [2]Sept. 1819.

Friendship is a disinterested commerce between equals; love, an abject intercourse between tyrants and slaves.

OLIVER GOLDSMITH

AT FIRST SIGHT

"Love at first sight", some say, misnaming
Discovery of twinned helplessness
Against the huge tug of procreation.

But friendship at first sight? This also
Catches fiercely at the surprised heart
So that the cheek blanches and then blushes.

ROBERT GRAVES

THE MUNICIPAL GALLERY REVISITED

Around me the images of thirty years:
An ambush; pilgrims at the water-side;
Casement upon trial, half hidden by the bars,
Guarded; Griffiths staring in hysterical pride;
Kevin O'Higgins' countenance that wears
A gentle questioning look that cannot hide
A soul incapable of remorse or rest;
A revolutionary soldier kneeling to be blessed.

An Abbot or Archbishop with an upraised hand
Blessing the Tricolour. "This is not", I say,
"The dead Ireland of my youth, but an Ireland
The poets have imagined, terrible and gay."
Before a woman's portrait suddenly I stand,
Beautiful and gentle in her Venetian way.
I met her all but fifty years ago
For twenty minutes in some studio.

Heart-smitten with emotion I sink down,
My heart recovering with covered eyes;
Wherever I had looked I had looked upon
My permanent or impermanent images:
Augusta Gregory's son; her sister's son,
Hugh Lane, "onlie begetter" of all these;
Hazel Lavery living and dying, that tale
As though some ballad-singer had sung it all.

Mancini's portrait of Augusta Gregory,
"Greatest since Rembrandt", according to John Synge;
A great ebullient portrait certainly;
But where is the brush that could show anything
Of all that pride and that humility?
And I am in despair that time may bring
Approved patterns of women or of men
But not that selfsame excellence again.

My mediaeval knees lack health until they bend,
But in that woman, in that household where
Honour had lived so long, all lacking found.
Childless I thought, "My children may find here

Deep-rooted things," but never foresaw its end,
And now that end has come I have not wept;
No fox can foul the lair the badger swept –

(An image out of Spenser and the common tongue.)
John Synge, I and Augusta Gregory, thought
All that we did, all that we said or sang
Must come from contact with the soil, from that
Contact everything Antaeus-like grew strong.
We three alone in modern times had brought
Everything down to that sole test again,
Dream of the noble and the beggar-man.

And here's John Synge himself, that rooted man,
"Forgetting human words", a grave deep face.
You that would judge me, do not judge alone
This book or that, come to this hallowed place
Where my friends' portraits hang and look thereon;
Ireland's history in their lineaments trace;
Think where man's glory most begins and ends,
And say my glory was I had such friends.

W. B. Yeats

FOLLOWER OF THE MUSES

But upon thee is grace of words, and within thee is a heart of wisdom.

The Odyssey, Book XI. Transl. by MAURICE BARING

The Gods had made him neither a delver, nor a ploughman, nor anything useful; he was master of no trade: a follower of the Muses and of the long-bowed Apollo.

Homeric epigram from the *Margites*. Transl. by MAURICE BARING

FOLLOWER OF THE MUSES

Introductory Note

THE link that binds together the passages in this section is a very simple one: they are all about people who have had an unconquerable addiction to one of the arts.

Maurice Baring, after quoting the epigram from the *Margites* quoted on page 127, also quotes a translation of the same epigram by Leconte de Lisle, in which τέχνη is translated by "*art*", though commenting that he thought the word "*métier*" would have been better. "The subject of the poem in question, was, in fact, an amateur," – and Baring goes on to quote Willmott, an actor-manager, and Giles, a critic and man of letters. They are discussing Rostand.

"Willmott: 'He's an amateur. He's never written professionally for his bread, but only for pleasure.'

Giles: 'But in that sense, God is an amateur.' "

It is writers who, for obvious reasons, have been most articulate about their addiction to their art, and it is from them that I have quoted most freely, but of course this does not mean that the disciples of the other arts have not been equally devoted. Not only Michelangelo, climbing up to the marble quarries of the Carrara mountains, to find slabs of exactly the right colour and grain for his tomb of Julius II, or Luca della Robbia, sculpting all day and drawing all night, and according to Vasari, "placing his feet into a basket of wood-shavings when they were numb with cold, rather than interrupt his work", but almost any minor craftsman of one of the Florentine *botteghe d'arte* of the Renaissance accepted a discipline as rigorous and gave to his art a devotion as unstinted as that of Flaubert or Leopardi. If I have quoted comparatively few passages from painters, sculptors, or musicians, it has been partly because there was so vast a choice of purely literary documents to draw upon, but chiefly because of the difficulties inherent in the attempt to discuss one art in the terms of another. "Taste and even genius", as Northcote remarked to Hazlitt, "is but a misfortune, without a correspondent degree of power of language to make it manifest."

This is especially true of the writings of musicians about their work. While there is scarcely one of Keats's letters that, in addition to enabling us to penetrate further into his mind, is not in itself a delight to read, the whole voluminous correspondence between Brahms and Elizabeth Herzogenberg (though almost exclusively concerned with music, and of considerable technical interest) does not even remotely equal the pleasure given us by hearing one of his compositions. Elizabeth herself was not unaware of this. "What a poor thing speech is!" she writes. "One seeks in vain for the right, the comprehensive word to relieve one's feelings after moments of real enjoyment." One of the few exceptions is Verdi's letters, in which we do really get an impression of the uncompromising character of the man, the difficulties he had to confront and the passion and strength of character which enabled him to impose his own views. But there is no letter of Mozart's which evokes the exquisitely lyrical quality of his works, while in Beethoven's letters the effect is *cumulative*. If one reads them as a whole, one is aware of the passion, strength, courage, torment, occasional rollicking humour, touchiness, vulnerability and total dedication to his art of this great Titan; but there is also a great deal about money-matters, law suits, slights fancied or real, ill-health and domestic tragedy, which makes it very difficult to quote any single letter in its entirety. Perhaps the most characteristic are the three letters to Wegler in 1801, in which, having fully realised the extent of his deafness, he rises above his affliction. "I will as far as possible defy my fate, though there must be moments when I shall be the most miserable of God's creatures . . . I will grapple with fate; it shall never drag me down." And again, in the same autumn, "I live only in my music, and no sooner is one thing done than another is begun. As I am now writing, I often work at three or four things at once . . ." Friendship, love, deafness, all were secondary to his dedication to his composition. The only letter, however, that I have quoted in full here belongs to a happier mood, and describes how the motif of a Canon for three voices came to him in a dream during a journey.

Many painters, too, when they have tried to describe the processes by which their work was created have suffered a similar bafflement. Leonardo was the first to admit it: "Thirst shall parch your tongue," he wrote in one of his note-books, "and your body shall waste through lack of sleep and sustenance, before you can describe in words that which painting instantly sets before the eye." Yet he himself is the outstanding contradiction of this statement. In the page from one of his note-books, for instance, quoted on p. 143 he conveys with complete success what he wishes the attitude of each of his figures to express in the "Last Supper", at the moment when each of the disciples has been struck dumb by Christ's words: "Verily I say unto you that one of you shall betray me." "*Farò una finzione*," he wrote, "*che significherà cose grandi*." (I shall produce an image which will hold a great meaning.)

Nature never set forth the earth in so rich a tapestry as divers poets have done, neither with so pleasant rivers, fruitful trees, sweet-smelling flowers, nor whatsoever else may make this too-much-loved world more lovely. Her world is brazen, the poets only deliver a golden.

SIR PHILIP SIDNEY

'Twill be a pretty thing, and I am glad you putt me on it. [John Aubrey's *Brief Lives.*] I doe it playingly. This morning being up by 10 I writt two lives: one was Sir John Suckling of whom I wrote a leafe and ½ in folio.

. . . .

My memoires of lives is now a book of two quires, close written: and after I begun it, I had such an impulse on my spirit that I could not be at quiet till I had done it.

. . . .

JOHN AUBREY: *Letter to Anthony Wood*

'A NATURAL STYLE'

When we see a natural style we are surprised and delighted, for we thought to see an author and found a man.

PASCAL: *Pensées*

Son art de plaire et de n'y penser pas.

LA FONTAINE

He walked much and contemplated, and he had in the head of his staff a pen and inke-horne, carried alwayes a note-booke in his pocket, and as soon as a thought darted, he presently entered it into his booke, or otherwise he might perhaps have lost it.

JOHN AUBREY

He laboured with the same tranquility of mind to his last hour; and with Bayle it was death alone which could interrupt the printer.

ISAAC DISRAELI

Men misacknowledge the natural infirmity of their mind. She doth but quest and ferret, and uncessantly goeth turning, winding, building, and entangling herself in her own work, as do our silkworms, and therein stifleth herself. "A mouse in pitch"

. . . .

There is no end in our inquisitions. Our end is in the other world... It is a sign his wits grow short when he is pleased, or a sign of weariness. No generous spirit stays and relies upon himself. He ever pretendeth and goeth beyond his own strength. He hath some vagaries beyond his effects. If he advance not himself, press, settle, shock, turn, wind and front himself, he is but half alive....

MONTAIGNE: *Of Experience*. Transl. by John Florio

'REAL PERFORMANCE'

Why, sir, what makes the difference between man and man is real performance and not genius or conception. There are a thousand Garricks, a thousand Giardinis, and Fischers and Abels. Why only one Garrick, with Garrick's eyes, voice, &c, &c? One Giardini with Giardini's fingers, &c, &c. But one Fischer with Fischer's dexterity, quickness &c? Or more than one Abel with Abel's feeling upon that instrument? All the rest of the world are but *hearers* and *see'rs.*

And, in another letter in the same year,

Garrick is the greatest creature living in every respect; he is worth studying in every action. Every view and every idea of him is worthy of being stored up for imitation, and I have ever found in him a generous and sincere friend. Look upon him, Henderson, for when he drops you'll have nothing but poor old Nature's book to look in. You'll be left to grope it out alone, scratching your pate in the dark, or by a farthing candle. Now is your time, my lively fellow.

THOMAS GAINSBOROUGH: *Letters to John Henderson*,
June 27 and July 18, 1773

*No one was quicker than Gainsborough at distinguishing the true servant of the Muses from the amateur. He could be civil – just – to his clients, but only provided that they showed themselves to him in their true colours. His treatment of Lord Sherburne is well-known. After two attempts to paint him, he threw away his brush, exclaiming, "I never could see through varnish, and there's an end!"

I know that This World is a World of Imagination and Vision. I see Every thing I paint In This World, but Every body does not see alike. To the Eyes of a Miser a Guinea is far more beautiful than the Sun, and a bag worn with the use of money has more beautiful proportions than a Vine filled with Grapes The tree which moves some to tears of joy is in the Eyes of others only a Green thing which stands in the way. Some see Nature all Ridicule and Deformity . . . and some scarce see Nature at all. But to the Eyes of the Man of Imagination, Nature is Imagination itself. As a man is, so he sees. As the Eye is formed, such are its Powers. You certainly Mistake, when you say that the Visions of Fancy are not to be found in This World. To Me This World is all One continued Vision of Fancy or Imagination, and I feel Flattered when I am told so.

. . . .

WILLIAM BLAKE: *Letter to the Rev. Dr. Trusler*

KEATS ON HIS OWN WRITINGS

. . . I feel assured I should write from the mere yearning and fondness I have for the Beautiful even if my night's labours should be burnt every morning, and no eye ever shine upon them. But even now I am perhaps not speaking from myself, but from some character in whose soul I now live . . .[1]

I have heard Hunt say and (I) may be asked – why endeavour after a long Poem? To which I should answer – Do not the Lovers of Poetry like to have a little Region to wander in where they may pick and choose, and in which the images are so numerous that many are forgotten and found new in a second Reading: which may be food for a Week's stroll in the Summer? Do they not like this better than what they can read through before Mrs. Williams comes down stairs?[2]

I think Poetry should surprise by a fine excess and not by Singularity – it should strike the Reader as a wording of his own highest thoughts, and appear almost a Remembrance . . . And this leads me on to another axiom. That if Poetry comes not as naturally as the Leaves to a tree it had better not come at all . . . [3]

[1]To Richard Woodhouse, Tuesday 27 Oct. 1818.
[2]To Benjamin Bailey, Wednesday 8 Oct. 1817.
[3]To John Taylor, Friday 27 Feb. (1818).

My own domestic criticism has given me pain without comparison beyond what Blackwood or the Quarterly could possibly inflict, and also when I feel I am right, no external praise can give me such a glow as my own solitary reperception and ratification of what is fine . . . The Genius of Poetry must work out its own salvation in a man: It cannot be matured by law and precept, but by sensation and watchfulness in itself. That which is creative must create itself – in Endymion, I leaped headlong into the Sea, and thereby have become better acquainted with the Soundings, the quicksands, & the rocks than if I had stayed upon the green shore, and piped a silly pipe, and took tea and comfortable advice.[1]

GIACOMO LEOPARDI ON POETRY

Everything has been perfected since Homer's time: not poetry.

Zibaldone

Often it has happened to me to fall asleep with some verses or words upon my lips, which I had often repeated to myself during the day, or in the hours before sleep; or else with the recollection of the air of some melody; and, having thought or dreamed during my sleep about quite other things, I would wake up repeating to myself the same verses or words, or the same air. It would seem that the soul, in falling asleep, lays down the thoughts and images it holds, as we lay down our clothes, in some place very near at hand, so as to find them once again on waking.

Zibaldone

To a sensitive and imaginative man, who lives as I have lived for a long time, constantly feeling and imagining, the world and its objects are, in a way, double. He sees with his eyes a tower, a landscape; he hears with his ears the sound of a bell; and at the same time his imagination sees another tower, another bell, and hears another sound.

Zibaldone

[1]To James August Hessey, Friday 9 Oct. 1818.

After reading a passage of true poetry of our own time, whether in verse or prose (but the most powerful impressions come from verse), one can say, even in these prosaic times, what Sterne said about a smile: that it adds a thread to the short canvas of our life.

Zibaldone

Poetry . . . a breath of the soul.

Zibaldone

ON WRITING A POEM

I have never followed anything but an inspiration (or frenzy) during which, in the course of two minutes, I conceived the plan and arrangement of the whole composition. This done, I usually wait until such another moment returns, and when it comes – which is usually not until some months later – I begin to compose, but so slowly that I cannot finish a poem, however short, in less than two or three weeks. This is my method, and if inspiration does not come of its own accord, water would spring out of a log more easily than a single verse from my brain.

GIACOMO LEOPARDI: *Letter to Giuseppe Melchiorri*

The good writer is the man who buries a word every day . . . For him, words are artesian wells.

LÉON-PAUL FARGUE

Of two words, always choose the lesser.

PAUL VALÉRY

If I had to have a kind of motto for my poetry, it would be something like, "In my poverty is my strength".

GEORGE SEFERIS to his translator, Rex Warner

HOW POETRY IS MADE

As many poets have said – Akhmatova in "Poem without a Hero" and Mandelstam among them – a poem begins with a musical phrase ringing insistently in the ears; at first inchoate, it later takes on a precise form, though still without words. I sometimes saw M[andelstam] trying to get rid of this kind of "hum", to brush it off and escape from it. He would toss his head as though it could be shaken out like a drop of water that gets into your ear when bathing. But it was always louder than any noise, radio or conversation in the same room.

Akhmatova told me that when "Poem without a Hero" came to her, she was ready to try anything just to get rid of it, even rushing to do her washing. At some point words formed behind the musical phrase, and then the lips began to move ... The "hum" sometimes came to M in his sleep, but he could never remember it on waking. I have a feeling that verse exists before it is composed. (M never talked of "writing" verse, only of "composing" it and then copying it out.) The whole process of composition is one of straining to catch and record something compounded of harmony and sense as it is relayed from an unknown source and gradually forms itself into words.

. . . .

I noticed that in his work on a poem there were two points at which he would sigh with relief – when the first words in a line or stanza came to him, and when the last of the foreign bodies was driven out by the right word ... Only then is there an end to the process of listening to oneself ... Io, the poor cow, escapes from the gadfly.

. . . .

In Voronezh he (Mandelstam) had absolutely no privacy when he was working. In none of the places we rented was there so much as a passage or a kitchen to which he could escape if he wanted to be completely alone. This is not to say that things were much better in Moscow, but at least there was always somewhere where I could go for an hour or so, leaving him alone at work. But in Voronezh there was nowhere to go, except out into the freezing streets ... Whenever a poem was approaching its final stage of "ripeness" I used to take pity on poor M, who was like a caged animal, and did what I could – lying down on the bed, for instance, and pretending to sleep.

. . . .

Everything suggested that the end was near and M was trying to take full advantage of his remaining days. He was possessed by the feeling that he must hurry or he would be cut short and not allowed to say what he still wanted to say. Sometimes I begged him to rest, to go out for a walk or have a nap, but he dismissed the idea: there was so little time left, and he must hurry.

. . . .

The poems poured out of him, one after another. He worked on several at once, and he often asked me to take down at one sitting two or three which he had already completed in his head. I could not stop him: "You must understand that I shan't have time otherwise"....

He drove himself so hard during the whole of that year that he became even more painfully short of breath: his pulse was irregular and his lips were blue. He generally had his attacks of angina on the street, and in our last year at Voronezh he could no longer go out alone. Even at home he was only calm when I was there. We sat opposite each other and I watched his moving lips as he tried to make up for lost time and hastened to record his last words.

Each time I copied out a new poem, M would count up the lines and decide how much he had "earned" at the highest current rates of payment... When we had thus added up his "earnings" for the day, we would go out to borrow money for our supper on the strength of them.

. . . .

Restlessness was the first sign that he was working on something and and the second was the moving of his lips. In one poem he says that his lips can never be taken away from him, and that they will still move when he is dead and buried. This has indeed happened.*

NADEZHDA MANDELSTAM: *Hope Against Hope*

*These deeply moving passages refer to the period when Josip Mandelstam – who had already been exiled with his wife to Siberia for six years and then released – was constantly expecting to be re-arrested. His wife never saw him again after his arrest, but devoted the rest of her life to trying to preserve his work. She had already started to do this during his lifetime, smuggling his poems out of Moscow sewn into cushions or into the linings of shoes, or copying them and distributing them to his friends for safe-keeping – and, after his death saying them aloud to herself, even when she was working on a night-shift in a factory. "There are many women," she writes, "like me, who have spent sleepless nights reciting the words of their dead husbands over and over again." Many? It is difficult to believe – but what a fine destiny!

OUR WORDS

When will you speak again?
They are children of many men, our words.
They are sown and brought forth like infants;
they take root and are nourished with blood.
As pines
keep the shape of the wind
even when the wind has fled and is no longer there,
so words
guard the shape of man
even when man has fled and is no longer there.
Perhaps the stars seek to speak
which trod upon your nakedness one night –
the Swan, the Archer, the Scorpion –
perhaps those.
But where will you be at the moment when,
here in this theatre, the light comes on?

GEORGE SEFERIS: *Three Secret Poems.*
Transl. by Walter Kaiser.

'TO ARRIVE'

I must only tell you that all these expressions – *to hurry up*, *it's high time*, *your chance gone*, *to settle down*, *out of the running*, constitute a vocabulary which has no meaning for me. It is as if you were speaking to a Red Indian. I don't understand.

To arrive – where? To the position of Messrs. Murger, Feuillet, Monselet etc. . . . Thank you.

To become known. That is not my chief concern, that only satisfies very mediocre vanities.

. . . .

I am aiming higher, at pleasing myself. Success can only be a result, not a goal.

. . . .

I have in mind a manner of writing and a delicacy (*gentillesse*) of language which I intend to achieve. When I think I have plucked the apricot, I shall not refuse to sell it, nor to be praised if it is good.

It may be that there are strokes of luck in commercial affairs, propitious moments for buying this ware or that. . . . But if your work of art is good, if it is *true*, it will have its echo, its place, in six months, six years, or after your time. What does it matter![1]

In addition there was also an absolute refusal to exploit his own private feelings, and a great distaste for the facile emotionalism of such poets as Lamartine and De Musset. To Louise Colet, who had accused him of describing emotions that he had never felt, he replied:

Personalised sentimentality, that it what will make a large part of our contemporary literature seem childish and foolish later on. So much sentiment, so much sentiment, such tenderness, so many tears!. . .The story of a blade of grass can be told with a deep love, the fable of *The Two Pigeons* has always moved me more than the whole of Lamartine – and not on account of its style. But if Lamartine had first expended all his faculty for loving in setting down his personal emotions, what would have been left over to describe the friendship of two birds? Beware of squandering in small change our golden coins.[2]

GUSTAVE FLAUBERT: *Correspondance*, II

THE COMPOSITION OF MADAME BOVARY

My novel makes me break out in a cold sweat; in five months, since the end of August, do you know how much I have written of it – sixty-five pages! . . . Each paragraph is good in itself and there are some pages, I am sure of it, that are perfect; but precisely on that account, *it won't do*. It is a series of rounded, immobile paragraphs, which do not run into each other; I shall have to unscrew them.

. . . .

La Bovary isn't going well, *two pages* in one week! sometimes it's enough to make one cut one's throat, with discouragement – if I can so express myself. Oh, I'll get there, I'll get there, but it will be tough. What this book will be like, I have no idea, but I can answer for it that it will be written.

. . . .

[1]To Maxime du Camp (1852).
[2]To Louise Colet (1854).

Here I've been for three days now, sinking down into all my chairs and into every possible position to find *something to say*! There are cruel moments in which the thread is broken, in which the reel seems bare. This evening, indeed, I begin to see light, but what a waste of time! how slowly I get on, and who will ever notice the complicated devices which so simple a book will have required? How much technique to produce naturalness, and how many tricks are needed to be true!

. . . .

I shall be left (this is weak and idiotic) with a great disgust for subjects in a vulgar setting. That's why I am having such trouble in writing this book. I must make a great effort to imagine my characters and then to make them speak, for they are profoundly repugnant to me. But when I write something from my own *guts*, it goes fast. Yet that is the danger, when one writes something from *inside oneself*, the sentence may be good in bursts and lyrical souls get their effects easily, following their natural bent; but there is not a whole . . . Details are terrible, especially when one loves detail as I do. A necklace is made of pearls, but it is the thread that holds it together; now to thread the pearls without losing a single one and always holding the thread in one's other hand, that's the trick.

. . . .

I am dizzy with boredom, with discouragement, with fatigue! I have spent four hours without being able to write one sentence. I haven't yet written a line today, or rather I have scribbled a hundred. What an atrocious job! Oh, art! art! What is this mad chimaera which eats up one's heart, and why?

GUSTAVE FLAUBERT to Louise Colet
Correspondance, II
(pp. 194–216–237–347–360)

THE WRITER

. . . .

No simple emotion exists any more for him. All that he sees, his joys, his pleasures, his despair, at once become subjects to be observed. In spite of everything, in spite of himself, endlessly, he analyses hearts, faces, gestures, intonations.

. . . .

Never to suffer, think, love, feel like everyone else, plainly, simply, without analysing oneself after every joy and every tear....

GUY DE MAUPASSANT

'L'ÉCRIVAIN'

When he writes, there is no gesture of his characters, no mannerism, no accent, which his memory has not bestowed upon his inspiration, there is no name of an imaginary character to which he could not give the names of sixty persons he has known, of whom one posed for [the character's] expression, another for his monocle, one for his anger, and yet another for the skilful sweep of his arm, etc. And thus the writer becomes aware that if his dream of becoming a painter was not consciously and deliberately realisable, it has yet come true, and that the writer, too, has made a sketch without knowing it.

MARCEL PROUST: *Le Temps retrouvé*

'THE GREATEST BOOK IN THE WORLD'

. . . .

I shall here write the first pages of the greatest book in the world. This is what the book would be that was made entirely, solely and with integrity of one's thoughts. Suppose one could catch them before they became "works of art"? Catch them hot and sudden as they rise in the mind – walking up Asheham hill for instance. Of course one cannot; for the process of language is slow and deluding. One must stop to find a word. Then, there is the form of the sentence, soliciting one to fill it.

What I thought was this: if art is based on thought, what is the transmuting process? I was telling myself the story of our visit to the Hardys, and I began to compose it; that is to say to dwell on Mrs. Hardy leaning on the table, looking out, apathetically, vaguely, and so would soon bring everything into harmony with that as the dominant theme. But the actual event was different.

. . . .

I might in the course of time learn what it is that one can make of this loose, drifting material of life; finding another use for it than the use I put it to, so much more consciously and scrupulously, in fiction. What sort of diary should I like mine to be? Something loose knit and yet not slovenly, so elastic that it will embrace anything, solemn, slight or beautiful that comes into my mind. I should like it to resemble some deep old desk, or capacious hold-all, in which one flings a mass of odds and ends without looking them through. I should like to come back, after a year or two, and find that the collection had sorted itself and refined itself and coalesced, as such deposits so mysteriously do, into a mould, transparent enough to reflect the light of our life, and yet steady, tranquil compounds with the alofness of a work of art.

. . . .

As for my next book, I am going to hold myself from writing till I have it impending in me: grown heavy in my mind like a ripe pear; pendant, gravid, asking to be cut or it will fall.

Indeed I am up against some difficultues. Fame to begin with. Orlando has done very well. Now I could go on writing like that – the tug and suck are at me to do it. People say this was so spontaneous, so natural. And I would like to keep those qualities if I could without losing the others. But those qualities were largely the result of ignoring the others. They came of writing exteriorly; and if I dig, must I not lose them? And what is my own position towards the inner and the outer? I think a kind of ease and dash are good; – yes: I think even externality is good; some combination of them ought to be possible. The idea has come to me that what I want now to do is to saturate every atom. I mean to eliminate all waste, deadness, superfluity: to give the moment whole; whatever it includes. Say that the moment is a combination of thought; sensation; the voice of the sea. Waste, deadness, come from the inclusion of things that don't belong to the moment; this appalling narrative business of the realist: getting on from lunch to dinner: it is false, unreal, merely conventional. Why admit anything to literature that is not poetry – by which I mean saturated? Is that not my grudge against novelists? that they select nothing? The poets succeeding by simplifying: practically everything is left out. I want to put practically everything in: yet to saturate.

VIRGINIA WOOLF: *A Writer's Diary*

THE CANON FOR THREE VOICES

Yesterday, when I was in a carriage on the road to Vienna, I was overcome by sleep . . . And while I dozed, I dreamed that I was going for a long journey, to nowhere less than Syria and India, and then was coming back, to Arabia, no less, and finally to Jerusalem. The Holy City made me think of the Holy Book, and so it is not surprising that Tobit came into my mind and also our Tobiasserl and Pertobiasser. So during my journey in my dream I was inspired to write the following Canon (a Canon follows, to the words "Oh Tobia Dominus Haslinger"). But as soon as I woke up, the Canon had fled, and nothing would come back again into my head. But when the day after I came back here with the same vehicle (which belonged to a poor Austrian musician) I went on, while awake, with the journey of my dream, and lo, by an association of ideas, the same Canon came back to my mind. Since I was awake, I grasped it tightly, as Menelaus did to Proteus, and only allowed him to transform himself into a Canon for three voices. Farewell!

LUDWIG VAN BEETHOVEN: *Letter to Tobias Haslinger*

STUDIES FOR THE LAST SUPPER

Verily I say unto you that one of you shall betray me.

One who was drinking has left the glass in its position and turned his head towards the speaker. Another, twisting the fingers of his hands together, turns with stern brows to his companion. Another, with hands spread open and showing the palms, shrugs his shoulders up to his ears, and makes a mouth of astonishment. Another speaks into his neighbour's ear, and he who listens to him turns towards him and lends an ear, holding a knife in one hand, and in the other the bread half cut through by the knife. Another in turning, holding a knife in his hand, upsets with his hand a glass over the table. Another lays his hand on the table and is looking. Another breathes hard from full mouth. Another leans forward to see the speaker, shading his eyes with his hand. Another draws back behind the one who leans forward, and sees the speaker between the wall and the man who is leaning.

From one of LEONARDO DA VINCI'S Notebooks
Transl. by Edward McCurdy

I am painting now with the rapture of a Marseillais eating bouillabaisse, which will not surprise you when you hear that the subject is big sunflowers.

. . . .

I really do not know how I paint. Armed with a white panel I take up a position in front of the spot that interests me, contemplate what lies before me and say to myself: "That white panel must be turned into something." Dissatisfied with my work I return home, put my panel out of sight, and after taking a little rest, go back to my work, almost with qualms to see what it looks like . . . I know that Nature told me something, that she spoke to me, and that I took down her message in shorthand. Perhaps my stenographic transcript contains words that are indecipherable; belike there are faults and omissions in it too; still it may possess something that the wood, the beach or the figures said. . . .

The symbol of St. Luke, the patron saint of painters, is as you know an ox. Thus one must be as patient as an ox if one would wish to cultivate the world of art. But how lucky oxen are to have nothing to do with this confounded business of painting! . . .

When one thinks how far one has to go and how much one must slave in order to paint an ordinary peasant and his cot, I almost believe that this journey is longer and more fatiguing than that which many painters undertake for their outlandish subjects . . . Fancy living the daily life of peasants in their cots and in the country, enduring the heat of summer and the snow and frost of winter – not indoors but out in the fields, and not for a leisurely walk – no! but for daily work like the peasants themselves.

. . . .

Apparently nothing is more simple than to paint a rag-picker, a beggar or any other kind of workman; but there are no subjects which are so difficult to paint as these everyday figures. I do not think there is a single academy where one can learn to draw or paint a man digging or sowing seed, a woman hanging a pot over the fire or doing needlework.

. . . .

I want to paint humanity, humanity and again humanity. I love nothing better than this series of bipeds, from the smallest baby in long clothes to Socrates, from the woman with black hair and a white skin to the one with golden hair and a brick-red sun-burnt face.

VINCENT VAN GOGH

I felt an extreme pleasure this morning, in seeing again a little picture of mine. There was nothing in it, but it was charming and seemed as if it had been painted by a bird.

COROT

MUSEÉ DES BEAUX ARTS

About suffering they were never wrong,
The Old Masters: how well they understood
Its human position; how it takes place
While someone else is eating or opening a window or just walking
dully along;
How, when the aged are reverently, passionately waiting
For the miraculous birth, there always must be
Children who did not specially want it to happen, skating
On a pond at the edge of the wood:
They never forgot
That even the dreadful martyrdom must run its course
Anyhow in a corner, some untidy spot
Where the dogs go on with their doggy life and the torturer's horse
Scratches its innocent behind on a tree.

In Brueghel's *Icarus*, for instance: how everything turns away
Quite leisurely from the disaster; the ploughman may
Have heard the splash, the forsaken cry,
But for him it was not an important failure; the sun shone
As it had to on the white legs disappearing into the green
Water; and the expensive delicate ship that must have seen
Something amazing, a boy falling out of the sky,
Had somewhere to get to and sailed calmly on.

W. H. AUDEN

THE FIRST STEP

The young poet Eumenes
complained one day to Theocritus:
"I have been writing for two years now
and I have done only one idyll.
It is my only finished work.
Alas, it is steep, I see it,
the stairway of Poetry is so steep;
and from the first step where now I stand,
poor me, I shall never ascend."
"These words," Theocritus said,
"are unbecoming and blasphemous.
And if you are on the first step,
you ought to be proud and pleased.
Coming as far as this is not little;
what you have achieved is great glory.
For even this first step
is far distant from the common herd.
To set your foot upon this step
you must rightfully be a citizen
of the city of ideas.
And in that city it is hard
and rare to be naturalized.
In her market place you find Lawmakers
whom no adventurer can dupe.
Coming as far as this is not little;
what you have achieved is great glory."

C. P. CAVAFY. Transl. by Rae Dalven

'I MADE MY SONG A COAT'

I made my song a coat
Covered with embroideries
Out of old mythologies
From heel to throat;
But the fools caught it,
Wore it in the world's eyes
As though they'd wrought it.
Song, let them take it
For there's more enterprise
In walking naked.

W. B. YEATS

. . . .

All I want is to speak simply; for this grace I pray.
For we have loaded even the song with so many kinds of music
That gradually it sinks.
And our art we so decorated that beneath the gilt
Its face is eaten away.
And it is now time for us to say the few words we have to say
Because tomorrow our soul sets sail.

GEORGE SEFERIS: *Three Secret Poems.*
Transl. by Rex Warner

Why not let your work be such that after death you become an image of immortality: as in life you become when sleeping like unto the hapless dead.

LEONARDO DA VINCI: *Codice Atlantico*, 76.

THE ART OF LIVING

Le grand et glorieux chef d'oeuvre de l'homme,
c'est vivre à propos.

MONTAIGNE: *De l'expérience*

THE ART OF LIVING

Introductory Note

THIS section really has two themes: the art of *living well*, which was what Montaigne meant when he said "My art and profession is to live", and that of enjoying oneself – which indeed is closely allied to the first, since it is not possible to feel pleasure for long without peace of mind. This state, however, is achieved by different men in very different ways: Pascal felt that to be "*en plein repos*" would drive a man mad, while Ser Lapo Mazzei, the fourteenth century notary of Prato, asked for nothing better than to be lulled to sleep by bag-pipes on his own threshing-floor, his enjoyment enhanced by the knowledge that his friend, the merchant, was toiling over his ledgers. Machiavelli liked to vary the "rustic pleasures" he had enjoyed during the day by drawing on, when he came home in the evening to his little villa at San Casciano, his lawyer's robes, and thus attired, to open his books and "enter the ancient courts of great men of the past", forgetful of anxiety, poverty and death, while Gainsborough, having become "sick of Portraits", would have liked "to take my viol da gamba and walk off to some sweet village where I can paint Landskips and enjoy the fag end of life in quietness and ease."

Here, too, I have been overwhelmed by an *embarras de richesses*. There are so many pleasant ways of enjoying oneself! – from the exquisite refinements of court life in Japan in the thirteenth century, as told in *The Pillow-Book of Sei Shonagon*, to the mild pleasures of a walk in the Tuileries with a cousin on a winter's day, as described by Gérard de Nerval. And then there are the pleasures of hospitality and of conversa-iton. Dr. Johnson, gilding the pill of existence by offering "three good meals and his company" to his poorer friends at every weekend, and treating them with "ceremonious civility", is one of the most agreeable instances. And I like, too, both his and Hazlitt's determination to avoid what would now be called highbrow conversation – Hazlitt firmly talking about the weather, and Dr. Johnson "removing his attention" when anyone spoke to him about the Punic wars, and "thinking of Tom Thumb".

The pleasures of food and drink have been celebrated so widely and so well that it was difficult to make a choice, but I have myself a par-ticular liking for Gainsborough's praise of John Henderson eating "pig and plumb sauce", and for Keats's taste for claret and "the breast of a

Partridge". And I like, too, the glimpse of Ronsard wandering in the fields to pick herbs for his salad, and then rolling up his sleeves to wash, salt and mix it.

Innumerable passages could, of course, also be devoted to various forms of appreciations of beauty. One which I have included here concerns the complex personality of the famous art-critic of our own time, Bernard Berenson, who transformed his rustic villa near Settignano, I Tatti, into as exquisite a quintessence of Tuscan art, architecture and landscape-gardening as only a non-Tuscan could have conceived, and who in his eighty-eighth year discovered, after his long pilgrimage of expertise and travel, that all the beauty he wanted could be found at his own door. Beside him I have placed the famous letter in which Colette's mother, at almost an equal age, gives up every other pleasure to wait for the flowering of her pink cactus – and, for contrast, Virginia Woolf's description of her own search for something that is not *only* beauty – "something one can lay one's hands on, and say, That is it!" And then there is T. E. Lawrence's escape into the world of books and Cyril Connolly's day-dream – which brings us back to Montaigne once again. Montaigne is never dazzled by that great illusion, unclouded happiness. Even when he is safely segregated in his tower among his books, he knows that this is "a pleasure not absolutely pure and neat, no more than all others." What he is seeking is one thing only: to be fully and consistently himself.

What egregious fools are we! "He hath passed his life in idleness," say we; "Alas I have done nothing this day." What; Have you not lived? It is not only the fundamental but the noblest of your occupation(s)."

. . . .

Have you known how to compose your manners? You have done more than he who hath composed books. Have you known how to take rest? You have done more than he who hath taken empires and cities. The glorious masterpiece of man is to live to the repulse.

. . . .

There is nothing so goodly, so fair, and so lawful, as to play the man well and duly; nor science so hard and difficult as to know how to live this life well. And of all the infirmities we have, the most savage is to despise our being.

. . . .

It is an absolute perfection, and as it were divine, for a man to know how to enjoy his being loyally. We seek for other conditions because we understand not the use of ours, and go out of ourselves forsomuch as we know not what abiding there is. We may long enough get upon stilts, for be we upon them, yet must we go with our own legs; and sit we upon the highest throne of the world, yet sit we upon our own tail.

MONTAIGNE: *Of Experience.* Transl. by John Florio

SONNET

O qu'heureux est celuy qui peult passer son aage
Entre pareils à soy! et qui sans fiction,
Sans crainte, sans envie, et sans ambition,
Regne paisiblement en son pauvre mesnage!

Le miserable soing d'acquérir d'avantage
Ne tyrannise point sa libre affection,
Et son plus grand désir, désir sans passion,
Ne s'estend plus avant que son propre héritage.

Il ne s'empesche point des affaires d'autry,
Son principal espoir ne dépend que de luy,
Il est sa cour, son roy, sa faveur, et son maistre.

Il ne mange son bien en païs estranger,
Il ne met pour autry sa personne en danger,
Et plus riche qu'il est ne voudroit jamais estre.

JOACHIM DU BELLAY

COSIMO DE' MEDICI AND THE AMBASSADORS FROM LUCCA

The audience was held in his own house, according to custom, and during discussions a small child, his grandson, came up to him with some oatsticks and a little knife for Cosimo to make him a whistle. Cosimo signified that the discussion was adjourned, devoted himself to the child and made the whistle, telling him then to run away and play. The ambassadors were somewhat offended. "Sir Cosimo, we are surprised at your behaviour. We have come to you on behalf of our Commune to treat of grave matters and you desert us for a child." With a laugh Cosimo flung his arms round their shoulders. "My brothers and lords, are you not fathers too? Don't you love your children and grandchildren? You are surprised that I should have made that whistle; it's as well that you didn't ask me to play it. Because I would have done that too."

L. CARBONE: *Facezie*, ed. Albdelkader (Livorno 1900).

'TO RUN UPON A HOBBY-HORSE'

. . . .

Nor anything more remarkable in Socrates, than when, being old and crazed, he would spare so much time as to be instructed in the art of dancing and playing upon instruments, and thought the time well bestowed; who notwithstanding hath been seen to continue a whole day and night in an ecstasy or trance, yea, even standing on his feet in presence of all the Greek army, as it were surprised and ravished by some deep and mind-distracting thought. . . . He hath continually been noted to march to the wars on foot, to break the ice with his bare feet, to wear one same garment in summer and winter, to exceed all his companions in patience of any labor or travail, to eat no more or otherwise at any banquet than at his ordinary. He hath been seen seven and twenty years together with one same undismayed countenance patiently to bear and endure hunger, poverty, the indocility and stubborness of his children, the forwardness and scratchings of his wife; and in the end, malicious detraction, tyranny, imprisonment, shackles and poison. . . . And yet he refused not nor disdained to play for nuts with children, nor to run with them upon a hobby-horse.

. . . .

MONTAIGNE: *Of Experience*. Transl. by John Florio

Tiribaldo de' Rossi, goldsmith, set down in his *Ricordanze* that one morning, as he was going to do the day's shopping, he saw that the foundations of the palace of Filippo Strozzi were being dug. And at once he sent someone home to bring his two boys to him, and his wife put on their Sunday clothes. "I brought them," he wrote, "to the foundations and lifted up Guarniero so that he could look down and told Damasco, who had a bunch of small roses in his hands, to throw them in. I said, 'Will you remember this?' And he said he would... May it be so, in God's name!"

Ricordanze of TIRIBALDO DE' ROSSI

THE NOTARY ON HIS FARM

Monna Margherita, I have come to the country to see to some work of Monna Bartola's [his mother]

. . . .

I am barefoot in the gay and sparkling air, and the sound of bagpipes lulls me to sleep, while the clean threshing-floor makes me feel inclined to jump and tumble like a juggler from Slavonia on the fat mounds of wheat which my empty granaries are awaiting. Here we have no cicadas nor horse-flies, nor tarantulas, which make me feel melancholy when I am at Il Palco. I am alone, and am not woken up nor called to the door by anyone. I hear that Francesco is toiling away, and I am enjoying myself.

SER LAPO MAZZEI*: *Letter to Margherita Datini* 1411

'UP AT THE VILLA'

. . . .

I am in my house in the country

. . . .

I rise every morning with the sun, and make my way to a wood which I am having cut down, where I stay for a couple of hours to inspect the

*Ser Lapo Mazzei was a close friend of the merchant of Prato, Francesco Datini, to whose wife this letter was addressed. He had a peevish, ailing wife and many children, a masterful mother and many cares, but sometimes, escaping from them all, he would ride up on his old nag to his little farm in the hills, and there, remembering the days when he himself had been a shepherd-boy, would prune his vines, and, taking off his toga and his shoes, would spend a few hours in happy idleness.

work of the preceding day and to pass the time with the woodcutters, who always have some trouble brewing, whether among themselves or their neighbours

. . . .

Having left the wood, I make my way to a spring, and thence to a fowling-hut of mine, taking with me a book, either Dante or Petrarch or one of the minor poets such as Tibullus, Ovid and their like. I read about their amorous passions and loves and remember my own; and find delight for a while in these thoughts. Then I turn up the road, to the inn, and talk to the passers-by, asking them for news of their homes; I learn many things, and observe the various tastes and fancies of mankind. Meanwhile the dinner hour has come, at which my company and I eat the food which my poor farm and meagre fortune provide. Having eaten, I go back to the inn, where the host generally is, and a butcher, a miller and two workmen from the kiln. With them I become a lazy lout all day, playing cards or backgammon, during which a thousand arguments arise and an exchange of insulting words; most often we are fighting over a farthing, and our shouts are heard as far as San Casciano.

. . . .

When evening comes, I go home again and enter my study, and on entering I cast off my every-day clothing, full of mud and clay, and put on a courtier's or a lawyer's gown; and thus decently clad, I enter the ancient courts of great men of the past, where, lovingly welcomed by them, I draw my sustenance from the food which is mine alone, and for which I was born. There I am not ashamed to speak with them and to ask them the reasons for their actions, and they, out of their courtesy, reply to me; and for four hours I know no tedium, remember no anxiety, fear no poverty, am not dismayed by death: I am wholly caught up in them. And since Dante says that there is no knowledge unless one holds fast to what one has understood, I have set down the essence of what I have drawn from their conversation, and have composed a little book*, *De principatibus.*

. . . .

NICCOLÒ MACHIAVELLI: *Letter to Francesco Vettori*,
from his country house in S. Andrea in Percussina,
December 10, 1513.

*The "little book" which Machiavelli set down in those evenings was *The Prince.*

. . . .

At home I betake me somewhat the oftener to my library, whence all at once I command and survey my household. It is seated in the chief entry of my house, thence I behold under me the garden, my base court, my yard, and look even into most rooms of my house. There, without order, without method, and by piecemeals I turn over and ransack now one book and now another. Sometimes I muse and rave; and walking up and down I indite and enregister these my humours, these my conceits.

It is placed on the third story of a tower. The lower-most is my chapel, the second a chamber with other lodgings, where I often lie, because I would be alone. Above it is a great wardrobe . . . Next unto it is a handsome neat cabinet, ample and large enough to receive fire in winter and very pleasantly windowed . . . The form of it is round and hath no flat side, but what serveth for my table and my chair; in which bending or circling manner, at one look it offereth me the full sight of all my books set around upon shelves or desks, five ranks upon one another. It hath three bay windows of a far-extending, rich and unresisted prospect and is one diameter sixteen paces void . . . There is my seat, there is my throne.

. . . .

Books have and contain divers pleasing qualities to those that can duly choose them. But no good without pains; no roses without prickles. It is a pleasure not absolutely pure and neat, no more than all others.

MONTAIGNE: *Of Three Commerces or Societies.*
Transl. by JOHN FLORIO

DR. JOHNSON ON HOSPITALITY

On Drink:

Mrs. Williams: "I wonder what pleasure men can take in making beasts of themselves."

Dr. Johnson: "*I* wonder, Madam, that you have not penetration enough to see the strong inducement of this excess; for he who makes a beast of himself gets rid of the pain of being a man."

On dining together:

Boswell: "Why, then, meet at table?"

Dr. Johnson: "Why, to eat and drink together, to *promote kindness.*"

Dr. Johnson's Saturday and Sunday Dinners

He [Dr. Johnson] loved the poor as I never yet saw any one else do, with an earnest desire to make them happy. – What signifies, says some one, giving halfpence to common beggars? they only lay it out in gin and tobacco. "And why should they be denied such sweeteners of their existence? (says Johnson). It is surely very savage to refuse them every possible avenue to pleasure, reckoned too coarse for our own acceptance. Life is a pill which none of us can bear to swallow without gilding; yet for the poor we delight in stripping it still barer, and are not ashamed to shew even visible displeasure, if ever the bitter taste is taken from their mouths." In consequence of these principles he nursed whole nests of people in his house, where the lame, the blind, the sick, and the sorrowful found a sure retreat from all the evils whence his little income could secure them: and commonly spending the middle of the week at our house, he kept his numerous family in Fleet-street upon a settled allowance; but returned to them every Saturday, to give them three good dinners, and his company, before he came back to us on the Monday night – treating them with the same, or perhaps more ceremonious civility, than he would have done by as many people of fashion.

HESTER LYNCH PIOZZI:
Anecdotes of the late Samuel Johnson, LL. DD.

TWO OPINIONS ABOUT CONVERSATION

The Punic Wars became a stock symbol to him [Dr. Johnson] of talk "that carried one away from common life" without extending "ideas".

He never desired to hear of the *Punic war* while he lived: such conversation was lost time (he said) . . . I [Mrs Thrale] asked him once concerning the conversational powers of a gentleman. . . . "He talked to me at the club one day . . . concerning Cataline's conspiracy – so I withdrew my attention and thought about Thom Thumb."

HESTER LYNCH PIOZZI:
Anecdotes of the late Samuel Johnson, LL. DD.

It is recorded in the life of some worthy (whose name I forget) that he was one of those "who loved hospitality and respect"; and I profess to belong to the same classification of mankind. Civility is with me a jewel. I like a little comfortable cheer, and careless, indolent chat. I hate to be always wise, or aiming at wisdom. I have enough to do with literary cabals, questions, critics, actors, essay-writing, without taking them out with me for recreation, and into all companies. I wish at these times to pass for a good-humoured fellow; and good-will is all I ask in return to make good company . . . I must occasionally lie fallow. The kind of conversation that I affect most is what sort of a day it is, and whether it is likely to rain or hold up fine for tomorrow. This I consider as enjoying the *otium cum dignitate*, as the end and privilege of a life of study . . . Would I indulge this feeling? In vain. They ask me what news there is, and stare if I say I don't know. If a new actress has come out, why must I have seen her? If a new novel has appeared, why must I have read it? . . . It was continually thrown in my teeth that I was *an author*.

William Hazlitt: *On the Disadvantages of Intellectual Superiority*

PIG AND PLUMB SAUCE

Do but recollect how many hard-featured fellows there are in the world that frown in the midst of enjoyment, chew with unthankfulness, and seem to swallow with pain instead of pleasure; now anyone who sees you eat pig and plumb sauce, immediately *feels that pleasure* which a plump morsel, smoothly gliding through a narrow glib passage into the regions of bliss and moistened with the dew of imagination, naturally creates.

Thomas Gainsborough: *Letter to John Henderson*, July 18, 1773

LA SALADE

Lave ta main, qu'elle soit belle et nette,
Resveille toy, apporte une serviette;
Une salade amasson, et faison
Part à nos ans des fruicts de la saison.

D'un vague pied, d'une veuë escartée
Deçà, delà en cent lieux rejettée
Sus une rive, et dessus un fossé,
Dessus un champ en paresse laissé
Du laboureur, qui de luy-mesme apporte
Sans cultiver herbes de toute sorte,
Je m'en iray solitaire à l'escart.
Tu t'en iras, Jamyn, d'une autre part
Chercher songneux la boursette toffue,
La pasquerette a la feuille menue
La pimprenelle heureuse pour le sang
Et pour la ratte, et pour le mal de flanc;
Je cueilleray, compagne de la mousse,
La responsette à la racine douce,
Et le bouton des nouveaux groiseliers
Qui le Printemps annoncent les premiers.

Puis, en lisant l'ingenieux Ovide
En ces beaux vers où d'amour il est guide,
Regagnerons le logis pas-à-pas.

Là, recoursant jusqu'au coude nos bras,
Nous laverons nos herbes à main pleine
Au cours sacré de ma belle fontaine:
La blanchirons de sel en mainte part,
L'arrouserons de vinaigre rosart,
L'engresserons de l'huile de Provence:
L'huile qui vient aux Oliviers de France
Rompt l'estomac, et ne vaut du tout rien.
Voylà, Jamyn, voylà mon souv'rain bien.
. . . .

PIERRE DE RONSARD

CLARET, PARTRIDGE AND WHITE CURRANTS

Now I like Claret whenever I can have Claret I must drink it – t'is the only palate affair that I am at all sensual in. Would it not be a good Speck to send you some vine roots – could i(t) be done? I'll enquire – If you could make some wine like Claret to drink on Summer evenings in an arbour! For really 'tis so fine – it fills the mouth one's mouth with a gushing freshness – then goes down cool and feverless – then you do not feel it quar(r)elling with your liver – no it is rather a Peace maker and lies as quiet as it did in the grape – then it is as fragrant as the Queen Bee; and the more ethereal part of it mounts into the brain . . . [and] walks like Aladin about his own enchanted palace so gently that you do not feel his step.

. . . .

I said this same Claret is the only palate-passion I have I forgot game – I must plead guilty to the breast of a Partridge, the back of a hare, the backbone of a grouse, the wing and side of a Pheasant and a Woodcock *passim*.

JOHN KEATS: *Letter to George and Georgina Keats*,
Sunday 14 Feb.–Monday 3 May 1819

I should like now to promenade round you(r) Gardens – apple tasting – pear-tasting – plumb judging – apricot-nibbling – peach-scrunching – Nectarine-sucking and Melon carving. I have also a great feeling for antiquated cherries full of sugar cracks – and a white currant tree kept for company. I admire lolling on a lawn by a water-lillied pond to eat white currants and see gold fish: and go to the Fair in the Evening if I'm good.

JOHN KEATS: *Letter to his sister Fanny*,
August 28 (1819)

It is Noon on a Summer Day

It is noon on a summer day and the weather is so hot that one does not know what to do with oneself. One keeps waving one's fan, but there is not a breath of cool air; then, just as one is hurrying to put one's hands in a bowl of iced water, a letter arrives. It is written on a sheet of fine, brilliantly red paper and attached to a Chinese pink in full bloom. Without thinking, one lays aside one's fan (which was not doing much good in any case) and imagines how deeply one's friend must feel to have taken all this trouble on such a suffocating day.

It is Delightful when there has been a Thin Fall of Snow

It is delightful when there has been a thin fall of snow; or again when it has piled up very high and in the evening we sit round a brazier at the edge of the verandah with a few congenial friends, chatting till darkness falls. There is no need for the lamp, since the snow itself reflects a clear light. Raking the ashes in the brazier with a pair of fire-tongs, we discuss all sorts of moving and amusing things.

It already seems to be quite late at night when we hear the sound of footsteps. We all look up, wondering who it may be. A man is approaching – the type of man that often visits us unannounced on such occasions. "I was wondering how you ladies were enjoying today's snow", he says. "I had intended to come and see you earlier, but I was held up all day some other place."

"Ah!" says one of us and quotes the poem about "the man who came today." Then, with a great deal of laughter, we begin talking about what has happened since the morning and about all sorts of other things. The visitor has been offered a round cushion, but he prefers to sit on the wooden verandah with one leg hanging over the edge.

The conversation goes on until the bell announces that dawn has come. The ladies sitting behind the blinds, and the man in front feel that they still have many things to tell each other; but he has to be off before daylight. As he gets ready to leave, he charmingly recites, "Snow lay upon such-and-such hills". Then he is gone. If he had not been there, we should certainly not have stayed up all night like this; it was he who made the occasion so delightful and now we start discussing what an elegant man he is.

During the Hot Months

During the hot months it is a great delight to sit on the veranda, enjoying the cool of the evening and observing how the outlines of objects gradually become blurred. At such a moment I particularly enjoy the sight of a gentleman's carriage, preceeded by outriders clearing the way. Sometimes a couple of commoners will pass in a carriage with the rear blinds slightly raised. As the oxen trot along, one has a pleasant sense of freshness. It is still more delightful when the sound of a lute or flute comes from inside the carriage, and one feels sorry when it disappears in the distance. Occasionally one catches a whiff of the oxen's leather cruppers; it is a strange, unfamiliar smell, but, absurd as it may seem, I find something rather pleasant about it.

On a very dark night it is delightful when the aroma of smoke from the pine-torches at the head of a procession is wafted through the air and pervades the carriage in which one is travelling.

From *The Pillow Book of Sei Shonagon.*
Transl. by Ivan Morris

LA COUSINE

L'hiver a ses plaisirs; et souvent, le dimanche,
Quand un peu de soleil jaunit la terre blanche,
Avec une cousine on sort se promener . . .
– Et ne vous faites pas attendre pour dîner,

Dit la mère. Et quand on a bien, aux Tuileries,
Vu sous les arbres noirs les toilettes fleuries,
La jeune fille a froid . . . et vous fait observer
Que le brouillard du soir commence à se lever.

Et l'on revient, parlant du beau jour qu'on regrette,
Qui s'est passé si vite . . . et de flamme discrète:
Et l'on sent en rentrant, avec grand appétit,
Du bas de l'escalier, – le dindon qui rôtit.

Gérard de Nerval (1808–1855)

LE RELAIS

En voyage, on s'arrête, on descend de voiture;
Puis entre deux maisons on passe à l'aventure,
Des chevaux, de la route et des fouets étourdi,
L'oeil fatigué de voir et le corps engourdi.

Et voici tout à coup, silencieuse et verte,
Une vallée humide et de lilas couverte,
Un ruisseau qui murmure entre les peupliers, –
Et la route et le bruit sont bien vite oubliés!

On se couche dans l'herbe et l'on s'écoute vivre,
De l'odeur du foin vert à loisir on s'enivre,
Et sans penser à rien on regarde les cieux . . .
Hélas! une voix crie: "En voiture, messieurs!"

GÉRARD DE NERVAL

. . . .

I had an idea that a Man might pass a very pleasant life in this manner – let him on a certain day read a certain Page of full Poesy or distilled Prose, and let him wander with it, and muse upon it, and reflect upon it, and bring home to it, and prophesy upon it, and dream upon it, until it becomes stale – but when will it do so? Never. When Man has arrived at a certain ripeness in intellect any one grand and spiritual passage serves him as a starting-post towards all 'the two-and-thirty Palaces'. How happy is such a voyage of conception, what delicious diligent Indolence! A doze upon a sofa does not hinder it, and a nap upon Clover engenders ethereal finger-pointings – the prattle of a child gives it wings, and the converse of middle-age a strength to beat them – a strain of music conducts to 'an odd angle of the Isle' and when the leaves whisper it puts a girdle round the earth.

. . . .

Now it appears to me that almost any Man may like the spider spin from his own inwards his own airy Citadel – the points of leaves and twigs on which the spider begins her work are few, and she fills the air with a beautiful circuiting. Man should be content with as few points to tip with the fine Web of his Soul, and weave a tapestry empyrean full of symbols for his spiritual eye, of softness for his spiritual touch, of space for his wandering, of distinctness for his luxury. . . . Minds would leave each other in contrary directions, traverse each other in numberless points, and at last greet each other at the journey's end. An old Man and a child would talk together and the old Man be led on his path and the child left thinking.

JOHN KEATS: *Letter to Reynolds*, 19 Feb. 1818

I have taken walks above my house hundreds upon hundreds of times, yet, on no two occasions does the landscape look the same. The distances are milky or silvery or pearly or golden yet ever varied and I hail every shade of difference as if I had never seen its like. So with the trunks and stems of the trees I pass. Their winter coats of jade and malachite, the tawny, russet and gilt bronze foliage are never the same. Little escapes my eye, but I can communicate scarcely any of it with the few and clumsy epithets at my disposal. If only I were like Adam who named the animals, roaming, creeping, flying, swimming over the earth, in the water or in the air; or like Solomon who could name all the flowers in the field!

. . . .

Colour is something that has been revealed to me, has grown upon me with the years. I was not born with a feeling for it, and in Boston sixty-five years ago there was little to generate and educate the sense of it. Of course I enjoyed it as the garment of the shapes I saw, but not sensually for its own sake. One summer morning tens of years later I wound my way up the staircase leading from the lower to the upper church of St. Francis at Assisi. I stepped suddenly into the nave and found myself wrapped in an atmosphere of disembodied colour. It did not belong to any shape. It was in the air, produced by reflections, from the stained glass, the frescoed walls and ceiling. I neither saw nor felt either. I was bathed in colour. I breathed it ... Since then I have got to enjoy colour as much as smell, almost as much as taste, and as sensuously.

. . . .

As I walk in the garden, I look at the flowers and shrubs and trees and discover in them an exquisiteness of contour, a vitality of edge or a vigour of spring as well as an infinite variety of colour than no artifact I have seen in the last sixty years can rival ... Each day, as I look, I wonder where my eyes were yesterday ... every morning ... as I go out of doors, I discover enough of newness to suffice for the day. I should still love real wandering—journeying where there are no inns, no railways and scarcely roads. I should love to re-visit all the scenery I have enjoyed in the last fifty years or more. But I don't hanker after it inordinately. I do not even have to look at pictures, for I have become my own painter . . . I require no sculpture, because my imagination has become so moulding that, having about me such models as the Tuscan peasantry, I can visualize them as statues in movement . . . The more I do a thing, the more I want to do it.

BERNARD BÉRENSON: *Sketch for a Self-Portrait*

THE PINK CACTUS

"Monsieur,

You have asked me to spend eight days or so in your house, that is with my daughter, whom I adore. You who live beside her, well know how seldom I see her, how much her presence enchants me, and I am touched that you should invite me to stay with her. Nevertheless I shall not accept your kind invitation – at least not now. This is why: my pink cactus is probably going to flower. It is a very rare plant which was given to me, and which, so I am told, only flowers in our climate once every four years. Now, I am already a very old woman; and if I went away while my cactus was going to flower, I am certain that I would not see it bloom again."

This note, signed, Sidonie Colette, *née* Landoy, was written by my mother to one of my husbands, the second. In the following year she died, at the age of seventy-seven.

During the hours in which I feel inferior to everything around me, threatened by my own mediocrity, afraid of discovering that a muscle has lost its vigour, a desire its intensity, or a grief the sharp edge of its blade, I can yet draw myself up and say: I am the daughter of the woman who wrote this letter – this and many others, which I have kept. This one, in ten lines, tells me that at seventy-six she was planning and taking journeys, but that the possible bloom, the expectation of a tropical flower, stopped everything else and reduced to silence even that heart born for love. . . . May I never forget that I am the daughter of such a woman, who hung trembling over the blades of a cactus, with all her wrinkles smoothed out, to seize the promise of a flower – a woman who herself never ceased to bloom, indefatigably, for three quarters of a century.

COLETTE: *La naissance du jour.*

. . . .

I enjoy epicurean ways of society; sipping and then shutting my eyes to taste. I enjoy almost everything. Yet I have some restless searcher in me. Why is there not a discovery in my life? Something one can lay hands on and say "This is it"? My depression is a harassed feeling. I'm looking: but that's not it – that's not it. What is it? And shall I die before I find it? Then (as I was walking through Russell Square last night) I see the mountains in the sky: the great clouds; and the moon which is risen over Persia; I have a great and astonishing sense of something there, which is "it". It is not exactly beauty that I mean. It is that the thing is in itself enough: satisfactory; achieved. A sense of my own strangeness, walking on the earth, is there too: of the infinite oddity of the human position; trotting along Russell Square with the moon up there and those mountain clouds. Who am I, what am I, and so on: these questions are always floating about in me: and then I bump against some exact fact – a letter, a person, and come to them again with a great sense of freshness. And so it goes on. But on this showing, which is true, I think I do fairly come upon this "it"; and then feel quite at rest.

VIRGINIA WOOLF: *A Writer's Diary*

'GETTING INTO A STRANGE COUNTRY'

You know, I think, the joy of getting into a strange country in a book; at home when I have shut my door and the town is in bed – and I know that nothing, not even the dawn, can disturb me in my curtains: only the slow crumbling of the coals in the fire: they get so red and throw such splendid glimmerings on the Hypnos and the brasswork. And it is lovely, too, after you have been wandering for hours in the forest with Percival or Sagramors le desirous, to open the door, and from over the Cherwell to look at the sun glowing through the valley-mists. Why does one not like things if there are other people about? Why cannot one make one's books live except in the night, after hours of straining? and you know they live to be your own books too, and you have to read them more than once. I think they take on something of your personality, and your environment also – you know a second-hand book sometimes is so much more flesh and blood than a new one – and it is almost terrible to think that your ideas, yourself in your books, may be giving life to generations of readers after you are forgotten . . . If you can get the right book at the right time you taste joys – not only bodily, physical, but spiritual also which pass on out above and beyond one's miserable self, as it were through a huge air, following the light of another man's thought. And you can never be quite the old self again. You have forgotten a little bit; or rather pushed it out with a little of the inspiration of what is immortal in someone who has gone before you.

T. E. LAWRENCE: *Letter to his mother*, 1910

'A DAY-DREAM'

A golden classical house, three stories high, with oeil-de-boeuf attic windows and a view over water. Outside a magnolia growing on the wall, a terrace for winter, a great tree for summer and a lawn for games; behind it a sheltered garden, indulgent to fig and nectarine, and in the corner a belvedere, book-lined like that of Montaigne, wizard of the Magic circle*, with this motto from him: "La liberté et l'oisiveté qui sont mes maîtresses qualités."

CYRIL CONNOLLY

'THINGS THAT GIVE A CLEAN FEELING'

An earthen cup. A new metal bowl.
A rush mat.
The play of the light on water as one pours into
a vessel.
A new wooden chest.

From *The Pillow Book of Sei Shonagon*
Transl. by IVAN MORRIS

*This "magic circle" enclosed most of the country between the Dordogne, the Lot and the Garonne.

LAND, SEA AND SKY

I was entertained like an Angel with the works in their splendour and glory.

THOMAS TRAHERNE

THE LOST WORLD OF ADONIS

. . . .

I lose the sunlight, lovely above all else;
Bright stars I loved the next, and the moon's face,
Ripe gourds, and fruit of apple-tree and pear.*

PRAXILLA. Transl. by T. F. Higham

INVERSNAID

. . . .

What would the world be, once bereft
Of wet and of wildness? Let them be left,
O let them be left, wildness and wet;
Long live the weeds and the wilderness yet.*

GERARD MANLEY HOPKINS

CICADA DAYS

When the cardoon flowers, and the loud cicada sings
perched on a tree, pouring from under his wings
a flood of shrillest music time and again:
when summer is ripe, and the heat a burden of pain,
then are the she-goats fattest, and wine is best,
and women most fain; but men are languidest,
for Sirius parches the heads and the knees of men
and burns their bodies with drouth. O give me then
the shade of a rock, with Biblis' wine set by,
and bread of the best, and the milk of goats drained dry!
Then be that heifer chosen to make my meat
that has not calved but feeds in the greenwood yet,
and firstling kids! Bright wine for my plenishment
I'd drink, in the shade, when food has brought content;
and there, as I sit, briskly the West should blow
meeting my brow; and from the unsullied flow
of some spring-water for ever running past
three cups to the gods I'd pour: of wine a last.

HESIOD: *Works and Days.*
Transl. by T. F. Higham

*These two quotations are as good an illustration as I know of the difference between the classical and the romantic visions of nature.

TO DEMETER AND THE SEASONS

To Demeter of the winnowing-fan and the Seasons whose feet are in the furrows Heronax lays here from a poor little plough-land their share of ears from the threshing-floor, and these mixed seeds of pulse on a slabbed table, the least of a little; for no great inheritance is this he has gotten him, here on the barren hill.

ZONAS. Transl. by J. W. Mackail

TO THE WEST WIND

Eudemus dedicates this shrine in the fields to Zephyrus, most bountiful of the winds, who came to aid him at his prayer, that he might right quickly winnow the grain from the ripe ears.

BACHYLIDES. Transl. by J. W. Mackail

THE OLD CORYCIAN'S ORCHARD

For I well remember
How once, under the high towers of Tarentum,
Where dark Galaesus moistens yellow cornfields,
I saw an old Corycian, who possessed
Some few acres of unclaimed land, a soil
Unfertile for the plough, for pasturage
Ill-suited, and unkindly to the vine.
Yet he, when among the bushes here and there
He had planted pot-herbs, and white lilies round them,
Vervain and slender poppy, would match in spirit
The wealth of kings, and coming home at night
Would load his table with an unbought feast.
He was the first in spring to pluck the rose,
Apples in autumn; and while gloomy winter
Was even yet splitting rocks with frost, and curbing
The running streams, there would he be already
Gathering flowers of delicate hyacinth,
Chiding the late spring and the tardy zephyrs.
Therefore he was the first to be enriched
With mother-bees and a big swarm; the first
From the squeezed comb to gather frothing honey.
Lime trees he had, and wild laurel in plenty;
And all the fruits wherewith each fertile tree

Had clothed itself in early flowering time,
So many in ripening autumn it still bore.
Moreover he had planted out in rows
Elm trees full-grown, and hard-wood pears, and thorns
Already bearing plums, and planes already
Ministering shade to thirsty wayfarers.

VIRGIL: *The Georgics*, Book IV. Transl. by R. C. Trevelyan

'L'ALBA VINCEVA L'ORA MATTUTINA'

L'alba vinceva l'ora mattutina
Che fuggía innanzi, sí che di lontano
Conobbi il tremolar della marina.

DANTE: *Purgatorio* I

The following is the version preferred by Maurice Baring:

The dawn was conquering the mists that flee
Before it, as the early shadows wane;
Afar I knew the trembling of the sea.

Transl. by MRS. RAMSAY

'ALL IN ORDER SWEET AND LOVELY'

First, e'er the morning breaks, joy opens in the flowery bosoms,
Joy even to tears, which the Sun rising dries; first the Wild Thyme
And Meadow-sweet, downy and soft, waving among the reeds,
Light springing on the air, lead the sweet Dance: they wake
The Honeysuckle sleeping on the Oak; the flaunting beauty
Revels along upon the wind; the White-thorn, lovely May
Opens her many lovely eyes; listening the Rose still sleeps;
None dare to wake her; soon she bursts her crimson curtain'd bed,
And comes forth in the majesty of beauty; every Flower,
The Pink, the Jessamine, the Wall-flower, the Carnation,
The Jonquil, the mild Lilly, opens her heavens; every Tree
And Flower and Herb soon fill the air with an innumerable Dance,
Yet all in order sweet and lovely

. . . .

WILLIAM BLAKE: *Milton*, Book the Second

ÉLOGE DE LA TERRE

Je te salue, ô terre, ô terre porte-grains
Porte-or, porte-santé, porte-habits, porte-humains,
Porte-fruits, porte-tours, alme, belle, immobile,
Patiente, diverse, odorante, fertile,
Vêtue d'un manteau tout damassé de fleurs,
Passementé de flots, bigarré de couleurs.
Je te salue, ô coeur, racine, base ronde,
Pied du grand animal qu'on appelle le Monde.

GUILLAUME DE SALUSTE DU BARTAS

PIED BEAUTY

Glory be to God for dappled things –
  For skies of couple-colour as a brinded cow;
    For rose-moles all in stipple upon trout that swim;
Fresh-firecoal chestnut-falls; finches' wings;
  Landscape plotted and pieced-fold, fallow, and
      plough;
    And áll trádes, their gear and tackle and trim.

All things counter, original, spare, strange;
  Whatever is fickle, freckled (who knows how?)
    With swift, slow; sweet, sour; adazzle, dim;
He fathers-forth whose beauty is past change:
          Praise him.

GERARD MANLEY HOPKINS

OF GARDENS

And because the breath of flowers is far sweeter in the air (where it comes and goes, like the warbling of music) than in the hand, therefore nothing is more fit for that delight, than to know what be the flowers and plants that do best perfume the air. Roses, damask and red, are fast flowers of their smells; so that you may walk by a whole row of them, and find nothing of their sweetness; yea, though it be in a morning's dew. Bays, likewise, yield no smell as they grow; rosemary little, nor sweet marjoram; that which, above all others, yields the sweetest smell in the air is the violet, specially the white double violet, which comes twice a year, about the middle of April, and about Bartholomew-tide. Next to that is the musk-rose; then the strawberry leaves dying with a most excellent cordial smell; then the flowers of the vines – it is a little dust, like the dust of a bent, which grown upon the cluster in the first coming forth. Then sweet briar; then wallflowers, which are very delightful to set under a parlour or lower chamber window; then pinks and gilliflowers, specially the matted pink, and clove gilliflower; then the flowers of the lime tree; then the honeysuckles, so they be somewhat afar off. Of bean flowers I speak not, because they are field flowers; but those which perfume the air most delightfully, not passed by as the rest, but being trodden upon and crushed are three-that is burnet, wild thyme, and water mints; therefore you are to set whole alleys of them, to have the pleasure, when you walk or tread.

FRANCIS BACON: *Of Gardens*

ECHO'S SONG

Slow, slow, fresh fount, keepe time with my salt teares;
Yet slower, yet; O faintly, gentle springs;
List to the heavy part the music beares;
Woe weepes out her division when shee sings.
Droupe hearbes and flowres;
Fall griefe in showres,
Our beauties are not ours;
O, I could still,
Like melting snow upon some craggie hill,
Drop, drop, drop, drop.
Since Nature's pride is now a wither'd daffodill.

BEN JONSON: From *Cynthias' Revels*

'THE UNTHRIFT SUN'

The unthrift sun shot vital gold,
  A thousand pieces,
And heaven it's azure did unfold
  Chequer'd with snowy fleeces.
The aire was all in spice,
  And every bush
A garland wore: thus fed my Eyes
  But all the Ear lay hush.

Only a little Fountain lent
  Some use for Eares
And on the dumbe shades language spent
  The Musick of her teares.

. . . .

Henry Vaughan

THE GARDEN

. . . .

What wondrous life in this I lead!
Ripe apples drop about my head;
The luscious clusters of the vine
Upon my mouth do crush their wine;
The nectarine and curious peach
Into my hands themselves do reach;
Stumbling on melons, as I pass,
Ensnared with flowers, I fall on grass.

Meanwhile the mind from pleasure less
Withdraws into its happiness;
The mind, that ocean where each kind
Does straight its own resemblance find;
Yet it creates, transcending these,
Far other worlds, and other seas;
Annihilating all that's made
To a green thought in a green shade....

. . . .

Andrew Marvell

'SABRINA FAIR...'

Sabrina fair
  Listen where thou art sitting
Under the glassie, cool, translucent wave,
  In twisted braids of Lillies knitting
The loose train of thy amber-dropping hair,
  Listen for dear honour's sake,
  Goddess of the silver lake,
      Listen and save!

Listen and appear to us,
In name of great *Oceanus*,
By the earth-shaking *Neptune's* mace
And *Tethys* grave majestick pace,
By hoary *Nereus* wrincled look,
And the *Carpathian* wisards hook,
By scaly *Tritons* winding shell,
And old sooth-saying *Glaucus* spell,
By *Leucothea's* lovely hands,
And her son that rules the strands,
By *Thetis* tinsel-slipper'd feet,
And the Songs of *Sirens* sweet,
By dead *Parthenope's* dear tomb,
And fair *Ligea's* golden comb,
Wherwith she sits on diamond rocks
Sleeking her soft alluring locks
By all the *Nymphs* that nightly dance
Upon thy streams with wily glance,
Rise, rise, and heave thy rosie head
From thy coral-pav'n bed,
And bridle in thy headlong wave,
Till thou our summons answered have.
      Listen and save!

JOHN MILTON

ULYSSES AND THE SYREN

Syren

Come worthy Greeke *Vlysses* come,
Possesse these shores with me,
The Windes and Seas are troublesome,
And here we may be free.
  Here may we sit, and view their toyle
That trauaile in the deepe,
And ioy the day in mirth the while,
And spend the night in sleepe . . .

SAMUEL DANIEL

ODE TO THE MEDITERRANEAN

Of thee the Northman by his beachèd galley
Dreamt, as he watched the never-setting Ursa
And longed for summer and thy light, O sacred
        Mediterranean.

Unseen he loved thee; for the heart within him
Knew earth had gardens where he might be blessed,
Putting away long dreams and aimless, barbarous
        Hunger for battle.

The foretaste of thy languors thawed his bosom,
A great need drove him to thy caverned islands
From the gray, endless reaches of the outer
        Desert of ocean.

He saw thy pillars, saw thy sudden mountains
Wrinkled and stark, and in their crooked gorges,
'Neath peeping pine and cypress, guessed the torrent
        Smothered in flowers.

Thine incense to the sun, thy gathered vapours,
He saw suspended on the flanks of Taurus,
Or veiling the snowed bosom of the virgin
        Sister of Atlas.

He saw the luminous top of wide Olympus,
Fit for the happy gods; he saw the pilgrim
River, with rains of Ethiopia flooding
Populous Egypt.

And having seen, he loved thee. His racked spirit,
By thy breath tempered and the light that clothes thee,
Forgot the monstrous gods, and made of Nature
Mistress and mother.

The more should I, O fatal sea, before thee
Of alien words make echoes to thy music;
For I was born where first the rills of Tagus
Turn to the westward,

And, wandering long, alas! have need of drinking
Deep of the patience of thy perfect sadness,
O thou that constant through the change of ages,
Beautiful ever,

Never wast wholly young and void of sorrows,
Nor even canst be old, while yet the morning
Kindles thy ripples, or the golden evening
Dyes thee in purple.

Thee, willing to be tamed but still untamable,
The Roman called his own until he perished,
As now the busy English hover o'er thee,
Stalwart and noble;

But all is naught to thee, while no harsh winter
Congeals thy fountains, and the blown Sahara
Chokes not with dreadful sand thy deep and placid
Rock-guarded havens.

Thou carest not what men may tread thy margin;
Nor I, while from some heather-scented headland
I may behold thy beauty, the eternal
Solace of mortals.

GEORGE SANTAYANA

'DRINKING THE SUN OF CORINTH'

Drinking the sun of Corinth
Reading the marble ruins
Striding across the vineyards and seas
Sighting along the harpoon
A votive fish that slips away
I found the leaves that the psalm of the sun memorizes
The living land that desire opens joyously.

I drink water, cut fruit,
Thrust my hand into the wind's foliage
The lemon trees irrigate the pollen of summer
The green birds tear my dreams
I leave with a glance
A wide glance in which the world is recreated
Beautiful from the beginning to the dimensions of the heart!

ODYSSEUS ELYTIS. Transl. by Edmund Keeley and Philip Sherrard

THE MEDITERRANEAN

quem das finem, rex magne, dolorum?

Where we went in the boat was a long bay
A slingshot wide, walled in by towering stone –
Peaked margin of antiquity's delay,
And we went there out of time's monotone:

Where we went in the black hull no light moved
But a gull white-winged along the feckless wave,
The breeze, unseen but fierce as a body loved,
That boat drove onward like a willing slave:

Where we went in the small ship the seaweed
Parted and gave to us the murmuring shore
And we made feast and in our secret need
Devoured the very plates Aeneas bore:

Where derelict you see through the low twilight
The green coast that you, thunder-tossed, would win,
Drop sail, and hastening to drink all night
Eat dish and bowl to take that sweet land in!

Where we feasted and caroused on the sandless
Pebbles, affecting our day of piracy,
What prophesy of eaten plates could landless
Wanderers fulfil by the ancient sea?

We for that time might taste the famous age
Eternal here yet hidden from our eyes
When lust of power undid its stuffless rage;
They, in a wineskin, bore earth's paradise.

Let us lie down once more by the breathing side
Of Ocean, where our live forefathers sleep
As if the Known Sea still were a month wide –
Atlantis howls but is no longer steep!

What country shall we conquer, what fair land
Unman our conquest and locate our blood?
We've cracked the hemispheres with careless hand!
Now, from the Gates of Hercules we flood

Westward, westward till the barbarous brine
Whelms us to the tired world where tasseling corn,
Fat beans, grapes sweeter than muscadine
Rot on the vine: in that land were we born.

ALLEN TATE

Just a little more
And we shall see the almond trees in blossom
The marbles shining in the sun
The sea, the curling waves.

Just a little more
Let us rise just a little higher.

GEORGE SEFERIS. Transl. by Rex Warner

L'INFINITO

Sempre caro mi fu quest'ermo colle,
E questa siepe, che da tanta parte
Dell'ultimo orizzonte il guardo esclude.
Ma sedendo e mirando, interminati
Spazi di là da quella, e sovrumani
Silenzi, e profondissima quiete
Io nel pensier mi fingo, ove per poco
Il cor non si spaura. E come il vento
Odo stormir tra queste piante, io quello
Infinito silenzio e questa voce
Vo comparando: e mi sovvien l'eterno,
E le morte stagioni, e la presente
E viva, e il suon di lei. Così tra questa
Immensità s'annega il pensier mio:
E il naufragar m'è dolce in questo mare.

GIACOMO LEOPARDI

INFINITY*

This lonely hill was ever dear to me,
And this green hedge, that hides so large a part
Of the remote horizon from my view.
But as I sit and gaze, my mind conceives
Unending spaces, silences unearthly,
And deepest peace, wherein the heart almost
Draws nigh to fear. And as I hear the wind
Rustling among the branches, I compare
That everlasting silence with this sound:
Eternity is mine, and all past ages,
And this age living still, with all its noise.
So in immensity my thought is drowned,
And sweet it is to founder in this sea.

*Leopardi's *Zibaldone* is rich in references to his "inclination for the infinite" – which he affirmed to be a taste as natural to children as it was to the poets of classical antiquity. It is allied to a child's perception of what he called "*il bello aereo*" – a beauty belonging not to the earth but to the sky. "For then it is our imagination that is at work, instead of our sight, and the fantastic takes the place of the real. The soul imagines what it cannot see, what is hidden by that tree, that bush, that tower, and goes off wandering into imaginary space . . . Thence the pleasure that I felt as a boy, and sometimes do even now, in seeing the sky through a window or a door or between two houses." (*Zibaldone*)

L'ÉTERNITÉ

. . . l'Éternité
C'est la mer mêlée
Au soleil.

ARTHUR RIMBAUD

NOON

Ivi, quando il meriggio in ciel si volve,
La sua tranquilla imago il Sol dipinge,
Ed erba o foglia non si crolla al vento,
E non onda incresparsi, e non cicala
Strider, nè batter penna augello in ramo,
Nè farfalla ronzar, nè voce o moto
Da presso nè da lunge odi nè vedi.
Tien quelle rive altissima quiete;
Ond'io quasi me stesso e il mondo obblio
Sedendo immoto; e già mi par che sciolte
Giaccian le membra mie, nè spirto o senso
Più le commova, e lor quiete antica
Co' silenzi del loco si confonda.

GIACOMO LEOPARDI: *La vita solitaria*

There, as the noon touches its high meridian
And as the Sun depicts its quiet image,
And neither leaf nor grass stir in the wind,
And no wave ripples nor cicada shrills
Nor bird upon the bough flutters a wing,
Nor hums the butterfly, nor can be seen
Movement nearby nor far nor voice be heard, –
Then deep tranquillity enfolds those shores,
And, sitting motionless, I nearly lose
Myself and all the world; it seems to me
My limbs are freed, no feeling and no breath
Will stir them more; and so their ancient peace
Is mingled with the silence of the place.

CANZONE

Le nuvole sono legate alla terra ed al vento.
Fin che ci saran nuvole sopra Torino
sarà bella la vita. Sollevo la testa
e un gran gioco si svolge lassù sotto il sole.
Masse bianche durissime e il vento vi circola
tutto azzurro – talvolta le disfa
e ne fa grandi veli impregnati di luce.
Sopra i tetti, a migliaia le nuvole bianche
copron tutto, la folla, le pietre e il frastuono.
Molte volte levandomi ho visto le nuvole
trasparire nell'acqua limpida di un catino.
Anche gli alberi uniscono il cielo alla terra.
Le città sterminate somiglian foreste
dove il cielo compare su su, tra le vie.
Come gli alberi vivi sul Po, nei torrenti
cosi vivono i mucchi di case nel sole.
Anche gli alberi soffrono e muoiono sotto le nubi,
l'uomo sanguina e muore, – ma canta la gioia
tra la terra ed il cielo, la gran meraviglia
di città e di foreste. Avrò tempo domani
a rinchiudermi e stringere i denti. Ora tutta la vita
son le nubi e le piante e le vie, perdute nel cielo.

CESARE PAVESE

SONG

Unto the earth and wind the clouds are bound.
So long as there are clouds over Turin
life will be wonderful. I lift my head
and watch the game up there under the sun –
Of white hard banks, which now an azure wind
blows round and round, and sometimes tears apart
making great billowing sails imbued with light.
Above the roofs, thousands of these white clouds
blanket the world: the crowd and stones and noise.
Often, when I get up, I see the clouds
reflected in the water of a pail.
Even the trees unite the earth and sky.

The endless towns resemble a great forest
in which you see the sky high up, between the glades.
As trees live on the Po and in the streams,
so live the houses clustered in the sun.
The trees too suffer, die; beneath the clouds
man bleeds and dies, – but sings a song of joy
between the earth and sky, and the great wonder
of towns and trees. I'll close my door tomorrow
and grit my teeth. But now the whole of life
is clouds and plants and streets, lost in the sky.

ON THE MOUNTAINS

Where, on the mountain peaks high up
Their torch-lit feasts the gods amuse,
Often you took a great gold cup,
A vessel such as shepherds use,
And milked a lioness with your hands, to make
A round of silver-bright cheese-cake.

ALCMAN. Transl. by C. M. Bowra

NIGHT

The far peaks sleep, the great ravines,
The foot-hills, and the streams,
Asleep are trees, and hivèd bees,
The mountain beasts, and all that dark earth teems,
The glooming seas, the monsters in their deeps:
And every bird, its wide wings folded, sleeps.

ALCMAN. Transl. by H. T. Wade-Gery

TO THE EVENING STAR

Thou fair-hair'd angel of the evening,
Now, whilst the sun rests on the mountains, light
Thy bright torch of love; thy radiant crown
Put on, and smile upon our evening bed!
Smile on our loves, and while thou drawest the
Blue curtains of the sky, scatter thy silver dew
On every flower that shuts its sweet eyes
In timely sleep. Let thy west wind sleep on
The lake; speak silence with thy glimmering eyes,
And wash the dusk with silver. Soon, full soon,
Dost thou withdraw; then the wolf rages wide,
And the lion glares thro' the dun forest:
The fleeces of the flocks are cover'd with
Thy sacred dew: protect them with thine influence.

WILLIAM BLAKE

NI BONJOUR NI BONSOIR*

SUR UN AIR GREC

Νὴ Καλημέρα νὴ Ὥρα καλή

Le matin n'est plus! le soir pas encore:
Pourtant de nos yeux l'éclair a pali.

Νὴ Καλημέρα νὴ Ὥρα καλή

Mais le soir vermeil ressemble à l'aurore,
Et la nuit plus tard amène l'oubli!

GÉRARD DE NERVAL

Neither good morning not yet goodnight.
The morn is gone by; the evening not yet.
But pale has become the shimmer of light.

Neither good morning nor yet goodnight.
But the crimson eve resembles the dawn,
And later oblivion comes with the night.

*Maurice Baring compared this poem to Byron's line, "The moon is up and yet it is not night."

'PAR LES SOIRS D'ÉTÉ'

Par les soirs d'été j'irai dans les sentiers,
Picoté par les blés, fouler l'herbe menue:
Rêveur, j'en sentirai la fraicheur à mes pieds.
Je laisserai le vent baigner ma tête nue.

Je ne parlerai pas; je ne penserai à rien.
Mais l'amour infini me montera dans l'âme;
Et j'irai loin, comme un bohémien,
Par la Nature – heureux comme avec une femme.

ARTHUR RIMBAUD

'DOLCE E CHIARA È LA NOTTE'

Dolce e chiara è la notte e senza vento,
E queta sovra i tetti e in mezzo agli orti
Posa la luna, e di lontan rivela
Serena ogni montagna. . . .

GIACOMO LEOPARDI: *La sera del dì di festa*

The night is soft and clear, and no wind blows;
The quiet moon stands over roofs and orchards
Revealing from afar each peaceful hill.*

Transl. by JOHN HEATH-STUBBS

*The following is R. C. Trevelyan's rendering of these lines:
Tender is the night and clear, and without wind;
And tranquilly on the roofs and o'er the gardens
The moon reposes, far away revealing
Each serene mountain-crest.

CREATURES GREAT AND SMALL

THE HORSES OF ACHILLES

Far from the conflict, the horses of Achilles had been weeping ever since they learnt that their charioteer had been brought down in the dust by the murderous Hector. Automedon, Diores' stalwart son, did all he could with them; he lashed them repeatedly with his whistling whip, he coaxed them, and he cursed them freely; but the pair refused either to go back to the ships and the broad Hellespont or into the battle after the Achaeans. Firm as a gravestone planted on the barrow of a dead man or woman, they stood motionless in front of their beautiful chariot with their heads bowed to the earth. Hot tears ran from their eyes to the ground as they mourned for their lost driver. . . .

The Iliad, Book XVII. Transl. by E. V. Rieu

ARGOS

As they were talking together, a hound that was lying there lifted his head and pricked up his ears. This was Argos, whom Odysseus himself had bred and trained: but he had not had much good of him before he went away to the war. Formerly the young men used to take him out to hunt wild goats or hares or deer: but there he was, lying neglected, his master gone, on the midden, where the mule-dung and cow-dung was heaped in front of the gates ready to be carted out to the fields. There lay Argos the hound, covered with vermin. When he knew that it was his old master near him, he wagged his tail and dropped both his ears; but he could not move to approach him. Odysseus saw, and secretly wiped a tear from his eye so that Eumaios did not notice: then he said to him:

"Eumaios, I am surprised to see this hound lying on a dung-heap. He looks a fine animal, but of course I don't know if he had speed to match his looks, or if he is just one of those table-dogs a man keeps, something for the master to show off."

Eumaios answered:

"Eh well, to be sure his master is dead and far away. If his looks and his powers were now what they were when the master went away and left him tha'd see his big strength and speed! Never a beast could escape him in the deep forest when he was on the track for he was a prime tracker. But now he has fallen on bad times: his master has perished far from his native land, and the women care nowt and do nowt for him. That's like your serfs: when the master's hand is gone, they'll not do an honest day's work. Aye, Zeus Allwise takes away half the good of a man when the day of slavery catches him."

So saying he entered the well-built mansion, made straight for the riotous pretenders in the hall. But Argos passed into the darkness of death, now that he had seen his master once more after twenty years.

The Odyssey, Book XVII. Transl. by W. H. D. Rouse

THE DOG FROM MALTA

He came from Malta; and Eumelus says
He had no better dog in all his days.
We called him Bull; he went into the dark.
Along those roads we cannot hear him bark.

Tymnes. Transl. by Edmund Blunden

THE FIELDS OF PERSEPHONE

No longer in the wealthy house of Alcis, O shrill grasshopper, shall the sun behold thee singing; for now thou art flown to the meadows of Clymenus and the dewy flowers of golden Persephone.

Aristodicus. Transl. by J. W. Mackail

SONNET ON THE GRASSHOPPER AND CRICKET

The Poetry of earth is never dead;
When all the birds are faint with the hot sun
And hide in cooling trees, a voice will run
From hedge to hedge about the new-mown mead.
That is the Grasshopper's, – he takes the lead
In summer luxury, – he has never done
With his delights; for, when tired out with fun
He rests at ease beneath some pleasnt weed.
The poetry of earth is ceasing never.
On a lone winter evening, when the frost
Has wrought a silence, from the stove there shrills
The Cricket's song, in warmth increasing ever,
And seems to one in drowsiness half lost,
The Grasshopper's among some grassy hills.

John Keats

THE RELEASE OF THE OX

The labouring ox, outworn with old age and labour of the furrow, Alcon did not lead to the butchering knife, reverencing it for its works; and loose in the deep meadow grass it rejoices with lowings over freedom from the plough.

ADDAEUS. Transl. by J. W. Mackail

A HOME FOR BEES

For a start you must find your bees a suitable home, a position
Sheltered from wind (for wind will stop them carrying home
Their forage), a close where sheep nor goats come butting in
To jump on the flowers, nor blundering heifer stray to flick
The dew from the meadow and stamp its springing grasses down.
Discourage the lizard, too, with his lapis-lazuli back,
From their rich folds, the bee-eater and other birds,
And the swallow whose breast was blooded once by a killer's hand:
For these wreak wholesale havoc, snap up your bees on the wing
And bear them off as a tit-bit for their ungentle nestlings.
But mind there's a bubbling spring nearby, a pool moss-bordered,
And a rill ghosting through the grass:
See, too, that a palm or tall oleaster shadow the entrance,
For thus, when the new queens lead out the earliest swarms –
The spring all theirs – and the young bees play, from hive unprisoned,
The bank may be handy to welcome them in out of the heat
And the tree meet them halfway and make them at home in its foliage.
Whether the water flows or is stagnant, fling in the middle
Willow boughs criss-cross and big stones,
That the bees may have plenty of bridges to stand on and dry their wings
At the summer sun, in case a shower has caught them loitering
Or a gust of east wind ducked them suddenly in the water.
Green spurge-laurel should grow round about, wild thyme that perfumes
The air, masses of savory rich-breathing, and violet beds
Sucking the channelled stream.

VIRGIL: *Georgics* IV, 11, 8–32. Transl. by C. Day Lewis

AUX MOUSCHES A MIEL

Où allez-vous, filles du Ciel,
Grand miracle de la Nature,
Où allez-vous, mousches à miel,
Chercher aux champs vostre pasture?
Si vous voulez cueillir les fleurs
D'odeur diverse et de couleurs,
Ne volez plus à l'avanture.

Autour de ma Dame halenée
De mes baisers tant bien donnez,
Vous trouverez la rose née,
Et les oeillets environnez
De fleurettes ensanglantées
D'Hyacinthe, et d'Ajax, plantées
Pres des liz sur sa bouche nez.

Les marjolaines y fleurissent,
L'amôme y est continuel,
Et les lauriers qui ne perissent
Pour l'Hyver, tant soit il cruel:
L'anis, le chévrefueil qui porte
La Manne qui vous reconforte,
Y verdoye perpetuel.

Mais je vous pri' gardez vous bien,
Gardez-vous qu'on ne l'eguillonne,
Vous apprendriez bien-tost combien
Sa poincture est trop plus felonne,
Et de ses fleurs ne vous soulez
Sans m'en garder, si ne voulez
Que mon âme ne m'abandonne.

PIERRE DE RONSARD

'FORGET NOT BEES IN WINTER'

. . . .

Forget not bees in winter, though they sleep,
For winter's big with summer in her womb,
And when you plant your rose-trees, plant them deep,
Having regard to bushes all aflame,
And see the dusky promise of their bloom
In small red shoots, and let each redolent name –
Tuscany, Crested Cabbage, Cottage Maid –
Load with full June November's dank repose;
See the kind cattle drowsing in the shade,
And hear the bee about his amorous trade,
Brown in the gipsy crimson of the rose.

. . . .

VITA SACKVILLE WEST: *The Land*

As when in the winter months Zeus brings fourteen days of calm, and mortals call it the sacred, windless breeding time of the many-coloured kingfisher.

SIMONIDES. Transl. by Maurice Baring

THE HALCYONS

No more, O maiden voices, sweet as honey, soft as love is,
No more my limbs sustain me. – A halcyon on the wing
Flying o'er the foam-flowers, in the halcyon coveys,
Would I were, and knew not care, the sea-blue bird of spring!

ALCMAN. Transl. by H. T. Wade-Gery

'THE SWALLOW COMES'

The swallow comes
From the white sea,
And sits and sings:
"March, my lovely March
And mournful February,
Even if it snows
Even if it rains,
You smell of spring".

FAURIEL: *Chants populaires de la Grèce moderne*, II.
Transl. by Walter Kaiser

THE LATE SWALLOW

Leave, leave your well-loved nest,
Late swallow, and fly away.
Here is no rest
For hollowing heart and wearying wing.
Your comrades all have flown
To seek their southern paradise
Across the great earth's downward sloping side,
And you are alone.
Why should you cling
Still to the swiftly ageing narrowing day?
Prepare;
Shake out your pinions long untried
That now must bear you there where you would be
Through all the heavens of ice;
Till falling down upon the homing air
You light and perch upon the radiant tree.

EDWIN MUIR

BIRDSONG

This I went wide-where, walking alone,
In a wide wilderness, by a wood side.
Bliss of the birds song made me abide there,
And on a lawn under a linden I leaned awhile
To listen to their lays, their lovely notes;
The mirth of their mouths made me to sleep,
And mid that bliss I dreamed marvellously.

WILLIAM LANGLAND: *Piers Plowman*

It were a heavenly health,
It were an endless wealth,
It were a life for God Himself,
To hear this Nightingale . . .

JOHN SKELTON

'SEE, SEE, MINE OWN SWEET JEWEL'

See, see mine own sweet jewel
What I have for my darling:
A robin-redbreast and a starling.
These I give both in hope to move thee;
Yet thou say'st I do not love thee.

ANON.

'THE LARK'

Thou hearest the Nightingale begin the Song of Spring.
The Lark sitting upon his earthy bed, just as the morn
Appears, listens silent; then springing from the waving Cornfield,
He leads the Choir of Day: trill, trill, trill, trill, [loud
Mounting upon the wings of light into the Great Expanse,
Re-echoing against the lovely blue & shining heavenly Shell,
His little throat labours with inspiration; every feather
On throat & breast & wings vibrates with the effluence Divine.
All Nature listens silent to him, & the awful Sun
Stands still upon the Mountain looking on this little Bird
With eyes of soft humility & wonder, love & awe.
Then loud from their green covert all the Birds begin their Song:
The Thrush, the Linnet & the Goldfinch, Robin & the Wren
Awake the Sun from his sweet reverie upon the Mountain.

WILLIAM BLAKE: *Milton*, Book the Second

THE AZIOLA

"Do you not hear the Aziola cry?
Methinks she must be nigh,"
Said Mary, as we sate
In dusk, ere stars were lit, or candles brought;
And I, who thought
This Aziola was some tedious woman,
Asked, "Who is Aziola?" How elate
I felt to know that it was nothing human,
No mockery of myself to fear or hate:
And Mary saw my soul,
And laughed, and said, "Disquiet yourself not;
'Tis nothing but a little downy owl." . . .

. . . .

PERCY BYSSHE SHELLEY

THE DOVE

I had a dove and the sweet dove died,
  And I have thought it died of grieving:
O, what could it grieve for? its feet were tied
  With a single thread of my own hands weaving.

Sweet little red feet why should you die?
Why should you leave me, sweet bird, why?
You lived alone in the forest tree.
Why, pretty thing! would you not live with me?
I kissed you oft, and gave you white peas;
Why not live sweetly, as in the green trees?

JOHN KEATS

NIGHTINGALES

Beautiful must be the mountains whence ye come,
And bright in the fruitful valleys the streams, wherefrom
    Ye learn your song:
Where are those starry woods? O might I wander there,
Among the flowers, which in that heavenly air
    Bloom the year long!

Nay, barren are those mountains and spent the streams:
Our song is the voice of desire, that haunts our dreams,
    A throe of the heart,
Whose pining visions dim, forbidden hopes profound,
No dying cadence nor long sigh can sound,
    For all our art.

Alone, aloud in the raptured ear of men
We pour our dark nocturnal secret; and then,
    As night is withdrawn
From these sweet-springing meads and bursting boughs of May,
Dream, while the innumerable choir of day
    Welcome the dawn.

ROBERT BRIDGES

THE WILD SWANS AT COOLE

The trees are in their autumn beauty,
The woodland paths are dry,
Under the October twilight the water
Mirrors a still sky;
Upon the brimming water among the stones
Are nine and fifty swans.

The nineteenth Autumn has come upon me
Since I first made my count;
I saw, before I had well finished,
All suddenly mount
And scatter wheeling in great broken rings
Upon their clamorous wings

I have looked upon those brilliant creatures,
And now my heart is sore.
All's changed since I, hearing at twilight,
The first time on this shore,
The bell-beat of their wings above my head,
Trod with a lighter tread.

Unwearied still, lover by lover,
They paddle in the cold,
Companionable streams or climb the air;
Their hearts have not grown old;
Passion or conquest, wander where they will,
Attend upon them still.

But now they drift on the still water
Mysterious, beautiful;
Among what rushes will they build,
By what lake's edge or pool
Delight men's eyes when I awake some day
To find they have flown away?

W. B. YEATS

PANGUR BÁN

I and Pangur Bán my cat,
'Tis a like task we are at:
Hunting mice is his delight,
Hunting words I sit all night....

'Tis a merry thing to see
At our tasks how glad are we,
When at home we sit and find
Entertainment to our mind....

'Gainst the wall he sets his eye,
Full and fierce and sharp and sly;
'Gainst the wall of knowledge I
All my little wisdom try....

So in peace our tasks we ply,
Pangur Bán, my cat, and I;
In our arts we find our bliss,
I have mine and he has his....

ROBIN FLOWER

PLAYING WITH MY CAT

When I am playing with my cat, who knows whether she have more sport in dallying with me than I have in gaming with her? We entertain one another with mutual apish tricks; if I have my hour to begin or refuse, so hath she hers.*

MONTAIGNE: *An Apology of Raymond Sebond.*
Transl. by John Florio

*This quotation comes from a famous passage, in which Montaigne declares that man, "the only forsaken and outcast creature, naked on the bare earth... having nothing to cover and arm himself withal but the spoil of others", is yet "the proudest and disdainfullest", and considers the world to be made for him. Yet why should not a goose say, too, – "All parts of the world belong to me; the earth serveth me to tread upon, the sun to give me light, the stars to inspire me with influence; this commodity I have of the winds, and this benefit of the waters... I am the favourite of nature...."

ON A CAT, AGEING

He blinks upon the hearth-rug,
And yawns in deep content,
Accepting all the comforts
That Providence has sent.

Loud he purrs and louder,
In one glad hymn of praise
For all the night's adventures,
For quiet restful days.

Life will go on for ever,
With all that cat can wish,
Warmth and the glad procession
Of fish and milk and fish.

Only – the thought disturbs him –
He's noticed once or twice
The times are somehow breeding
A nimbler race of mice.

ALEXANDER SELKIRK

THE WHITE HARE

At the field's edge,
In the snow-furred sedge,
Couches the white hare;
Her stronghold is there.

Brown as the seeding grass
In summer she was,
With a creamed belly soft as ermine;
Beautiful she was among vermin.
Silky young she had,
For her spring was glad;
On the fell above
She ran races with love.
Softly she went
In and out of the tent
Of the tasselled corn;
Till the huntsman's horn
Raised the bogey death
And she was gone, like breath.

Thanks to her senses five
This charmer is alive:
Who cheated the loud pack,
Biting steel, poacher's sack;
Among the steep rocks
Outwitted the fanged fox.

And now winter has come;
Winds have made dumb
Water's crystal chime;
In a cloak of rime
Stands the stiff bracken;
Until the cold slacken
Beauty and terror kiss;
There is no armistice.
Low must the hare lie;
With great heart and round eye.

Wind-scoured and sky-burned
The fell was her feet spurned
In the flowery season
Of her swift unreason;
Gone is her March rover;
Now noon is soon over;
Now the dark falls
Heavily from sheer walls
Of snow-cumbering cloud,
And Earth shines in her shroud.
All things now fade
That were in love's image made.

She too must decrease
Unto a thorny peace,
Who put her faith
In this flesh, in this wraith.
A hoar habit borrows
Our light lady of sorrows,
Nor is her lot strange;
Time rings a snow-change.

LILIAN BOWES LYON

THE FALLOW DEER AT THE LONELY HOUSE

One without looks in tonight
  Through the curtain-chink
From the sheet of glistening white;
One without looks in tonight
  As we sit and think
  By the fender-brink.

We do not discern those eyes
  Watching in the snow;
Lit by lamps of rosy dyes
We do not discern those eyes
  Wondering, aglow,
  Fourfooted, tiptoe.

THOMAS HARDY

HUMMING-BIRD

I can imagine, in some other-world
Primeval-dumb, far back
In that most awful stillness, that only gasped and hummed,
Humming-birds raced down the avenues.

Before anything had a soul,
While life was a heave of Matter, half inanimate,
This little bit chipped off in brilliance
And went whizzing through the slow, vast, succulent stems.

I believe there were no flowers then,
In the world where the humming-bird flashed ahead of creation.
I believe he pierced the slow vegetable veins with his long beak.

Probably he was big
As mosses, and little lizards, they say, were once big.
Probably he was a jabbing, terrifying monster.

We look at him through the wrong end of the long telescope of Time,
Luckily for us.

D. H. LAWRENCE

BEAUTY SHOW, CLIFDEN, CO. GALWAY

They're come to town from each dot on the compass, they're
Wild as tinkers and groomed to an eyelash,
And light of foot as a champion featherweight
Prance on the top of the morning.

They walk the ring, so glossy and delicate
Each you'd think was a porcelain masterpiece
Come to life at the touch of a raindrop,
Tossing its mane and its halter.

The shy, the bold, the demure and the whinnier,
Grey, black, piebald, roans, palominos
Parade their charms for the tweedy, the quite un-
Susceptible hearts of the judges.

Now and again at the flick of an instinct,
As if they'd take off like a fieldful of rooks, they will
Fidget and fret for the pasture they know, and
The devil take all this competing.

The light is going, the porter is flowing,
The field a ruin of paper and straw.
Step neatly home now, unprized or rosetted,
You proud Connemara ponies.

C. Day Lewis

TORTOISE, DROMEDARY, CARP, CRAB

La tortue

Du Thrace magique, o délire!
Mes doigts surs font sonner la lyre.
Les animaux passent aux sons
De ma tortue, de mes chansons.

Le dromadaire

Avec ses quatre dromadaires
Don Pedro d'Alfaroubeira
Courut le monde et l'admira.
Il fit ce que je voudrais faire
Si j'avais quatre dromadaires.

La Carpe

Dans vos viviers, dans vos étangs,
Carpes, que vous vivez longtemps!
Est-ce que la mort vous oublie,
Poissons de la mélancolie.

L'écrevisse

Incertitude, o mes délices
Vous et moi nous nous en allons
Comme s'en vont les écrevisses,
A reculons, à reculons.

GUILLAUME APOLLINAIRE

'THAT VAIN ANIMAL'

. . . .

Were, I (who to my cost already am,
One of those strange, prodigious Creatures *Man*),
A Spirit free, to chuse for my own share,
What case of Flesh, and Blood, I pleas'd to weare,
I'd be a *Dog*, a *Monkey* or a *Bear*,
Or any thing, but that vain *Animal*,
Who is so proud of being rational.

JOHN WILMOT, Earl of Rochester.

IN TIME OF WAR

Non vi si pensa quanto sangue costa.

DANTE: Paradiso

Introductory Note

THIS section was nearly omitted from this anthology, since, when I first looked again at the commonplace books of my youth. I found that the poems which seemed most dated, most impossible to include today, were the romantic or heroic visions of "the fighting man" which I had set down in my teens, by some of the poets of the First World War. Nor did it seem possible (quite apart from their familiarity) to print once again the classical set-pieces about patriotism and valour that have moved so many past generations: Pericles' famous speech, for instance, or Henry V before Agincourt, or the epitaph of the Lacaedemonian dead. War has come to bear for us a different face.

What then can be set down about war that still seems valid? There is a good deal and – though said in many different languages, over a wide period of time – the feelings expressed are generally very much the same. These poems are a lament, a dirge – both for the living and the dead – for all who, down the centuries, have lived in times of war, revolution or strife. They are sometimes a protest against violence and futility. They are the voice of compassion.

The conviction that civilian populations have never been as much involved in the suffering caused by war, as in this generation, is so widespread as to have become a commonplace. But the evidence here inclines one to question its accuracy. It is of course true that fewer people, in terms of sheer numbers, were involved in the battles of the past; but that is true of soldiers as well as of civilians. The population itself was smaller and the actual field of action was restricted by the ground that could be covered by men's or horses' legs. But within that area, how general was the suffering! Besieged cities. from which "useless mouths" were often driven out to starve in the no-man's land between two armies; countrysides laid waste; raped women, stolen cattle, burning castles and farms – these we find in the chronicles of the Middle Ages or the records of strife between the tyrants of the Renaissance, as much as in the descriptions of war in ancient China or in the Europe of the Hundred Years' War. Even in the *Iliad*, the "poem of might", in which valour and skill in arms are mostly highly exalted, the triumph of Achilles' victory over Hector is not allowed to obscure the bereavement of Andromache and little Astyanax. For one epitaph in the Greek Anthology which exalts the courage of the fallen, there are at least three dwelling upon their misfortune, dying so far from their native land. Even in Aeschylus' description of the destruction of the Persian fleet at Salamis, the pride in the Hellenic victory is muted by sorrow at its cost. "Never yet 'twixt sunrise and sunset perished so vast a multitude of men," and twenty-four centuries later, another Greek poet, George Seferis, was meditating and mourning upon another "desolate and cloudy beach", laid waste by war.

Since writing this, I have seen the section on War in W. H. Auden's commonplace book, *A Certain World*. He maintains that there has been "a radical change in attitude towards War and the military profession since World War I" and that until then "it was generally assumed that war was glorious and the warrior a hero". I do not think that this is confirmed by the evidence in the passages quoted here, nor indeed in those quoted by Auden himself. War has always been well spoken of by rulers, generals, and a few brave, restless or ambitious young men, tolerated by others who considered it their duty, and abhorred by the vast majority. It is true, however, that, since the poems on this theme in Ancient China, some of which are quoted here, few periods have produced as many eloquent protests against war as those written by soldiers during the First and Second World Wars. Yet it is still possible for humanity to behave today as described in the most terrible poem in this section, *Toy on Target*.

In addition to the direct sufferings of war, there are its consequences: homelessness and exile. In the Middle Ages in Italy it was taken for granted that when one political faction had ousted another or one tyrant had captured his neighbour's city, the vanquished should be deprived of all their possessions and sent – often for ten or twenty years or the rest of their life – into banishment, to eat "salt bread" and tread on "other men's stairs". They could, however, always have the hope that Fortune's wheel might turn again; theirs was not the utter hopelessness and dispossession of Chen Tzu-Lung's husband and wife, flying before the advancing Manchus with their "Little Cart", of the "displaced persons" during and after both World Wars, of the thousands of Russians who, in the 1920's and 30's, disappeared forever into Siberia, or of the prisoners today in the Greek Islands. Exile, indeed, whether for individuals or for whole "ethnic unities", seems to have become the blight of our century, as the Black Death was in the 13th century and smallpox in the 18th.

Ares is equitable: he kills those who kill.

The Iliad

Ares is blind, and with unseeing eyes
Set in a swine's face stirs up all to evil.

SOPHOCLES. Transl. by C. M. Bowra

ANDROMACHE MOURNS HECTOR'S DEATH

Andromache, with palpitating heart, rushed out of the house like a mad woman, and her maid-servants went with her. When they came to the wall, where the men had gathered in a crowd, she climbed up on the battlements, searched the plain, and saw them dragging her husband in front of the town – the powerful horses were hauling him along at an easy canter towards the Achaean ships . . .

"Alas, Hector; alas for me!" she cried . . . "For you are on your way to Hades and the unknown world below, leaving me behind in misery, a widow in your house. And your son is no more than a baby, the son we got between us, we unhappy parents. You, Hector, now that you are dead, will be no joy to him, nor he to you." Even if he escapes the horrors of the Achaean war, nothing lies ahead of him but hardship and trouble, with strangers eating into his estate. An orphaned child is cut off from his playmates. He goes about with downcast looks and tear-stained cheeks. In his necessity he looks in at some gathering of his father's friends and plucks a cloak here and a tunic there, till someone out of charity holds up a wine-cup to his mouth, but only for a moment, just enough to wet his lips and leave his palate dry. Then comes another boy, with both his parents living, who beats him with his fists and drives him from the feast and jeers at him. "Out you go!" he shouts. "You have no father dining here." So the child runs off in tears to his widowed mother – little Astyanax, who used to sit on his father's knees and eat nothing but marrow and mutton fat, and when he was sleepy and tired of play, slept in a bed, softly cradled in his nurse's arms, full of good cheer. But now, with his father gone, evils will crowd in on Astyanax, Protector of Troy, as the Trojans called him, seeing in you the one defence of their long walls and gates. And you, by the beaked ships, far from your parents, will be eaten by the wriggling worms when the dogs have had their fill. . . .

Thus Andromache lamented through her tears, and the women joined in her lament.

The Iliad, Book XXII. Transl. by E. V. Rieu

SALAMIS IN CYPRUS

"... and Salamis, the mother-city of which
is the cause of our present woes."

AESCHYLUS: *The Persians*

At times the sun of midday, at times the handfuls of light rain
And the beach full of fragments of ancient sherds.
The columns, unimportant. There is only Saint Epiphanios
Dimly radiant of that absorbed might of the golden Empire.
The flesh and blood of the young, loved and loving, have passed here;
Those beating hearts, rose-pink of shells, the light feet
Fearlessly skimming the water,
And arms opened for the joining of desire.
The Lord upon many waters,
Here upon this place of passing.

Then I heard footsteps upon the pebbles
I saw no faces. They had gone when I turned my head.
Still that voice heavy upon me like the treading of cattle
Stayed in the pulses of the sky and in the sea's roll
Over upon the shingle again and again:

"The earth has no handles
For them to lift it on their shoulders and take it away.
They are not able, however thirsty,
To sweeten the salt sea with half a cup-full of water.
And those bodies
Created from a land unknown to them
Have their own souls.

Now they assemble tools to change these souls.
It will not be possible. They will only undo them,
If souls can be undone.
It does not take long for the corn to ripen
No time is needed
For the yeast of bitterness to rise,
No time is needed
For evil to raise its head,
And the sick mind drained empty,
No time is needed
For the filling of this with madness.
There is an island."

Friends of the other war,
On this desolate and cloudy beach
I call you to mind, as the day is turning –
Who fell in the fighting, who fell long after the battle,
Who saw the dawn rising through the mist of death,
Or, in the wild solitude below the stars,
Felt upon their skin the great dark eyes
Of absolute disaster;
And, once again, those who prayed
When the ships were being sawn by the burning steel:
"O Lord, help us to keep in mind
How this murder came about;
Greed, dishonesty, selfishness,
The drying up of love.
Lord help us to root out these things."

– Now, among these pebbles, it is better to forget;
It does no good to speak.
What the powerful have determined, who can change it?
And who can make himself heard?
Each has his dreams apart; unknown to him the nightmares
That vex the others' sleep.
– True. But the messenger is on his way
And, however long his journey, he will bring
To those who tried to put fetters on the Hellespont
The fearful message that came from Salamis.

Voice of the Lord upon the waters.
There is an island.

November 1953

GEORGE SEFERIS: *Poems*. Transl. by Rex Warner

Salamis in Cyprus – the prayer in this poem is based on one composed by Commander Lord Hugh Beresford, R.N., who fell in the Battle of Crete: "O God our loving Father . . . Help us to keep in mind the real causes of war: dishonesty greed, selfishness and lack of love, and to drive them out of this ship."

THE ERETRIAN DEAD

Euboeans we, men of Eretria city,
  Here lying, overseen
By Persian Susa. O for pity,
  How long the road between!

PLATO. Transl. by T. F. Higham

THE ATHENIAN DEAD

On Dirphys' wrinkled side we fell;
And where the Narrow Waters drift
Our countrymen, to mark us well,
Raised up this cairn, their gift.

A gift deserved; for youth is sweet,
And youth we gave, nor turned away,
Though sharp the storm of battle beat
That darkened all our day.

SIMONIDES. Transl. by T. F. Higham

THE PRISONER

Tartars led in chains,
Tartars led in chains!
Their ears pierced, their faces bruised—they are driven into the land of Ch'in.
The Son of Heaven took pity on them and would not have them slain.
He sent them away to the south-east, to the lands of Wu and Yüeh.
A petty officer in a yellow coat took down their names and surnames;
They were led from the city of Ch'ang-an by relays of armed guards.
Their bodies were covered with the wounds of arrows, their bones stood out from their cheeks.
They had grown so weak they could only march a single stage a day.
In the morning they must satisfy hunger and thirst with neither plate nor cup;
At night they must lie in their dirt and rags on beds that stank with filth.

Suddenly they came to the Yangtze River and remembered the waters of Chiao.[1]
With lowered hands and levelled voices they sobbed a muffled song.
Then one Tartar lifted up his voice and spoke to the other Tartars,
"*Your* sorrows are none at all compared with my sorrows."
Those that were with him in the same band asked to hear his tale;
As he tried to speak the words were choked by anger.
He told them "I was born and bred in the town of Liang-Chou;[2]
In the frontier wars of Ta-li[3] I fell into the Tartar's hands.
Since the days the Tartars took me alive, forty years ago,
I have had to wear a coat of skins tied with a fur belt.
Only on the first of the first month might I wear my Chinese dress.
As I put on my coat and arranged my cap, how fast the tears flowed!
I made in my heart a secret vow I would find a way home:
I hid my plan from my Tartar wife and the children she had borne me in the land.
I thought to myself, "It is well for me that my limbs are still strong",
And yet, being old, in my heart I feared I should never live to return.
The Tartar chieftains shoot so well that the birds are afraid to fly:
From the risk of their arrows I escaped alive and fled swiftly home.
Hiding all day and walking all night, I crossed the Great Desert,[4]
Where clouds are dark and the moon black and the sands eddy in the wind.
Frightened, I sheltered at the Green Grave,[5] where the frozen grasses are few;
Stealthily I crossed the Yellow River, at night, on the thin ice
Suddenly I heard Han[6] drums and the sound of soldiers coming;
I went to meet them at the road-side, bowing to them as they came.
But the moving horsemen did not hear that I spoke the Han tongue;
Their Captain took me for a Tartar born and had me bound in chains.
They are sending me away to the south-east, to a low and swampy land
Provided with hardly any kit and no protective drugs.
Thinking of this my voice chokes and I ask of Heaven above,
Was I spared from death only to spend the rest of my years in sorrow?

[1]In Turkestan.
[2]In Kansu.
[3]The period Ta-li, A.D. 766–780.
[4]The Gobi Desert.
[5]The grave of Chao-chun, a Chinese girl who in 33 B.C. was "bestowed upon the Khan of the Hsiung-nu as a mark of Imperial regard" (Giles). Hers was the only grave in this desolate district on which grass would grow.
[6]i.e. Chinese.

My native village of Liang I shall not see again;
My wife and children in the Tartars' land I have fruitlessly deserted.
When I fell among Tartars and was taken prisoner, I pined for the land of Han;
Now that I am back in the land of Han, they have turned me into a Tartar.
Had I but known what my fate would be, I would not have started home!
For the two lands, so wide apart, are alike in the sorrow they bring.
Tartar prisoners in chains!
Of all the sorrows of all the prisoners mine is the hardest to bear!
Never in the world has so great a wrong befallen the lot of man,
A Han heart and a Han tongue set in the body of a Turk."

Po Chü-I. Transl. by Arthur Waley

They come like sacrifices in their trim,
And to the fire-eyed maid of smoky war,
All hot and bleeding will we offer them:
The mailed Mars shall on his altar sit
Up to the ears in blood.

SHAKESPEARE: *Henry IV*, IV

THE SOLDIER'S DEATH

Trail all your pikes, dispirit every drum,
March in a slow procession from afar,
Be silent, ye dejected Men of War!
Be still the hautboys, and the flute be dumb!
Display no more, in vain, the lofty banner;
For see! where on the bier before ye lies
The pale, the fall'n, the untimely Sacrifice
To your mistaken shrine, to your false idol Honour.

ANNE FINCH, Countess of Winchelsea

STRANGE MEETING

It seemed that out of battle I escaped
Down some profound dull tunnel, long since scooped
Through granites which titanic wars had groined.
Yet also there encumbered sleepers groaned,
Too fast in thought or death to be bestirred.
Then, as I probed them, one sprang up, and stared
With piteous recognition in fixed eyes,
Lifting distressful hands as if to bless.
And by his smile, I knew that sullen hall;
By his dead smile I knew we stood in Hell
With a thousand pains that vision's face was grained;
Yet no blood reached there from the upper ground,
And no guns thumped, or down the flues made moan.
"Strange friend," I said, "here is no cause to mourn."
"None", said that other, "save the undone years,
The hopelessness. Whatever hope is yours,
Was my life also; I went hunting wild
After the wildest beauty in the world,
Which lies not calm in eyes, or braided hair,
But mocks the steady running of the hour,
And if it grieves, grieves richlier than here.
For of my glee might many men have laughed,
And of my weeping something had been left,
Which must die now. I mean the truth untold,
The pity of war, the pity war distilled.
Now men will go content with what we spoiled.
Or, discontent, boil bloody, and be spilled.
They will be swift with swiftness of the tigress,
None will break ranks, though nations trek from progress.
Courage was mine, and I had mystery;
Wisdom was mine, and I had mastery;
To miss the march of this retreating world
Into vain citadels that are not walled.
Then, when much blood had clogged their chariot-wheels,
I would go up and wash them from sweet wells,
Even with truths that lie too deep for taint.
I would have poured my spirit without stint
But not through wounds; not on the cess of war.
Foreheads of men have bled where no wounds were.
I am the enemy you killed, my friend.

I knew you in the dark; for so you frowned
Yesterday through me as you jabbed and killed.
I parried; but my hands were loath and cold.
Let us sleep now. . . ."

WILFRED OWEN

MEMORIAL RAIN

AMBASSADOR PUSER the ambassador
Reminds himself in French, felicitous tongue,
What these (young men no longer) lie here for
In rows that once, and somewhere else, were young –

All night in Brussels the wind had tugged at my door:
I had heard the wind at my door and the trees strung
Taut, and to me who had never been before
In that country it was a strange wind blowing
Steadily, stiffening the walls, the floor,
The roof of my room. I had not slept for knowing
He too, dead, was a stranger in that land
And felt beneath the earth in the wind's flowing
A tightening of roots and would not understand,
Remembering lake winds in Illinois,
That strange wind. I had felt his bones in the sand
Listening.

– Reflects that these enjoy
Their country's gratitude, that deep repose,
That peace no pain can break, no hurt destroy,
That rest, that sleep –

At Ghent the wind rose.
There was a smell of rain and a heavy drag
Of wind in the hedges but not as the wind blows
Over fresh water where the waves lag
Foaming and the willows huddle and it will rain:
I felt him waiting.

– Indicates the flag
Which (may he say) enisles in Flanders' plain
This little field these happy, happy dead
Have made America –

In the ripe grain
The wind coiled glistening, darted, fled,
Dragging its heavy body: at Waereghem
The wind coiled in the grass above his head:
Waiting – listening –

– Dedicates to them
This earth their bones have hallowed, this last gift
A grateful country –

Under the dry grass stem
The words are blurred, are thickened, the words sift
Confused by the rasp of the wind, by the thin grating
Of ants under the grass, the minute shift
And tumble of dusty sand separating
From dusty sand. The roots of the grass strain,
Tighten, the earth is rigid, waits – he is waiting –

And suddenly, and all at once, the rain!

The living scatter, they run into houses, the wind
Is trampled under the rain, shakes free, in again
Trampled. The rain gathers, running is thinned
Spurts of water that ravel in the dry sand
Seeping in the sand under the grass roots, seeping
Between cracked boards to the bones of a clenched hand:
The earth relaxes, loosens; he is sleeping,
He rests, he is quiet, he sleeps in a strange land.*

ARCHIBALD MACLEISH

*This poem was written in memory of Archibald MacLeish's brother Kenneth, killed in the First World War in Flanders.

THE LITTLE CART

The little cart jolting and banging through the yellow haze of dusk;
  The man pushing behind, the woman pulling in front.
They have left the city and do not know where to go.
"Green, green those elm-tree leaves; *they* will cure my hunger,
If only we could find some quiet place and sup on them together."

The wind has flattened the yellow mother-wort;
Above it in the distance they see the walls of a house.
"*There* surely must be people living who'll give you something to eat."
They tap at the door, but no one comes; they look in, but the kitchen
  is empty.
They stand hesitating in the lonely road and their tears fall like rain.

CH'ÉN TZU-LUNG
Transl. by Arthur Waley;

TWELVE SONGS – I

Say this city has ten million souls,
Some are living in mansions, some are living in holes:
Yet there's no place for us, my dear, yet there's no place for us.

Once we had a country and we thought it fair,
Look in the atlas and you'll find it there:
We cannot go there now, my dear, we cannot go there now.

In the village churchyard there grows an old yew,
Every spring it blossoms anew:
Old passports can't do that, my dear, old passports can't do that.

The consul banged the table and said;
"If you've got no passport you're officially dead";
But we are still alive, my dear, but we are still alive.

Went to a committee; they offered me a chair;
Asked me politely to return next year:
But where shall we go today, my dear, but where shall we go today?

Came to a public meeting; the speaker got up and said:
"If we let them in, they will steal our daily bread";
He was talking of you and me, my dear, he was talking of you and me.

Thought I heard the thunder rumbling in the sky;
It was Hitler over Europe, saying: "They must die";
O we were in his mind, my dear, O we were in his mind.

Saw a poodle in a jacket fastened with a pin,
Saw a door opened and a cat let in:
But they weren't German Jews, my dear, but they weren't German
Jews.

Went down the harbour and stood upon the quay,
Saw the fish swimming as if they were free:
Only ten feet away, my dear, only ten feet away.

Walked through a wood, saw the birds in the trees;
They had no politicians and sang at their ease:
They weren't the human race, my dear, they weren't the human race.

Dreamed I saw a building with a thousand floors,
A thousand windows and a thousand doors;
Not one of them was ours, my dear, not one of them was ours.

Stood on a great plain in the falling snow;
Ten thousand soldiers marched to and fro:
Looking for you and me, my dear, looking for you and me.

W. H. Auden

A REFUSAL TO MOURN THE DEATH, BY FIRE, OF A CHILD IN LONDON

Never until the mankind making
Bird beast and flower
Fathering and all humbling darkness
Tells with silence the last light breaking
And the still hour
Is come of the sea tumbling in harness

And I must enter again the round
Zion of the water bead
And the synagogue of the ear of corn
Shall I let pray the shadow of a sound
Or sow my salt seed
In the least valley of sackcloth to mourn

The majesty and burning of the child's death.
I shall not murder
The mankind of her going with a grave truth
Nor blaspheme down the stations of the breath
With any further
Elegy of innocence and youth.

Deep with the first dead lies London's daughter,
Robed in the long friends,
The grains beyond age, the dark veins of her mother,
Secret by the unmourning water
Of the riding Thames.
After the first death, there is no other.

DYLAN THOMAS

IN THE SHELTER

In a shelter one night, when death was taking the air
Outside, I saw her, seated apart – a child
Nursing her doll, to one man's vision enisled
With radiance which might have shamed even death to its lair.

Then I thought of our Christmas roses at home – the dark
Lanterns comforting us a winter through
With the same dusky flush, the same bold spark
Of confidence, O sheltering child, as you.

Genius could never paint the maternal pose
More deftly than accident had roughed it there,
Setting amidst our terrors, against the glare
Of unshaded bulb and whitewashed brick, that rose.

Instinct was hers, and an earthquake hour revealed it
In flesh – the meek-laid lashes, the glint in the eye
Defying wrath and reason, the arms that shielded
A plaster doll from an erupting sky.

No argument for living could long sustain
These ills: it needs a faithful eye, to have seen all
Love in the droop of a lash and tell it eternal
By one pure bead of its dew-dissolving chain.

Dear sheltering child, if again misgivings grieve me
That love is only a respite, an opal bloom
Upon our snow-set fields, come back to revive me
Cradling your spark through blizzard, drift and tomb.

C. Day Lewis

SEAFRONT

Here like the maze of our bewilderment
the thorn-crowned wire spreads high along the shore,
and flowers with rust, and tears our common sun;
and where no paths of love may reach the sea
the shut sands wait deserted for the drowned.

On other islands similarly barbed
mankind lies self-imprisoned in his fear,
and watches through the black sights of a gun
the winging flocks of migratory birds
who cannot speak of freedom, yet are free.

Laurie Lee

THE GRAVES OF THE PARTISANS

The graves of the partisans lie asleep
among the birch groves and wild raspberries.
Death works his magic.
Oh may you who are burdened
come to these graves under the weight you carry,
it will be sad and light,
you too will see clearly
distantly.

I read the names.
Nastya Kevstova.
Pyotr Belomestnykh. Maxim Kuzmichov.
Over them all this solemn lettering:
"Who died courageously for Marxism."
Consider this inscription.
Long ago in the year 1919
some simple man who could read and write
spelt slowly out his universal truth.
They none of them read Marx:
they believed in the existence of a God:
they went to war and thrashed the upper classes,
as things turned out Marxists is what they were . . .
Who died for a new, young world;
Siberian peasants, cross around their necks,
lying dead not under the cross
but a proletarian red-painted star.
And I stand here with my shoes in the dew,
ageing in one morning. I have passed
the whole examination in Marxism.
Or not the whole of it.
Say goodbye to the graves of the partisans.
You have helped me in every way you can.
And I have still to search, still to suffer;
the world is waiting for this,
its birds are whistling in the wet branches,
expecting courage.
The world is everlasting.
The living, thinking of the dead,
the dead, of the living.

YEVGENY YEVTUSHENKO
Transl. by Peter Levi and R. Milner-Gulland

NON GRIDATE PIÙ

Cessate d'uccidere i morti,
Non gridate più, non gridate
Se li volete ancora udire,
Se sperate di non perire.

Hanno l'impercettibile sussurro,
Non fanno più rumore
Del crescere dell'erba,
Lieta dove non passa l'uomo.

GIUSEPPE UNGARETTI

CRY NO MORE

Cease from killing the dead,
Cry no more, do not cry
If you still wish to hear them,
If you hope not to perish.

Theirs is an imperceptible murmur,
They make no more noise
Than the grass growing,
Happy where man does not tread.

LAST STOP

. . . .

. . . Again and again the same things, you will tell me, friend;
Yet the thought of the exile, the thought of the prisoner, the thought
Of man, when man has become a commodity, –
Try to alter it, you cannot.
Perhaps, even, he would like to remain King of the Cannibals,
Using up powers which no one wants to buy,
To walk among broad fields of agapanthi,
To hear the drums beneath the bamboo tree
As the courtiers, wierdly masked, step in the dance.
Nevertheless the country under the axe, chopped, burned like pine, and
    you see it,
Whether in the dark compartment, without water, the windows broken,
    night after night,
Or in the red-hot ship which, according to statistics, will sink –
These things are fixed in the mind; they do not change;
These things have planted images, like those trees
Which drop their shoots down in the virgin forest,
And these take root in the earth then rise and then
Throw down more shoots and again rise, bestriding
League after league.
Our mind is a virgin forest of murdered friends.
And if I speak to you in fables and parables
It is for your smoother hearing, and horror
Cannot be spoken because it is alive,
Because it is silent and is going forward;
It drips into the day and it drips into sleep
Sorrow-recalling pain.

To speak of heroes, to speak of heroes. Michael
Who with open wounds fled from the hospital, –
Perhaps he spoke of heroes when, that night,
As he dragged his feet along through blacked-out streets,
He howled groping over our pain, "Into the darkness
We go, into the darkness we go forward . . ."
Heroes go forward into darkness.

Not many moon-lit nights have given me pleasure.

George Seferis. Transl. by Rex Warner

GEZIELTES VON SPIELZEUG

Abwurf
von Spielzeug
statt Bomben
zum Fest der Kinder

sagten die Marktforscher
das
macht zweifellos
grossen Eindruck

Es hat sehr grossen
Eindruck
gemacht
auf die ganze Welt

Hätte das Flugzeug
lieber vor vierzehn Tagen
Spielzeug heruntergeworfen
und jetzt erst die Bomben

Hätten meine zwei Kinder
noch vierzehn Tage
durch eure Güte
etwas zum Spielen gehabt

ERICH FRIED

TOY ON TARGET

Dropping
toys
instead of bombs
for the Festival of the Children

that,
the market researchers said,
will doubtlessly make
an impression

It has made
a great
impression
on the whole world

If the aeroplane
had dropped the toys
a fortnight ago
and only now the bombs

my two children
thanks to your kindness
would have had something to play with
for those two weeks.*

Transl. by G. Rapp

*On the day of the Vietnamese "Festival of the Children", U.S. bombers dropped toys, even on villages where shortly before children had been killed by their bombs.

REMEMBRANCE

Passons, passons, puisque tout passe
Je me retournerai souvent,
Les souvenirs sont cors de chasse
Dont meurt le bruit parmi le vent.

GUSTAVE APOLLINAIRE

REMEMBRANCE

Introductory Note

THERE is very little to be added here to the text itself. Remembrance has a colour of its own, and its edges need no sharpening. The first quotations in this section are given up to the most poignant grief that can befall any man or woman: the early death of their child. There could have been many more of this kind – taken from poets of every century, from the Greek Anthology until our own time – but since each one of those I have chosen has seemed to me to say exactly what its writer had to say, I was reluctant to add any others. Moreover, unless an emotion as painful as this one is expressed with the utmost restraint, it moves one to embarrassment, rather than grief. "Poetry", said Flaubert, "must not be the scum of the heart; that is neither serious nor *right*."

The only other poems here directly concerned with the loss of a loved person are the lines by the Emperor Wu-Ti (157–87 B.C.), sixth emperor of the Han dynasty, when his mistress Li Fu-jên died; two sonnets by Petrarch, and, in a very different vein, the passage from St. Augustine's *Confessions* about the death of his mother, which I have included chiefly for the sake of his naive hope that if, in his grief, he went and bathed his sorrow would be healed – and the tears that he shed when he found it was not so. In the fragment from Rilke's *First Elegy*, on the other hand, we have the other side of human loss: "They've finally no more need of us, the early-departed . . . but we . . . could we exist without them?"

The other memories evoked here are not directly connected with death, but only with its prelude, absence, or with nostalgia: remembered youth, remembered joy, remembered love – and sometimes, the joy that these too can bring.

ON A BOY OF TWELVE

Philip his father laid here the twelve-years-old child, his high hope, Nicoteles.

CALLIMACHUS. Transl. by J. W. Mackail

ON A WAYSIDE TOMB

Sit beneath the poplars, wayfarer, when thou art weary, and drawing nigh drink of our spring; and even far away remember the fountain that Simus sets by the side of Cillus his dead child.

NICIAS. Transl. by J. W. Mackail

EPITAPH FOR A LITTLE SLAVE-GIRL

Hanc tibi, Fronto pater, genitrix Flaccilla, puellam
Oscula commendo deliciasque meas
Parvola ne nigras horrescat Erotion umbras
Oraque Tartarei prodigiosa canis.
Impletura fuit sextae modo frigora brumae
Vixiesset totidem ni minus illa dies.
Inter tam veteres ludat lasciva patronos
Et nomen blaeso garriat ore meum.
Mollia non rigidus cespes tegat ossa nec illi
Terra, gravis fueris: non fuit illa tibi.

MARTIAL: *Epigrammaton* V, XXXIV

To thee, father Fronto, and thee, mother Flaccilla, I commend this little girl, on whom I bestowed my kisses and my delight. She-Erotion-is so small! Let her not fear the dark shades and the monstrous jaws of the hound of Tartarus. She lacked six days, had she lived so long, to reach her sixth birthday this winter. May she play happily with you, her revered guardians, and prattle in her childish voice, calling my name. Let no rough bush cover her tender bones, and, thou, Earth, lie lightly upon her: she did not weigh on thee.*

*This epitaph refers to the death of a little slave-girl of Martial's, whom he commended after her death to the care of his own dead parents, Fronto and Flaccilla. She died in A.D. 89, but Martial was still remembering her nine years later, and requested that whoever should own his Italian land after his return to Spain, should keep on tending her grave. (Epigram, X, 61.)

LAGGE FILI BENE QUIESCAS
MATER TUA ROGAT TE
UT ME AD TE RECIPIAS.
VALE.

Laggus, my son, rest in peace.
I thy mother beseech thee
To take me to thee.
Farewell.

(Undated Roman epitaph)

Grief fills the room up of my absent child.

SHAKESPEARE: *King John*

Farewell, thou child of my right hand and joy . . .
Rest in soft peace, and, ask'd, say here doth lye
Ben Jonson, his best piece of *poetrie*.

BEN JONSON

Deare Sir, I am in some little disorder by reason of the death of a little child of mine, a boy that lately made us very glad: but now he rejoyces in his little orbe, while we thinke, and sigh, and long to be as safe as he is.

JEREMY TAYLOR: *Letter to John Evelyn*

AFTER THE DEATH OF LAURA

I

Oimè il bel viso, oimè il soave sguardo,
Oimè il leggiadro portamento altero;
Oimè il parlar ch'ogni aspro ingegno e fero
Facevi umile, ed ogni uom vil gagliardo!

E oimè il dolce riso, onde uscío'l dardo
Di che morte, altro bene omai non spero!
Alma real, dignissima d'impero,
Se non fossi fra noi scesa sí tardo!

Per voi convien ch'io arda, e'n voi respire
Ch'i pur fui vostro; ese di voi son privo,
Via men d'ogni sventura altra mi dole.

Di speranza m'empieste, e di desire
Quand'io parti' dal sommo piacer vivo;
Ma'l vento ne portava le parole.

II

La vita fugge, e non s'arresta una ora,
E la morte vien dietro a gran giornate;
E le cose presenti, e le passate,
Mi danno guerra, e le future ancora.

E'l rimembrare e l'aspettar m'accora,
Or quinci, or quindi, sì che'n veritate
Se non ch'i' ò di me stesso pietate
I' sarei già di questi pensier fòra.

Tornami avanti, s'alcun dolce mai
Ebbe 'l cor tristo; e poi da l'altra parte
Veggio al mio navigar turbati i venti:

Veggio fortuna in porto, e stanco omai
Il mio nocchier, e rotte arbore e sarte,
E i lumi bei, che mirar soglio, spenti.

FRANCESCO PETRARCA: *Sonetti*, CCLXVII e CCLXXII

I

Alas, that gentle look, and that fair face!
  Alas, for the body's beauty when you wended
  Your gracious way! Alas, your words that mended
  the brutal, and taught honour to the base!
Alas, that smile of yours, whose wounding grace
  has come to death, and all my hope is ended!
  You'd have been queen of earth, had you descended
  to a younger world, to a less evil race.

Still I must burn in you, in you respire!
  I was yours utterly; my stricken heart
  can feel no other hurt, after today.
You showered hope upon me and desire
  in our last moment, ere we came to part;
  And then the wind blew all your words away.

II

Life hurries on, a frantic refugee,
  and death, with great forced marches, follows fast;
  and all the present leagues with all the past
  and all the future to make war on me.
Anticipation joins to memory
  tearing my soul in torment; and at last,
  Did not damnation set me so aghast,
  I'd put an end to thinking, and be free.

The few glad moments that my heart has known
  return to me; and now I watch in dread
  the winds upgathering against my ways
storm in the harbor, and the pilot prone,
  the mast and rigging down; and dark and dead
  the lovely lights whereon I used to gaze.

Transl. by MORRIS BISHOP

LI FU-JÊN

The sound of her silk skirt has stopped.
On the marble pavement dust grows.
Her empty room is cold and still.
Fallen leaves are piled against the doors.
Longing for that lovely lady
How can I bring my aching heart to rest?.*

WU-TI (157–87 B.C.). Transl. by Arthur Waley

*The Translator adds:
This poem was written by Wu-Ti, sixth emperor of the Han dynasty, when his mistress, Li Fu-jên died. Unable to bear his grief, he sent for wizards from all parts of China, hoping that they would be able to put him into communication with her spirit.

At last one of them managed to project her shape on to a curtain. The emperor cried:

Is it or isn't it?
I stand and look.
The swish, swish of a silk skirt.
How slow she comes!

ST. AUGUSTINE MOURNS THE DEATH OF HIS MOTHER

I closed her eyes, and a great tide of sorrow surged into my heart and would have run over in weeping. Yet my eyes by a strong effort of will drove back the tears even unto dryness, and in that struggle it went very hard with me. As she drove her last breath, the boy Adeodatus broke out into lamentations; but we all rebuked him, and he was silent again . . . For we judged it not seemly that such a death should be attended by weeping, and those cries of grief wherewith the world bewails what it counts the misery or utter extinction of the departed. She was not miserable nor was she wholly dead. This we knew for certain from the life she had led, from faith unfeigned, from reasons which we could not doubt.

What then was that aching pain in my heart? What but the bleeding wound, caused by the sudden tearing away of that sweet and precious intercourse? I treasured up her praise, for in her last illness, when I was rendering her some little service, she caressed me and called me "her good son", and said with great emotion that she had never heard from my lips an angry or disrespectful word.

We went [to the burial] and returned without a tear . . . But all that day I sorrowed in secret, and with troubled mind besought Thee, as best I could, to heal my grief . . . I determined even to go and bathe; for I had heard that the bath derives its name from the Greek word βαλανανειον, because it drives away sorrow from the mind. Behold, this also I confess to Thy mercy, O Father of the fatherless that I went and bathed, and was the same after the bath as before! For the bitterness of my trouble could not be washed away from my heart.

Then I slept and woke, and found my sorrow diminished not a little . . . I came back to my former thoughts of Thy handmaid and her life . . . And as I dwelt upon that sudden loss, I wept freely in Thy sight over her and for her, over myself and for myself. I gave my pent up tears licence to flow as they would, and laid them as a bed for my heart. And it found rest upon them; for Thy ears alone could hear my weeping, not man, who might have scorned me.

And now, O Lord, I confess it unto Thee in my book. Let anyone that will read it, and make of it what he will. And if he count it a sin that for a fraction of an hour I should have wept for my mother, the mother who in my sight for a while was dead, who had wept for so many years for me that I might live in Thy sight, yet let him not scoff at me; but rather, if his charity be large, let him weep for my sins unto Thee, the Father of all the brethren of Thy Christ.

ST. AUGUSTINE: *Confessions*, IX, 12. Transl. by C. Bigg

DREAMING THAT I WENT WITH LI AND YÜ TO VISIT YUAN CHÊN PO

At night I dreamt I was back in Ch'ang-an;
I saw again the faces of old friends.
And in my dreams, under an April sky,
They led me by the hand to wander in the spring winds.
Together we came to the village of Peace and Quiet;
We stopped our horses at the gate of Yüan Chên.
Yüan Chên was sitting all alone;
When he saw me coming, a smile came to his face.
He pointed back at the flowers in the western court;
Then opened wine in the northern summer-house.

He seemed to be saying that neither of us had changed;
He seemed to be regretting that joy will not stay;
That our souls had met only for a little while,
To part again with hardly time for greeting.
I woke up and thought him still at my side;
I put out my hand: there was nothing there at all.*

Po Chü-I. Transl. by Arthur Waley

ON HEARING SOMEONE SING A POEM BY YÜAN CHÊN

No new poems his brush will trace;
Even his fame is dead.
His old poems are deep in dust
At the bottom of boxes and cupboards.
Once lately, when someone was singing,
Suddenly I heard a verse –
Before I had time to catch the words
A pain had stabbed my heart.

Po Chü-I. Transl. by Arthur Waley

PARTHENOPHIL

Parthenophil is lost and I would see him,
For he is like to something I remember
A great while since, a long, long time ago.

John Ford

*After Yüan Chên's death, Po Chü-I's last years were spent in retirement in an unoccupied part of the Hsiang-shan monastery, spending part of his time in collecting his complete works. The translator adds: "There is a story that he was in the habit of reading his poems to an old peasant woman and altering any expression that she could not understand."

'STIMMEN, STIMMEN'

. . . .

Stimmen, Stimmen. Höre, mein Herz, wie sonst nur
Heilige hörten: dass sie der riesige Ruf
aufhob vom Boden; sie aber knieten,
Unmögliche, weiter und achtetens nicht:
So waren sie hörend. Nicht dass du Gottes ertrügest
die Stimme, bei weitem. Aber das Wehende höre,
die ununterbrochene Nachricht, die aus Stille sich bildet.
Es rauscht jetzt von jenen jungen Toten zu dir.
Wo immer du eintratst, redete nicht in Kirchen
zu Rom und Neapel ruhig ihr Schicksal dich an?
Oder es trug eine Inschrift sich erhaben dir auf,
wie neulich die Tafel in Santa Maria Formosa.
Was sie mir wollen? leise soll ich des Unrechts
Anschein abtun, der ihrer Geister
reine Bewegung manchmal ein wenig behindert.

Freilich is es seltsam, die Erde nicht mehr zu bewohnen,
kaum erlernte Gebräuche nicht mehr zu üben,
Rosen, und andern eigens versprechenden Dingen
nicht die Bedeutung menschlicher Zukunft zu geben;
das, was man war in unendlich ängstlichen Händen,
nicht mehr zu sein, und selbst den eigenen Namen
wegzulassen wie ein zerbrochenes Spielzeug.
Seltsam, die Wünsche nicht weiterzuwünschen. Seltsam,
alles, was sich bezog, so lose im Raume
flattern zu sehen. Und das Totsein ist mühsam
und voller Nacholn, dass man allmählich ein wenig
Ewigkeit spürt. – Aber Lebendige machen
alle den Fehler, dass sie zu stark unterscheiden.
Engel (sagt man) wüssten oft nicht, ob sie unter
Lebenden gehn oder Toten. Die ewige Strömung
reisst durch beide Bereiche alle Alter
Immer mit sich übertönt sie in beiden.

Schliesslich brauchen sie uns nicht mehr, die Früheentrückten,
man entwöhnt sich des Irdischen sanft, wie man den Brüsten
milde der Mutter entwächst. Aber wir, die so grosse
Geheimnisse brauchen, denen aus Trauer so oft
seliger Fortschritt entspringt – : könnten wir sein ohne sie?

Ist die Sage umsonst, dass einst in der Klage um Linos
wagende erst Musik dürre Erstarrung durchdrang,
dass erst im erschrockenen Raum, dem ein beinah göttlicher Jüngling
plötzlich für immer enttrat, das Leere in jene
Schwingung geriet, die uns jetzt hinreisst und tröstet und hilft.

RAINER MARIA RILKE: From *Die Erste Elegie*

. . . .

Voices, voices. Hear, O my heart, as only
saints have heard: heard till the giant-call
lifted them off the ground; yet they went impossibly
on with their kneeling, in undistracted attention:
so inherently hearers. Not that you could endure
the voice of God – far from it. But hark to the suspiration,
the uninterrupted news that grows out of silence.
Rustling towards you now from those youthfully-dead.
Whenever you entered a church in Rome or in Naples
were you not always being quietly addressed by their fate?
Or else an inscription sublimely imposed itself on you,
as, lately, the tablet in Santa Maria Formosa.
What they require of me? I must gently remove the appearance
of suffered injustice, that hinders
a little, at times, their purely-proceeding spirits.

True, it is strange to inhabit the earth no longer,
to use no longer customs scarcely acquired,
not to interpret roses, and other things
that promise so much, in terms of a human future;
to be no longer all that one used to be
in endlessly anxious hands, and to lay aside
even one's proper name like a broken toy.
Strange, not to go on wishing one's wishes. Strange,
to see all that was once relation so loosely fluttering
hither and thither in space. And it's hard, being dead,
and full of retrieving before one begins to espy
a trace of eternity. – Yes, but all of the living
make the mistake of drawing too sharp distinctions.
Angels (they say) are often unable to tell
whether they move among living or dead. The eternal
torrent whirls all the ages through either realm
for ever, and sounds above their voices in both.

They've finally no more need of us, the early-departed,
one's gently weaned from terrestrial things as one mildly
outgrows the breasts of a mother. But we, that have need of
such mighty secrets, we, for whom sorrow's so often
source of blessedest progress, could we exist without them?
Is the story in vain, how once, in the mourning for Linos,
venturing earliest music pierced barren numbness, and how,
in the horrified space an almost deified youth
suddenly quitted for ever, emptiness first
felt the vibration that now charms us and comforts and helps?

Transl. by J. B. Leishman and Stephen Spender

'L'ORA CHE VOLGE IL DISIO'

Era già l'ora che volge il disio
  ai navicanti e 'ntenerisce il core
  lo dí c'han detto ai dolci amici addio;
e che lo novo peregrin d'amore
  punge, se ode squilla di lontano
  che paia il giorno pianger che si more;
. . . .

DANTE: *Purgatorio*, VIII, 1-6

Now was the hour which longing backwards bends
  In those that sail, and melts their heart in sighs,
  The day they have said farewell to their sweet friends,
And pricks with love the outsetting pilgrim's eyes
  If the far bell he hears across the land
  Which seems to mourn over the day that dies. . . .

Transl. by Laurence Binyon

'IMMEASURABLE PAIN'

Immeasurable pain!
My dreaming soul last night was king again.
As in past days
I wandered through the Palace of Delight,
And in my dream
Down grassy garden-ways
Glided my chariot, smoother than a summer stream;
There was moonlight,
The trees were blossoming,
And a faint wind softened the air of night
For it was spring.

LI HOU-CHU (last Emperor of the Southern
T'ang Dynasty; *c.* A.D. 975). Transl. by Arthur Waley

LE RICORDANZE

Frammenti

Vaghe stelle dell'Orsa, io non credea
Tornare ancora per uso a contemplarvi
Sul paterno giardino scintillanti,
E ragionar con voi dalle finestre
Di questo albergo ove abitai fanciullo
E delle gioie mie vidi la fine.
Quante immagini un tempo, e quante fole
Creommi nel pensier l'aspetto vostro
E delle luci a voi compagne! allora
Che, tacito, seduto in verde zolla,
Delle sere io solea passar gran parte
Mirando il cielo, ed ascoltando il canto
Della rana rimota alla campagna!
E la lucciola errava appo le siepi
E in su l'aiuole, susurrando al vento
I viali odorati, ed i cipressi
Là nella selva; e sotto al patrio tetto
Sonavan voci alterne, e le tranquille
Opre de' servi. E che pensieri immensi,
Che dolci sogni mi spirò la vista

Di quel lontano mar, quei monti azzurri,
Che di qua scopro, e che varcare un giorno
Io mi pensava, arcani mondi, arcana
Felicità fingendo a viver mio!

. . . .

Viene il vento recando il suon dell'ora
Dalla torre del borgo. Era conforto
Questo suon, mi rimembra, alle mie notti,
Quando fanciullo, nella buia stanza,
Per assidui terrori io vigilava,
Sospirando il mattin. Qui non è cosa
Ch'io vegga o senta, onde un' immagin dentro
Non torni, e un dolce rimembrar non sorga.
Dolce per se; ma con dolor sottentra
Il pensier del presente, un van desio
Del passato, ancor tristo, e il dire: io fui.

. . . .

O speranze, speranze, ameni inganni
Della mia prima età! sempre, parlando,
Ritorno a voi; che per andar di tempo,
Per variar d'affetti e di pensieri,
Obbliarvi non so. Fantasmi, intendo,
Son la gloria e l'onor; diletti e beni
Mero desio; non ha la vita un frutto,
Inutile miseria. E sebben vóti
Son gli anni miei, sebben deserto, oscuro
Il mio stato mortal, poco mi toglie
La fortuna, ben veggo. Ahi, ma qualvolta
A voi ripenso, o mie speranze antiche,
E a quel caro immaginar mio primo;

. . . .

O Nerina! e di te forse non odo
Questi luoghi parlar? caduta forse
Dal mio pensier sei tu? Dove sei gita
Che qui sola di te la ricordanza
Trovo, dolcezza mia? Più non ti vede
Questa Terra natal: quella finestra,
Ond'eri usata favellarmi, ed onde
Mesto riluce delle stelle il raggio,
E' deserta. Ove sei, che più non odo
La tua voce sonar, siccome un giorno,

Quando soleva ogni lontano accento
Del labbro tuo, ch'a me giungesse, il volto
Scolorarmi? Altro tempo. I giorni tuoi
Furo, mio dolce amore. Passasti. Ad altri
Il passar per la terra oggi è sortito,
E l'abitar questi odorati colli.
Ma rapida passasti: e come un sogno
Fu la tua vita.

. . . .

GIACOMO LEOPARDI

O you bright stars of the Bear, I did not think
That I should come once more, as was my custom,
To gaze upon you glittering above
My father's garden, or converse with you
From the windows of this house, where as a boy
I lived, and saw the end of happiness.
Time was, how many mad imaginings
I fashioned in the thought of your bright aspect,
And your companion stars. For then I used
To pass away the most part of the evening
Quietly sitting on the green turf, watching
The sky, and listening to the frogs' remote
Song, from the open country. The firefly wandered
About the hedgerows and above the flowerbeds,
And the wind sighed among the fragrant alleys
And through the cypress trees there in the wood;
While sounded from the house at intervals
Voices of servants at their ordered tasks.
But what vast thoughts and what sweet visions then
That distant sea called forth, and those blue mountains
Discerned from far away! – which then I thought
To cross some day, inventing for myself
An unknown world, and unknown happiness

. . . .

The tolling of the hour comes on the wind
From the town belfry. A sound which was my comfort,
As I remember, in those fearful nights
Of boyhood, when I lay in my dark room,
Beset by terrors, longing for the dawn.

There is no object here that meets my sense
Which does not bring some image back again,
Or raise some sweet remembrance – sweet in itself,
But then creeps in, with pain, thought of the present,
And so, an empty longing for the past,
Though it was sad, and these words: "I have been"

. . . .

O dreams, O dreams, O you the dear illusions
Of my young years, always I turn again
To you, in musing; though time goes, and though
Our thoughts and passions change, forget you not.
Phantoms – I know it now – are glory and honour;
All good and all delight are mere desire;
The waste and misery of life bear at the last
No single fruit. And though my years are empty,
And this, my life's condition, desert and dark,
Fortune has taken little – too well I see it
But oh, as often as I think of you,
My early hopes, the dear imaginings
I once possessed

. . . .

But O Nerina, does not this place speak
Of you, and can it be that you indeed
Are faded from my thoughts? Where are you gone?
For memories. O sweetness of my life,
Are all I find of you. This countryside
Where you were born knows you no more. That window
Where once you used to talk with me is empty,
Reflecting the sad glitter of the stars.
Where are you? For the echo of your voice
Is heard no more – whose distant accents once
Falling upon my ears, made me turn pale.
That was another time. Your days are over,
My sweet beloved. You have passed. To others
Is given now to go about the land
And find a dwelling in these fragrant hills.
But swiftly you passed by, and all your life
Was like a dream . . .

Transl. by John Heath-Stubbs

LE MANCHY

Sous un nuage frais de claire mousseline,
  Tous les dimanches, au matin,
Tu venais à la ville en manchy de rotin,
  Par les rampes de la colline.

La cloche de l'église alertement tintait;
  Le vent de mer bercait les cannes:
Comme une grêle d'or, aux pointes des savanes,
  Le feu du soleil crépitait.

Le bracelet aux poings, l'anneau sur la cheville,
  Et le mouchoir jaune aux chignons,
Deux Telingas portaient, assidus compagnons,
  Ton lit aux nattes de Manille.

Ployant leur jarret maigre et nerveux et chantant,
  Souples dans leurs tuniques blanches,
Le bambou sur l'épaule et les mains sur les hanches,
  Ils allaient le long de l'Étang.

Le long de la chaussée et des varangues basses
  Ou les vieux créoles fumaient,
Par les groupes joyeux des Noirs, ils s'animaient
  Au bruit des bobres Madécasses.

Dans l'air léger flottait l'odeur des tamarins;
  Sur les houles illuminées
Au large, les oiseaux, en d'immenses traînées,
  Plongeaient dans les brouillards marins.

Et, tandis que ton pied, sorti de la babouche,
  Pendait, rose, au bord du manchy,
A l'ombre des Bois-noirs touffus, et du Letchi
  Aux fruits moins pourprés que ta bouche;

Tandis qu'un papillon, les deux ailes en fleur,
  Teinté d'azur et d'écarlate,
Se posait par instants sur ta peau délicate
  En y laissant de sa couleur;

On voyait, au travers du rideau de batiste,
Tes boucles dorer l'oreiller;
Et, sous leurs cils mi-clos, feignant de sommeiller,
Tes beaux yeux de sombre améthyste.

Tu t'en venais ainsi, par ces matins si doux,
De la montagne à la grand'messe,
Dans ta grace naïve et ta rose jeunesse,
Au pas rythmé de tes Hindous.

Maintenant, dans le sable aride de nos grêves,
Sous les chiendents, au bruit des mers,
Tu reposes parmi les morts qui me sont chers,
O charme de mes premiers rêves!

LECONTE DE LISLE

THE VOICE

Woman much missed, how you call to me, call to me,
Saying that now you are not as you were
When you had changed from the one who was all to me,
But as at first, when our day was fair.

Can it be you that I hear? Let me view you, then,
Standing as when I drew near to the town
Where you would wait for me: yes, as I knew you then,
Even to the original air-blue gown!

Or is it only the breeze, in its listlessness
Travelling across the wet mead to me here
You being ever dissolved to wan wistlessness
Heard no more again far or near?

Thus I; faltering forward,
Leaves around me falling,
Wind oozing thin through the thorn from norward
And the woman calling.

THOMAS HARDY

IN MEMORY OF EVA GORE-BOOTH AND CON MARKIEWICZ

The light of evening, Lissadell,
Great windows open to the south,
Two girls in silk kimonos, both
Beautiful, one a gazelle.
But a raving autumn shears
Blossom from the summer's wreath;
The older is condemned to death,
Pardoned, drags out lonely years
Conspiring among the ignorant.
I know not what the younger dreams –
Some vague Utopia – and she seems,
When withered old and skeleton-gaunt,
An image of such politics.
Many a time I think to seek
One or the other out and speak
Of that old Georgian mansion, mix
Pictures of the mind, recall
That table and the talk for youth,
Two girls in silk kimonos, both
Beautiful, one a gazelle

. . . .

W. B. YEATS

CALYPSO'S ISLAND

I know very well, goddess, she is not beautiful
As you are: could not be. She is a woman,
Mortal, subject to the chances: duty of

Childbed, sorrow that changes cheeks, the tomb –
For unlike you she will grow grey, grow older,
Grey and older, sleep in that small room.

She is not beautiful as you, O golden!
You are immortal and will never change
And can make me immortal also, fold

Your garment round me, make me whole and strange
As those who live forever, not the while
That we live; keep me from those dogging dangers –

Ships and the wars – in this green, far-off island,
Silent of all but sea's eternal sound
Or sea-pine's when the lull of surf is silent.

Goddess, I know how excellent this ground
What charmed contentment of the removed heart
The bees make in the lavender where pounding

Surf sounds far off and the bird that darts
Darts through its own eternity of light,
Motionless in motion, and the startled

Hare is startled into stone, the fly
Forever golden in the flickering glance
Of leafy sunlight that still holds it. I

Know you, goddess, and your caves that answer
Ocean's confused voices with a voice:
Your poplars where the storms are turned to dances;

Arms when the heart is turned. You give the choice
To hold forever what forever passes,
To hide from what will pass, forever. Moist,

Moist are your well-stones, goddess, cool your grasses!
And she – she is a woman with that fault
Of change that will be death in her at last!

Nevertheless I long for the cold, salt,
Restless, contending sea and for the island
Where the grass dies and the seasons alter:

Where that one wears the sunlight for a while.

ARCHIBALD MACLEISH

*'UN BONHEUR EST PASSÉ'

Un bonheur est passé,
Furtif, leger.
Comme on voit bien que c'est
Un étranger.

Un bonheur est passé
Sur le chemin.
O coeur, et c'est assez
Jusqu'à demain.

Un bonheur est passé
Tout à côté,
Loin et comme espacé
D'éternité.

CHARLES PÉGUY

ESCALES

Orages de souffrance
Mer sans bords du passé –
Aux rives de l'enfance
Mon coeur est amarré.

Amour de la vie:
Espoir desoeuvré –
Aux bords de ton âme
Mon coeur est amarré.

ANON.

L'ADIEU

J'ai cueilli ce brin de bruyère
L'automne est morte souviens t'en
Nous ne nous verrons plus sur terre
Odeur du temps brin de bruyère
Et souviens-toi que je t'attends.

GUILLAUME APOLLINAIRE: *Alcools*

*These quatrains refer to a lady – whom Péguy always called "*l'Innominata*" – with whom he maintained for many years an *amitié amoureuse* which developed, on his side, into a deep but unfufilled passion. Finally, she married someone else, and it was soon after this that these lines were written. In a letter to a friend, at much the same time, Péguy wrote: "In the Lord's Prayer there are those terrible words, 'Thy Will be done'. I couldn't get them through my teeth."

ACCORDING TO ANCIENT FORMULAS OF GRECOSYRIAN MAGI

"What extract can be discovered from
witching herbes," said an aesthete,
"what extract prepared according to the
formulas of ancient Grecosyrian magi
that, for a day (if its potency
can last no longer), or even for an hour,
can evoke for me my twenty-three years;
can evoke again for me my friend
when he was twenty-two – his beauty, his love?

"What extract can be found according to the formulas
prepared by the ancient Grecosyrian magi which,
along with this return to the past,
can also evoke for me our little room?"

C. P. CAVAFY. Transl. by Rae Dalven

ORPHEUS' DREAM

And she was there. The little boat
Coasting the perilous isles of sleep,
Zones of oblivion and despair,
Stopped, for Eurydice was there.
The foundering skiff could scarcely keep
All that felicity afloat.

As if we had left earth's frontier wood
Long since and from this sea had won
The lost original of the soul,
The moment gave us pure and whole
Each back to each, and swept us on
Past every choice to boundless good.

Forgiveness, truth, atonement, all
Our love at once – till we could dare
At last to turn our heads and see
The poor ghost of Eurydice
Still sitting in her silver chair,
Alone in Hades' empty hall.

EDWIN MUIR

MEMORY I

"*And there was no more sea*"

And I with my hands holding nothing but a reed;
The night was desolate, the moon was on the wane
And the earth smelling of the last shower of rain.
I whispered: memory, wherever you touch it, gives pain,
There is little sky and there is no more sea,
They cart off what they kill by day and dispose of it behind the ridge.
My fingers were playing with this pipe absentmindedly.
I wished an old shepherd good evening and he gave it to me.
The others have done away with every greeting;
They wake, they shave, they start the day's work of killing,
Like pruning or surgery, with method and with no feeling;
Pain is a corpse like Patroclus and nobody makes a mistake.

I thought of playing a tune, and then I was shamed of the other world
The one that sees me from beyond the night from within my light
Which is woven from living bodies, from naked hearts,
And the love which belongs also to those Dread Goddesses
Just as to man and to stone, to the waters and to the grasses,
And to the animal staring in death's eyes as death comes to take it.

So I went up the dark path. I turned in
At my garden gate. I dug and buried the reed.
And again I whispered: one dawn will come the Resurrection,
As trees shine in the spring, so will gleam the dew of that morning,
Once more the sea, and again Aphrodite shaken out from the wave's
 foam;
We are the seed that dies. And I went into my empty home.

GEORGE SEFERIS. Transl. by Rex Warner

NEWS FROM A FOREIGN COUNTRY

News from a foreign Country came
As if my Treasure and my Joys lay there;

THOMAS TRAHERNE

. . . Man is one world, and hath
Another to attend him.

GEORGE HERBERT

Where ask is have, where seek is find,
Where knock is open wide.

CHRISTOPHER SMART

NEWS FROM A FOREIGN COUNTRY

Introductory Note

THESE selections have one quality in common: they are all concerned with "another world than this". Indeed I have tried to include no lines that did not seem to me to hold the qualities that open the door to that world: awe and wonder. Martin Buber, the great Semitic philosopher and scholar, once said to Ignazio Silone, with whom he was talking about the difficulties he was encountering in translating the Bible, that the word Jahweh, Jehovah, cannot be translated. "God is not a *name* – the word is an exclamation, a cry: THOU!"

TO THE CHRISTIANS

I give you the end of a golden string,
   Only wind it into a ball,
It will lead you in at Heaven's gate
   Built in Jerusalem's wall.

WILLIAM BLAKE: *Jerusalem*, IV

'CE MATIN'

Ce matin
J'ai vu dans le lointain
Frémir au vent des banderolles claires.
Ce matin
J'ai vu dans le lointain
Venir des gens
Vêtus de frais satin.
Sur leurs habits
Perles et rubis,
Partout de l'or
Aux harnais des dromadaires.
Sur leurs habits
Perles et rubis
Turbans de soie
Et casques bien fourbis.

(Carol sung on Twelfth Night by the children of Bonneval in the French Alps)

LA SACRA FAMIGLIA

Maria lavava
Giuseppe stendeva
Il figlio piangeva
Dal freddo che aveva.
– Sta zitto mio figlio
Che adesso ti piglio.
Del latte ti ho dato
Del pan' un ce n'è.
La neve sui monti
Cadeva dal cielo
Maria col suo velo
Copriva Gesù.

Tuscan Lullaby

THE HOLY FAMILY

Mary was washing,
Joseph hung up the clothes,
The little boy was wailing,
He was so very cold.
  Now hush you, my baby,
  I'll take you up soon,
  I've given you milk
  And bread there is none.
The snow on the mountains
Fell down from the sky
And Mary's blue veil
Lay over the child.

CHRISTMAS STAR

It was winter.
The wind blew from the steppe
And it was cold for the child
In the cave on the hillside.

He was warmed by the breath of an ox.
The farm animals
Were stabled in the cave,
And a warm haze drifted over the manger.

Shaking from their sheepskins
The wisps of straw and hay-seeds of their bedding,
Half asleep, the shepherds gazed
From a rock ledge into the midnight distance

. . . .

A crowd had gathered by the stone at the entrance.
Day was breaking. The trunks of the cedars were plain.
"Who are you?" asked Mary.
"We are a company of shepherds and envoys from heaven.
We have come to praise you both".
"You can't all come in at once. Wait a little by the door."

Shepherds and herdsmen stamped about
In the ashy dusk before the dawn.
By the wooden water trough
Men on foot and horsemen swore at each other,
Camels roared and asses kicked.

Day was breaking. The dawn swept the remaining stars
Like cinders from the sky.
Out of all the great gathering Mary allowed
Only the Wise Men through the opening in the rock.

He slept in the oak manger,
Radiant as moonlight in the hollow of a tree.
Instead of a sheepskin,
The lips of the ass and the nostrils of the ox kept him warm.

The Magi stood in the shadow,
Whispering, scarcely finding words.
All at once, a hand stretched out of the dark
Moved one of them aside to the left of the manger.
He looked round. Gazing at the Virgin from the doorway.
Like a guest, was the Christmas Star.

BORIS PASTERNAK. Transl. by Manya Harari and Max Hayward

'ETERNAL LIFE'

We said then: "If the tumult of the flesh were hushed; hushed these shadows of earth, sea, sky; hushed the heavens and the soul itself, so that it should pass beyond itself and not think of itself; if all dreams were hushed, and all sensuous revelations, and every tongue and every symbol; if all that comes and goes were hushed – They all proclaim to him that hath an ear: 'We made not ourselves: He made us who abideth for ever' – But suppose that, having delivered their message,. they held their peace, turning their ear to Him who made them, and that He alone spoke, not by them but for Himself, and that we heard His word, not by any fleshly tongue, nor by any angel's voice, nor in the thunder, nor in any similitude, but His voice whom we love in these His creatures – Suppose we heard Him without any intermediary at all – Just now we reached out, and with one flash of thought touched the Eternal Wisdom that abides above all – Suppose this endured, and all other far inferior modes of vision were taken away, and this alone were to ravish the beholder, and absorb him, and plunge him in mystic joy, might not eternal life be like this moment of comprehension for which we sighed? Is not this the meaning of "Enter thou into the joy of thy Lord?"

ST. AUGUSTINE: *Confessions*, IX, 10. Transl. by C. Bigg

DIC CHRISTI VERITAS

Dic Christi Veritas,
dic cara raritas,
dic rara Caritas,
ubi nunc habitas?
aut in valle Visionis,
aut in throno Pharaonis,
aut in alto cum Nerone,
aut in antro cum Timone,
vel in viscella scirpea,
cum Moyse plorante,
vel in domo Romulea
cum bulla fulminante?

. . . .

Respondit Caritas:
homo, quid dubitas,
quid me sollicitas?
non sum quod usitas
nec in euro nec in austro
nec in foro nec in claustro,
nec in bysso nec in cuculla,
nec in bello nec in bulla.
de Iericho sum veniens,
ploro cum sauciato,
quem duplex Levi transiens
non astitit grabato.

MS. of BENEDICTBEUERN (13th century)

O Truth of Christ,
O most dear rarity,
O most rare Charity,
Where dwell'st thou now?
In the valley of Vision?
On Pharaoh's throne?
On high with Nero?
With Timon alone?
In the bulrush ark
Where Moses wept?
Or in Rome's high places
With lightning swept?

. . . .

Then Love replied,
"Man, wherefore didst thou doubt
Not where thou wast wont to find
My dwelling in the southern wind
Not in court and not in cloister
Not in casque nor yet in cowl,
Not in battle nor in Bull,
But on the road from Jericho
I come with a wounded man."

Transl. by Helen Waddell

TOUS LES CORPS, LE FIRMAMENT...

All bodies, the firmament, the stars, the earth and its kingdoms, are not worth as much as the smallest soul; for the soul knows them all, and himself; and the bodies (know) nothing.

All bodies put together, and all souls put together, and all that they have produced, are not worth as much as the slightest movement of charity. That is of an infinitely higher order.

Out of all bodies put together, you could not produce the smallest thought. That is impossible, it is of a different order.

From all bodies and minds, one could not draw forth a single movement of true charity; that is impossible, it is of another supernatural order.

PASCAL: *Pensées*

'QUAL È COLUI CHE SOMNÏANDO VEDE'

Qual è colui che somnïando vede,
che dopo il sogno la passione impressa
Rimane, e l'altro a la mente non riede,

cotal son io, ché quasi tutta cessa
mia visione, ed ancor mi distilla
nel core il dolce che nacque da essa.

Cosí la neve al sol si disigilla;
cosí al vento nelle foglie levi
si perdea la sentenza di Sibilla.

DANTE: *Paradiso*, XXXIII

As he who dreams sees, and when disappears
  The dream, the passion of its print remains,
  And naught else to the memory adheres,

Even such am I; for almost wholly wanes
  My vision now, yet still the drops I feel
  Of sweetness it distilled into my veins.

Even so the sunbeam doth the snow unseal;
  So was the Sibyl's saying lost inert
  Upon the thin leaves for the wind to steal.

Transl. by Laurence Binyon

Ogni cosa è fatta con misterio e per amore.

S. CATERINA DA SIENA

All things are done with mystery and because of love.

THE FLOWER

How fresh, O Lord, how sweet and clean
Are thy returns! ev'n as the flowers in spring,
To which, besides their own demean,
The late-past frosts tributes of pleasures bring.
Greif melts away
Like snow in May,
As if there were no such cold thing.

Who could have thought my shrivel'd heart
Could have recovered greennesse? it was gone
Quite underground: as flowers depart
To see their mother-root, when they have blown;
Where they together
All the hard weather,
Dead to the world, keepe house unknown.

These are thy wonders, Lord of power,
Killing and quickning, bringing down to hell,
And up to heaven in an houre;
Making a chiming of a passing bell.
We say amisse,
This or that is,
Thy word is all, if we could spell.

. . . .

And now in age I bud again.
After so many deaths I live and write,
I once more smell the dew and rain,
And relish versing: O my onely light
It cannot be
That I am he
On whom thy tempests fell all night.

. . . .

GEORGE HERBERT

'WHAT CAN IT MEAN'

. . . .

What can it mean
But that below the purling stream
Some unknown joys there be
Laid up in store for me,
To which I shall, when that thin skin
Is broken, be admitted in.

THOMAS TRAHERNE

'THE SKIN AND SHELL OF THINGS'

The skinne, and shell of things
Though faire
are not
Thy wish nor pray'r
but got
By meer Despair
of wings.

HENRY VAUGHAN

'THE GLORY OF THE PLACE'

By this time the Pilgrims had a desire to go forward, and the Shepherds a desire they should; so they walked together towards the end of the Mountains. Then said the Shepherds one to another, Let us here shew to the Pilgrims the gates of the Celestial City, if they have skill to look through our Perspective Glass. The Pilgrims then lovingly accepted the motion; so they had them to the top of a high Hill, called *Clear*, and gave them their Glass to look. Then they essayed to look, but the remembrance of that last thing that the Shepherds had shewed them made their hands shake, by means of which impediment, they could not look steadily through the Glass; yet they thought they saw something like the Gate, and also some of the Glory of the place.

. . . .

JOHN BUNYAN: *The Pilgrim's Progress*

PEACE

My Soul, there is a Countrie
  Far beyond the stars,
Where stands a winged centrie
  All skilfull in the wars:
There above noise, and danger
  Sweet peace sits crown'd with smiles,
And one born in a Manger
  Commands the Beauteous files.
He is thy gracious friend
  And (O my soul awake!)
Did in pure love descend
  To die here for thy sake.
If thou canst get but thither
  There grows the flowre of peace
The Rose that cannot wither,
  Thy fortresse, and thy ease.
Leave then thy foolish ranges,
  For none can thee secure
But One who never changes –
  Thy God, thy life, thy Cure.

HENRY VAUGHAN

ASCENSION HYMN

They are all gone into the world of light!
And I alone sit ling'ring here;
Their very memory is fair and bright,
And my sad thoughts doth clear.

It glows and glitters in my cloudy brest
Like stars upon some gloomy grove,
Or those faint beams in which this hill is drest,
After the Sun's remove.

I see them walking in an Air of glory,
Whose light doth trample on my days:
My days, which are at best but dull and hoary,
Meer glimmering and decays.

O holy hope! and high humility,
High as the Heavens above!
These are your walks, and you have shewed them me
To kindle my cold love.

Dear, beauteous death! the Jewel of the Just,
Shining nowhere, but in the dark;
What mysteries do lie beyond thy dust,
Could man outlook that mark!

He that hath found some fledg'd birds nest, may know
At first sight, if the bird be flown;
But what fair Well, or Grove he sings in now,
That is to him unknown.

And yet, as Angels in some brighter dreams
Call to the soul, when man doth sleep:
So some strange thoughts transcend our wonted theams,
And into glory peep.

. . . .

HENRY VAUGHAN

'HARK! ALOUD THE BLACKBIRD WHISTLES

. . . .

Hark! aloud the blackbird whistles
  With surrounding fragrance blest
And the goldfinch in the thistles
  Makes provision for her nest.

Ev'n the hornet hives for honey
  Blue-cap builds his stately dome,
And the rocks supply the coney
  With a fortress and a home.

But the servants of the Saviour
  Which with Gospel peace are shod
Have no bed but what the paviour
  Makes them in the porch of God.

. . . .

CHRISTOPHER SMART

WHO IS AT MY WINDOW?

Who is at my window? Who? Who?
Go from my window! Go! Go!
Who calls there, like a stranger,
Go from my window! Go!

– Lord, I am here, a wretched mortal,
That for thy mercy doth cry and call
Unto thee, my lord celestial,
See who is at thy window, who? –

Remember the sin, remember the smart,
And also for thee what was my part,
Remember the spear that pierced my heart,
And in at my door thou shalt go.

I ask no thing of thee therefore,
But love for love, to lay in store.
Give me thy heart; I ask no more,
And in at my door thou shalt go.

Who is at my window? Who?
Go from my window! Go!
Cry no more there, like a stranger,
But in at my door thou go!

ANON. (John Wedderburn? 1540)

'GOD COMING'

. . . .

Kamante showed his good will towards me, outside of the kitchen as well. He wanted to help me, in accordance with his own ideas of the advantages and dangers in life.

One night, after midnight, he suddenly walked into my bedroom with a hurricane-lamp in his hand, silent, as if on duty. It must have been only a short time after he first came into my house, for he was very small; he stood by my bedside like a dark bat that had strayed into the room, with very big spreading ears, or like a small African Will-o'-the-wisp, with his lamp in his hand. He spoke to me very solemnly, "Msabu," he said, "I think you had better get up." I sat up in bed bewildered; I thought that if anything serious had happened, it would have been Farah who would have come to fetch me, but when I told Kamante to go away again, he did not move. "Msabu," he said again, "I think that you had better get up. I think that God is coming." When I heard this, I did get up, and asked him why he thought so. He gravely led me into the dining-room which looked West, towards the hills. From the door-windows I now saw a strange phenomenon. There was a big grass-fire going on, out in the hills, and the grass was burning all the way from the hill-top to the plain; when seen from the house it was a nearly vertical line. It did indeed look as if some gigantic figure was moving and coming towards us. I stood for some time and looked at it, with Kamante watching by my side, then I began to explain the thing to him. I meant to quiet him, for I thought that he had been terribly frightened. But the explanation did not seem to make much impression on him one way or the other; he clearly took his mission to have been fulfilled when he had called me. "Well yes," he said, "it may be so. But I thought that you had better get up in case it was God coming."

KAREN BLIXEN: *Out of Africa*

NIGHT

The sun descending in the west,
The evening star does shine;
The birds are silent in their nest,
And I must seek for mine.
The moon like a flower
In heaven's high bower,
With silent delight
Sits and smiles on the night.

Farewell, green fields and happy groves,
Where flocks have took delight.
Where lambs have nibbled, silent moves
The feet of angels bright;
Unseen they pour blessing
And joy without ceasing,
On each bud and blossom,
And each sleeping bosom.

They look in every thoughtless nest,
Where birds are cover'd warm;
They visit caves of every beast,
To keep them all from harm.
If they see any weeping
That should have been sleeping,
They pour sleep on their head
And sit down by their bed.

When wolves and tygers howl for prey,
They pitying stand and weep;
Seeking to drive their thirst away,
And keep them from the sheep.
But if they rush dreadful,
The angels, most heedful,
Receive each mild spirit,
New worlds to inherit.

And there the lion's ruddy eyes
Shall flow with tears of gold,
And pitying the tender cries,
And walking round the fold,

Saying "Wrath, by his meekness,
And by His health, sickness
Is driven away
From our immortal day.

"And now beside thee, bleating lamb,
I can lie down and sleep;
Or think on him who bore thy name,
Graze after thee and weep.
For, wash'd in life's river,
My bright mane for ever
Shall shine like the gold
As I guard o'er the fold."

WILLIAM BLAKE

. . . .

Tho' thou art Worship'd by the Names Divine
Of Jesus & Jehova, thou art still
The Son of Morn in weary Night's decline,
The lost Traveller's Dream under the Hill.

WILLIAM BLAKE: *The Gates of Paradise*

OUR JOURNEY HAD ADVANCED

Our journey had advanced;
Our feet were almost come
To that odd fork in Being's road,
Eternity by term.

Our pace took sudden awe,
Our feet reluctant led.
Before were cities, but between,
The forest of the dead.

Retreat was out of hope, –
Behind, a sealéd route,
Eternity's white flag before,
And God at every gate.

EMILY DICKINSON

No room in history is large enough
To hold man's greatness. Even the most spacious
Church is too small for all the hankering
After eternity and love.

. . . .

DEMETRIOS CAPETENAKIS

And what I was seeking upon the roads was not so much an inn as my own hunger.

PAUL VALÉRY: *Nourritures*

I SEE HIS BLOOD UPON THE ROSE

I see his blood upon the rose
And in the stars the glory of his eyes,
his body gleams amid eternal snows
his tears fall from the skies.

I see his face in every flower,
The thunder and the singing of the birds
Are but his voice and carven by his power
Rocks are his written words.

All pathways by his feet are worn,
His strong heart stills the ever-beating sea,
His crown of thorns is twined with every thorn,
His cross is every tree.

JOSEPH PLUNKETT

THE ANTEROOM

For the night is already at hand, and it is well to yield to the night.

Iliad, VII. Transl. by MAURICE BARING

Since I am comming to that Holy roome
Where, with thy Quire of Saints, for evermore
I shall be made thy music; As I come
I tune the Instrument here at the door,
And what I must doe then, thinke here before.

JOHN DONNE: *Hymn to God, my God, in my sicknesse*

THE ANTEROOM

Introductory Note

CONFUCIUS used to say that it was not until sixty that "his ears obeyed him", and therefore, according to Po-Chü-I, the years after sixty were called in China "the time of obedient ears". Certainly the later years of life are the time when men may acquire a greater delicacy as well as firmness of taste, and sometimes also a greater capacity to pay attention – not only to works of art, but to their fellow-creatures and the universe. This attention is due not only to experience, but to a greater detachment: one's own self is no longer so much in the way. "God knocks at every door", wrote Julian Green, "but who ever opens? The place is taken. By whom? By ourselves".

Simone Weil called this kind of attention "creative attention" and believed that no real understanding of other human beings is possible without it. "Creative attention," she wrote, "consists in truly paying attention to what is not there. Humanity is not there in an anonymous lifeless body by the side of the road, but the Samaritan who stops to look is yet paying attention to that humanity, and his subsequent actions show that his attention was real . . . In that moment of attention faith is present as well as love."

Yet another prerogative of old age may be – though not always, since mind, senses and heart may also be dulled by illness, or by that daily companion, fatigue – an increase of a different sort of awareness. Proust referred to it, when speaking of memories of his childhood, as a return to his upper consciousness of certain events, certain emotions, which in reality had never stopped. "Of late", he wrote, "I have been increasingly able to catch, if I listen attentively, the sound of the sobs which broke out only when I found myself alone with Mama. Actually, their echo has never ceased; it is only because life is now growing more and more quiet round about me that I hear them afresh, like those convent bells which are so effectively drowned during the day by the noises of the streets that one would suppose them to have been stopped for ever, until they sound out again through the silent evening air . . .

The "beauty of the physical world", too, may in old age recover some of the clear intensity that it had for us in childhood. What we shall, perhaps, not often see again becomes as marvellous as when it first met our sight. And sometimes, also, the human scene takes on a fresh pathos. "Happiness" – I am quoting again from Simone Weil – "is an object for compassion for the same reason as misfortune, because it is earthly – that is to say, incomplete and fleeting . . . Compassion for fragility is always bound to a love for true beauty, for we feel intensely that things which are truly beautiful should be granted an eternal existence, and they are not."

Reflections such as these give a fresh perspective to a man's knowledge that his days are numbered, and may lead some people, according to their turn of mind, to "tune the instrument here at the door." The last words of Socrates, the serene and astringent passages from Epictetus, the gentle and humorous resignation of the Chinese sages, have all a close affinity of spirit, which seems to linger in many of the later passages quoted here, particularly in those by La Fontaine and Montaigne.

For the practising Christian there are other hopes, deeper certainties. Yet these, too, sometimes falter, and I have personally found it consoling to read that even Père Teilhard de Chardin, "*le grand imaginatif*", wrote a few days before his death: "The difficulty in old age is to fit one's interior life to a life without a *future* for oneself. (One has one's face to the wall.)" He added, however, soon after, " 'To be ready' has never seemed to me to signify anything else than 'to be stretching forward'."

There are some "last sayings" which I had thought of quoting in the text – since they used to please me, and a good many are set down in my commonplace books. But on re-reading, there are only a few that I now find credible – at least with the high-flown significance generally attributed to them. Goethe's "*Mehr Licht*", for instance, may surely have had no deeper meaning than that his sight was failing, and there is something too pat about Heine's famous phrase: "*Dieu me pardonnera: c'est son métier.*" To Beethoven's saying to two old friends, "*Plaudite amici, comoedia finita est*" (Applaud, my friends, the comedy is over) – I prefer the simpler remark on his last day, when two bottles of wine were placed beside his bed: "A pity, a pity, too late." I also like Madame de Pompadour's remark to the priest about to leave her bedside: "*Un moment, Monsieur le curé, nous partirons ensemble*".

A touch of irony, too, is often more moving than edifying phrases. I like Lady Violet Bonham Carter's reply when her daughter bent over her and asked how she felt: "Amphibious". And, especially, I enjoy the comment of the Englishman who, surrounded by a circle of anxious friends, opened one eye and said: "A watched pot never boils."

ODYSSEUS IN THE KINGDOM OF THE DEAD

At once she knew me, and made her meaning clear with lamentable words:

"My love, how did you come down to the cloudy West, and you alive? It is hard for the living to see this place. . . ."

I answered: "Dear mother, necessity has brought me to the house of Hades. . . . But do tell me, really and truly, what was the cause of your death? how did you die? Was it a long disease? or did Artemis Archeress kill you with her gentle shafts? . . ."

My beloved mother answered at once: ". . . This is how I sickened and died. The Archeress did not shoot me in my own house with those gentle shafts that never miss; it was no disease that made me pine away; but I missed you so much, and your clever wit and your gay merry ways, and life was sweet no longer, so I died."

The Odyssey, Book XI. Transl. by W. H. D. Rouse

OLD AGE

Let my spear lie down for the spider to weave its thread;
May Peace dwell with me at home when I grow old.
May I sing with garlands bound on my whitening head;
Let the pillared shrine of Pallas Athene hold
My buckler from Thrace, while in books I unfold
Sweet words which the wise have said.

EURIPIDES: *Erechtheus*. Transl. by C. M. Bowra

THE SIGNAL OF RETREAT

When God fails to provide for you, then he is giving the signal of retreat. He has opened the door and says to you, "Come". "Where?" – "To nothing fearful, but thither whence you were born, to things friendly and akin to you, the Elements. . . ."

. . . .

When Ulysses was shipwrecked and cast away, did his helpless condition at all deject him? Did it break his spirit? No. But how did he go to Nausicaa and her attendants, to ask those necessaries which it seems most shameful to beg from another?

"As the fierce lion, on the mountain bred, confiding in his strength." Confiding in what? Not in glory nor in riches, nor in dominion, but

in his own strength: that is in his principles concerning what things are in our own power, what not. For these alone are what render us free. . . .
But what if I should be sick?
You will be as sick as you ought.
Who will take care of me?
God; your friends.
I shall lie in a hard bed.
But like a man.
I shall not have a convenient room.
You will be sick in an inconvenient one then.
But, besides, what will be the conclusion of my sickness? Any other than death?

Why, do you not know, then, that the origin of all human evils and of mean-spiritedness and cowardice is not death, but rather the fear of death? Fortify yourself, therefore, against this. Hither let all your discourses, readings, exercises, tend. And then you will know that thus alone are men made free.

EPICTETUS: *Discourses*. Transl. by Elizabeth Carter

ILLNESS

Dear friends, there is no cause for so much sympathy.
I shall certainly manage from time to time to take my walks abroad.
All that matters is an active mind, what is the use of feet?
By land one can ride in a carrying-chair; by water, be rowed in a boat.

PO CHÜ-I
(Written *c.* A.D. 842 when he was paralysed)

LAST POEM

. . . .

They have put my bed beside the unpainted screen;
They have shifted my stove in front of the blue curtain.
I listen to my grandchildren reading me a book;
I watch the servants heating up my soup.
With rapid pencil I answer the poems of friends,
I feel in my pocket and pull out medicine-money.
When this superintendence of trifling affairs is done,
I lie back upon my pillows and sleep with my face to the South.

PO CHÜ-I. Transl. by Arthur Waley

'AN AFTER DINNER'S SLEEP'

Thou hast nor youth nor age,
But, as it were, an after dinner's sleep,
Dreaming on both.

SHAKESPEARE: *Measure for Measure*

BEATA L'ALMA

. . . .

Beata l'alma, ove non corre tempo,
per te s'è fatta a contemplare Dio.

MICHELANGELO BUONARROTI (1475–1564)

Blessed the soul in which Time leaves no mark
By you, 't is brought to contemplate our God.

'THE LEAVES, THE BLOSSOMS AND THE FRUIT''

Such as we especially, who live a private life not exposed to any gaze but our own, ought in our hearts establish a touchstone and thereto touch our deeds and try our actions, and accordingly now cherish and now chasten ourselves.

. . . .

That is an exquisite life which even in his own private keepeth itself in awe and order. Everyone may play the juggler and represent an honest man upon the stage, but within, and in bosom, where all things are lawful, where all is concealed, to keep a due rule or formal decorum, that's the point. . . . To gain a battle, perform an ambassage, and govern a people are noble and worthy actions. To chide, laugh, sell, pay, love, hate and mildly and justly to converse both with his own and with himself, not to relent, and not gainsay himself, are things more rare, more difficult and less remarkable.

. . . .

For my part, I may in general wish to be other than I am; I may condemn and mislike my universal form; I may beseech God to grant me an undefiled reformation and excuse my natural weakness. But meseemeth I ought not to term this repentance no more than the displeasure of being neither angel nor Cato. My actions are squared to what I am and conformed to my condition.

. . . .

Moreover I hate that accidental repentance which old age brings with it . . . I shall never give impuissance thanks for any good it can do me.

. . . .

I will present myself and make a general muster of my whole, everywhere uniformly. Were I to live again, it should be as I have already lived. I neither deplore what is past nor dread what is to come. And if I be not deceived, the inward parts have merely resembled the outward. It is one of the chiefest points wherein I am beholden to fortune, that in the course of my body's estate, each thing hath been carried in season. I have seen the leaves, the blossoms and the fruit; and now see the drooping and withering of it. Happily, because naturally.

MONTAIGNE: III: *Of Repenting*

'HUMAN LIFE'

. . . .

When all is done, Human Life is, at the greatest and the best, but like a froward Child, that must be Play'd with, and Humour'd a little to keep it quiet, till it falls asleep, and then the Care is over.

. . . .

SIR WILLIAM TEMPLE: *Essays*

AFTERWARDS

When the Present has latched its postern behind my tremulous stay,
And the May month flaps its glad green leaves like wings,
Delicate-filmed as new-spun silk, will the neighbours say,
"He was a man who used to notice such things"?

If it be in the dusk when, like an eyelid's soundless blink,
The dewfall-hawk comes crossing the shades to alight
Upon the wind-warped upland thorn, a gazer may think,
"To him this must have been a familiar sight."

If I pass during some nocturnal blackness, mothy and warm,
  When the hedgehog travels furtively over the lawn,
One may say, "He strove that such innocent creatures should come to
    no harm,
  But he could do little for them; and now he is gone."

If, when hearing that I have been stilled at last, they stand at the door,
  Watching the full-starred heavens that winter sees,
Will this thought rise on those who will meet my face no more,
  "He was one who had an eye for such mysteries"?

And will any say when my bell of quittance is heard in the gloom,
  And a crossing breeze cuts a pause in its outrollings,
Till they rise again, as they were a new bell's boom,
  "He hears it not now, but used to notice such things?"

THOMAS HARDY

TOLSTOY IN OLD AGE

The illness dried him up still more, burnt something out of him. Inwardly he seemed to become lighter, more transparent, more resigned. His eyes are still keener, his glance piercing. He listens attentively as though recalling something which he has forgotten or as though waiting for something new and unknown. . . . If he were a fish, he would certainly swim only in the ocean, never coming to the narrow seas, and particularly not to the flat waters of earthly rivers. Around him here there rest or dart hither and thither the little fishes; what he says does not interest them, is not necessary to them, and his silence does not frighten or move them. Yet his silence is impressive, like that of a real hermit driven out from this world. . . . Surely he has some thoughts of which he is afraid.

. . . .

With God he has very suspicious relations; they sometimes remind me of the relations of "two bears in one den".

GORKY: *Reminiscences of Tolstoy*

'WHILE I AM SETTING MY CABBAGES'

I am now, by the meane of the mercy of God, in such a taking, that without regret or grieving at any worldly matter, I am prepared to dislodge whensoever he shall please to call me. I am everywhere free. My farewell is soone taken of all my friends, except of myselfe. . . .

I would have a man to be doing, and to prolong my life's offices, as much as lieth in him, and let death seize upon me whilst I am setting my cabiges, carelesse of her dart, but more of my unperfect garden. . . .

Your death is but a piece of the world's order, and but a parcell of the world's life.

MONTAIGNE: *That to Philosophy is to learn how to die.*
Transl. by John Florio

THE SILVER SWANNE

The silver Swanne, who living had no Note,
When death approached unlockt her silent throat,
Leaning her breast against the reedie shore,
Thus sung her first and last, and sung no more:
Farewell, all joyes; O death come close mine eyes;
More Geese than Swannes now live, more fooles than wise.

ANON.

It would be interesting to know whether the writer of this madrigal, first published by Orlando Gibbons in 1612, was familiar with the lines of Cecco d'Ascoli (1268–1327), the astrologer, physicist and poet, who was sentenced to death on the pyre by the Inquisition:

El cigno è bianco senza alcuna macchia
e dolcemente canta nel morire
enfino che la morte non l'abbacchia.

L'Acerba

The swan* is white without a stain, and sings
in pain while he is dying, and does not cease
until death overtakes him.

*The swan was, in Cecco d'Ascoli's "Bestiary", the symbol of Confession.

'WHEN TIMELY DEATH'

When timely death my life and fortune ends,
Let not my hearse be vext with mourning friends,
But let all lovers, rich in triumph, come,
And with sweet pastimes grace my happie tombe.
And, Lesbia, close up thou my little light,
And crowne with love my ever-during night.

THOMAS CAMPION: *Book of Ayres*

'LA MORT AVAIT RAISON'

La Mort avait raison. Je voudrais qu'à cet age
On sortit de la vie ainsi que d'un banquet,
Remerciant son hôte. et qu'on fit son paquet;
Car de combien peut-on retarder le voyage?
Tu murmures, vieillard! Vois ces jeunes courir
A des morts, il est vrai, glorieuses et belles,
Mais sures cependant, et quelquefois cruelles.

LA FONTAINE

TO SLEEP AT EASE

Some in good health digged already their graves; othersome yet living did goe into them. And a day-labourer of mine, as he was dying, with his own hands and feet pulled earth upon him, and so covered himselfe. Was not this a lying downe in the shade to sleepe at ease?

MONTAIGNE: *Of Physiognomy*. Transl. by John Florio

Caius Gallus . . . in a good Old Age, as he was sitting in his Study, with his Head and his Hands full of his *Astronomy*, *went away* as peaceably as an Infant; and as it happen'd, while I was in the Room with him.

CICERO: *De Senectute*. Transl. by Samuel Parker

THE CHARIOT

Because I could not stop for Death,
He kindly stopped for me;
The carriage held but just ourselves
And Immortality.

We slowly drove, he knew no haste,
And I had put away
My labour, and my leisure too,
For his civility.

We passed the school where children played,
Their lessons scarcely done;
We passed the fields of gazing grain,
We passed the setting sun.

We paused before a house that seemed
A swelling on the ground;
The roof was scarcely visible,
The cornice but a mound.

Since then 'tis centuries; but each
Feels shorter than the day
I first surmised the horses' heads
Were toward eternity.

EMILY DICKINSON

We talked with fertility; never working a seam dry. Do you suppose then that we are now coming like the homing rooks back to the tops of our trees? and that all this cawing is the beginning of settling in for the night? I seem to notice in several of my friends some endearing and affecting cordiality; and a pleasure in intimacy; as if the sun were sinking. Often that image comes to me with some sense of my physical state being colder now, the sun just off one; the old disc of one's being growing cooler – but it is only just beginning; and one will turn cold and silver like the moon.*

VIRGINIA WOOLF: *A Writer's Diary*

*This was written just after a talk with Desmond MacCarthy.

‘SOLO UNA PIUMA’

. . . .

Or v’è solo una piuma, che all’invito
Del vento esita, palpita leggera:
Qual sogno antico in anima severa
Fuggente sempre e non ancor fuggito.

GIOVANNI PASCOLI: *Il Nido*

Now there’s one feather which by breezes bidden
Is wavering and trembling frail and light
As in a soul austere a dream lies hidden,
About to fly, and yet not taking flight.

Transl. by Maurice Baring

He is so young, my child,
He cannot know the track.
O Guide from that strange world,
Hearken, I’ll pay thee, but
Take him upon thy back.

From the Japanese (author unknown)

YEARS END

Sweep up dust and green
Sweep up rust and sorrow,
What is unseen
May shape tomorrow.

Walk toward the moon
It will come no nearer,
Nothing is soon
Nothing is clearer,

Than the heart's void
The mind's measure
The burden of love
Laid down forever.

Laid down to keep
Till the heart gives over
And death joins
Lover and lover.

KATHERINE GARRISON CHAPIN

'WHEN IT IS ALL OVER'

When it is all over and the blood
Runs out, do not bury this man
By the far river (where never stood
His fathers) flowing to the West,
But take him East where life began.
O my brothers, there is rest
In the depths of an eastward river
That I can understand; only
Do not think the truth we hold
I hold the slighter for this lonely
Reservation of the heart:
Men cannot live forever
But they must die forever
So take this body at sunset
To the great stream whose pulses start
In the blue hills, and let
These ashes drift from the Long Bridge
Where only a late gull breaks
That deep and populous grave.

ALLEN TATE: From *Emblems*

A SONG FOR SIMEON

Lord, the Roman hyacinths are blooming in bowls and
The winter sun creeps by the snow hills;
The stubborn season has made stand.
My life is light, waiting for the death wind,
Like a feather on the back of my hand.
Dust in sunlight and memory in corners
Wait for the wind that chills towards the dead land.

Grant us thy peace.
I have walked many years in this city,
Kept faith and fast, provided for the poor,
Have given and taken honour and ease.
There went never any rejected from my door.
Who shall remember my house, where shall live my
    children's children
When the time of sorrow is come?
They will take to the goat's path, and the fox's home,
Fleeing from the foreign faces and the foreign swords.

Before the time of cords and scourges and lamentation
Grant us thy peace.
Before the stations of the mountain of desolation,
Before the certain hour of maternal sorrow,
Now at this birth season of decease,
Let the Infant, the still unspeaking and unspoken Word,
Grant Israel's consolation
To one who has eighty years and no tomorrow.

According to thy word.
They shall praise Thee and suffer in every generation
With glory and derision,
Light upon light, mounting the saints' stair.
Not for me the martyrdom, the ecstasy of thought and
prayer,
Not for me the ultimate vision.
Grant me thy peace.
(And a sword shall pierce thy heart,
Thine also.)

I am tired with my own life and the lives of those after me,
I am dying in my own death and the deaths of those after me
Let thy servant depart,
Having seen thy salvation.

T. S. ELIOT

E'n la sua volontade é nostra pace.

DANTE: *Paradiso* III, 85

His will: our peace.

CHUANG TZU ON DEATH

How do I know that wanting to be alive is not a great mistake? How do I know that hating to die is not like thinking one has lost one's way, when all the time one is on the path that leads to home? Li Chi was the daughter of the frontier guardsman at Ai. When first she was captured and carried away to Chin, she wept till her dress was soaked with tears. But when she came to the king's palace, sat with him on his couch and shared with him the dainties of the royal board, she began to wonder why she had wept. How do I know that the dead do not wonder why they should ever have prayed for long life? It is said that those who dream of drinking wine will weep when day comes; and that those who dream of weeping will next day go hunting. But while a man is dreaming, he does not know that he is dreaming; nor can he interpret a dream till the dream is done. It is only when he wakes, that he knows it was a dream. Not till the Great Wakening can he know that all this was one Great Dream. . . .

Once Chuang Chou dreamt that he was a butterfly. He did not know that he had ever been anything but a butterfly and was content to hover from flower to flower. Suddenly he woke and found to his astonishment that he was Chuang Chou. But it was hard to be sure whether he really was Chou and had only dreamt that he was a butterfly, or was really a butterfly, and was only dreaming that he was Chou.

. . . .

Tzu-Lai fell ill. He was already at the last gasp; his wife and children stood weeping and wailing round his bed. "Pst," said Tzu-li, who had come to call, "stand back! a great Change is at work; let us not disturb it!" "Mighty are the works of the Changer! What is he about to make of you, to what use will he put you? Perhaps a rat's liver, perhaps, a beetle's claw?" "A child," said Tzu-lai, "at its parents' bidding must go north and south, east or west; how much the more when those parents of all Nature, the great powers Yin and Yang, command him, must he go where they will . . . In this life I have had the luck to be fashioned in human form. But were I now to say to the Great Transformer, "I refuse to let anything be made out of me but a man," he would think that it was indeed an unmannerly being that had come into his hands.

ARTHUR WALEY: Extract from *Three Ways of Thought in Ancient China*

'I TO DIE AND YOU TO LIVE'

Wherefore, O judges, be of good cheer about death, and know of a certainty, that no evil can happen to a good man, either in life or after death. He and his are not neglected by the gods; nor has my own approaching end happened by mere chance. But I see clearly that the time had arrived when it was better for me to die and be released from trouble; wherefore the oracle gave no sign. For which reason, also, I am not angry with my condemners, or with my accusers; they have done me no harm, although they did not mean to do me any good; and for this I may gently blame them.

Still I have a favour to ask of them. When my sons are grown up, I would ask you, O my friends, to punish them; and I would have you trouble them, as I have troubled you, if they seem to care about riches, or anything, more than about virtue; or if they pretend to be something when they are really nothing – then reprove them, as I have reproved you, for not caring about that for which they ought to care, and thinking that they are something when they are really nothing. And if you do this, both I and my sons will have received justice at your hands.

The hour of departure has arrived, and we go our ways – I to die, and you to live. Which is better God only knows.

PLATO: *The Apology*. Transl. by BENJAMIN JOWETT

All life is but a wandering to find home,
When we're gone, we're there.

JOHN FORD

ACKNOWLEDGEMENTS

I am grateful to many friends – in particular, to Colin Mackenzie, Archibald MacLeish and William Hughes – who at different times have introduced me to letters or poems quoted here. I should also like to say how much this book owes to the encouragement, taste and sometimes astringent advice of C. Day Lewis, without which I do not think it would ever have got pruned or finished.

I should like to express my gratitude to Enzo Crea for his design of the jacket, to Joan St. George Saunders for her unequalled gift for ferretting out and restoring to their pristine form even the most recondite quotations, and to Miss Mary Manus and Miss Patricia Prout for their patience with my handwriting and their skill in reproducing it in a legible form.

The extent of my debt to Elsa Dallolio and Aileen Meade is implied, I hope, in the dedication.

Acknowledgements are also due to the following copyright owners and publishers for permission to quote from copyright material:

Mr. Morris Bishop: translations of Petrarch; Basil Blackwell Ltd., Jonathan Cape Ltd., Mr. A. W. Lawrence and the T. E. Lawrence Letters Trust: a letter from *The Home Letters of T. E. Lawrence and His Brothers;* The Bodley Head and Little Brown & Co.: from *Poems* by George Seferis trans. by Rex Warner. English translation © Rex Warner 1960; Cambridge University Press: from Vergil's *Georgics* trans. by R. C. Trevelyan, and for a fragment of Sappho transl. by Walter Headlam; Jonathan Cape Ltd.: the poem by Damagetus trans. by R. A. Furness from *Translations from the Greek Anthology;* Jonathan Cape Ltd. and Harcourt Brace Jovanovich, Inc.: from *The Notebooks of Leonardo da Vinci* ed. Edward McCurdy; Jonathan Cape Ltd., The Hogarth Press, the Executors of the Estate of C. Day Lewis, and Harold Matson, Inc.; from *Collected Poems* 1954 by C. Day Lewis and from *The Georgics of Virgil* trans. by C. Day Lewis; Jonathan Cape Ltd. and the Executors of the Estate of C. Day Lewis and Harper & Row, Publishers, Inc.: from *The Whispering Roots and Other Poems.* © 1970 by C. Day Lewis, and from *Selected Poems* (Harper & Row, Publishers, Inc.). © 1957 by C. Day Lewis; Jonathan Cape Ltd. and the Executors of the Viola Meynell Estate: from *Alice Meynell: A Memoir;* Jonathan Cape Ltd., The Estate of Robert Frost and Holt, Rinehart and Winston, Inc.: from *The Poetry of Robert Frost* ed. Edward Connery. © 1923, 1930, 1939, © 1969 by Holt, Rinehart and Winston, Inc. © 1951, © 1958 by Robert Frost, © 1967 by Lesley Frost Ballantine; Jonathan Cape Ltd. and the Executors of the Lilian Bowes Lyon Estate and E. P. Dutton & Co. Inc.: from *Collected Poems* by Lilian Bowes Lyon. © 1948 by Lilian Bowes Lyon; Ceskoslovensky spisovatel and the Dilia Agency, Prague, representing the author's Estate: a poem by Frana

Sramek trans. from the Czech; Mrs. Katherine Garrison Chapin for her poem, 'Year's End'; The Executors of the Estate of Mr. Harold Owen, Chatto & Windus Ltd. and New Directions Publishing Corporation: from *The Collected Poems of Wilfred Owen.* © Chatto & Windus Ltd. 1946, © 1963; The Clarendon Press; Oxford: from *The Poetical Works of Robert Bridges* and from *The Oxford Book of Greek Verse in Translation* ed. T. F. Higham and C. M. Bowra; Collins Publishers and Pantheon Books: from *Dr. Zhivago* by Boris Pasternak trans. by Max Hayward and Manya Harari. © 1958 by William Collins Ltd. and Pantheon Books, a Division of Random House, Inc.; Collins Publishers and Atheneum Publishers: from *Hope Against Hope* by Nadezhda Mandelstam trans. by Max Hayward. © 1970 by Atheneum Publishers. English translation © 1970 by Atheneum Publishers; Collins Publishers and Hill & Wang, Inc., a division of Farrar, Straus & Giroux, Inc.: from *Yevtushenko: Poems Chosen By The Author* trans. by Peter Levi and Robin Milner-Gulland. © in the English translation, The Harvill Press, London; Constable Publishers: from *The Letters of a Post-Impressionist* by Vincent Van Gogh trans. and ed. by Anthony M. Ludovici, and from *Medieval Latin Lyrics* trans. by Helen Waddell; Constable Publishers and the Literary Estate of George Santayana: from *Sonnets and Other Verses* by George Santayana; J. M. Dent & Sons Ltd.: from *Greek Social Life* by F. A. Wright; J. M. Dent & Sons Ltd. and E. P. Dutton & Co. Inc.: from *Moral Discourses, The Enchiridion and Fragments by Epictetus* trans. by Elizabeth Carter, ed. by W. H. D. Rouse, Everyman's Library Edition; J. M. Dent & Sons Ltd., the Trustees for the Copyrights of the late Dylan Thomas, and New Directions Publishing Corporation: from *Collected Poems* by Dylan Thomas and *The Poems of Dylan Thomas* (© 1946 by New Directions Publishing Corporation); Andre Deutsch Ltd. and The Swallow Press, Inc., Chicago: from *On Pain of Seeing* by Erich Fried trans. by George Rapp. © 1969 by The Swallow Press; Giulio Einaudi Editore, Turin, Peter Janson-Smith Ltd. and Peter Owen Ltd.: from *Poesie del Disamore* by Cesare Pavese; Faber & Faber Ltd. and Random House, Inc.: from *Collected Shorter Poems 1927–1957* by W. H. Auden, © 1940 and renewed 1968 by W. H. Auden; Faber & Faber Ltd. and Harcourt Brace Jovanovich, Inc.: from *Collected Poems 1909–1962* by T. S. Eliot. ©1936 by Harcourt, Brace Jovanovich, Inc. © 1963, 1964 by T. S Eliot; Faber & Faber Ltd. from *The Hungry Grass* by Donagh MacDonagh; Mr. Gavin Muir, Faber & Faber Ltd. and Oxford University Press, Inc., N.Y.: from *Collected Poems 1921–1958* by Edwin Muir. © 1960 by Willa Muir; Faber & Faber Ltd. and Mrs. Myfanwy Thomas: from *Collected Poems* by Edward Thomas; The Estate of Dr. Robin Flower: from *Poems and Translations* by Robin Flower; Editions Gallimard, Paris: from *Calligrammes* and *Alcools* by G. Apollinaire; for 'l'Enfant et la Rivière' by Supervielle, 'On ne peut me connaître' by Paul Eluard, and 'Un bonheur est passé' by Charlse Péguy; Mr. Robert Graves and A. P. Watt & Son: from *Poems* 1965; Mr. John Lehmann for a poem by the late Demetrios Capetanakis; Harvard University Press: from *Three Secret Poems* by George Seferis trans. by Walter Kaiser. © 1969 by the President and Fellows of Harvard College and 1969 by George Seferis; the translator, the Hogarth Press and Harcourt Brace Jovanovich, Inc.: from *The Complete Poems of Cavafy* trans. by Rae Dalven. © 1961 by Rae Dalven; St. John's College, The Hogarth Press, and New Directions Publishing Corporation: from *Selected Works*, Vol. II, by Rainer Maria Rilke trans. by J. B. Leishman. © The Hogarth Press 1960; The Hogarth Press and W. W. Norton and Company, Inc. for part of 'The First Elegy' by Rainer Maria Rilke trans. by J. B. Leishman and Stephen Spender. © 1939 by W. W. Norton & Company, Inc. © renewed 1967 by Stephen Spender and J. B. Leishman; the author's literary estate, The Hogarth Press and Harcourt Brace Jovanovich, Inc.: from *A Writer's Diary* by Virginia Woolf. © 1953, 1954 by Leonard Woolf; Mr. Laurie Lee, The Hogarth Press and Wesleyan University Press: from *The Sun My Monument* by Laurie Lee; the Translators' Literary Estate, The Hogarth Press and Viking Press, Inc.: from *Reminiscences of Tolstoy, Chekhov and Andreev* by Maxim Gorky, trans. by Katherine Mansfield, S. S. Koteliansky and Leonard Woolf. © 1920 by The Freeman Inc., 1920 by B. W. Huebsch, Inc., 1948 by S. S. Koteliansky and Leonard Woolf; Houghton Mifflin Company: from Professor Walter Kaiser's Introduction to John Florio's translation of Montaigne's *Selected Essays* and from H. A. Mason's trans. of *Gilgamesh*. © 1970 by H. A. Mason; Prof. Kaiser for his translation from Fauriel's *Chants Populaires de la Grèce Moderne;* the author and Houghton Mifflin Company: from *Collected Poems of Archibald MacLeish 1917–1952*. © 1952 by Archibald MacLeish; Insel Verlag, Frankfurt: from 'Die Erste Elegie' by Rainer Maria Rilke and the German text of three other poems by Rilke; Longman Group Ltd.: from *The Greek Anthology* trans. by J. W. Mackail; McGibbon & Kee (Granada Publishing Ltd.) for 'the first of all my dreams was of' and 'lady will you come with me into' from *Complete Poems* by e. e. cummings; Harcourt Brace Jovanovich, Inc. for 'the first of all my dreams was of' from 73 *poems* by e. e. cummings. © 1963 by Marion Morehouse Cummings, and for 'lady will you come with me into' from *Poems 1923–1954* by e. e. cummings. © 1931, 1959, by e. e. cummings; The Trustees of the Hardy Estate, Macmillan & Co. Ltd., London and Basingstoke, The Macmillan and Company, N.Y. and The Macmillan Company of Canada: from *Collected Poems* by Thomas Hardy. © 1925 by The Macmillan Company; Mr. M. B. Yeats, Macmillan & Co. Ltd., London and Basingstoke, The Macmillan and Company, N.Y., and A. P. Watt & Son: from the *Collected Poems* by W. B. Yeats: 'A Coat', © 1916 by The Macmillan Company, renewed 1944 by Bertha Georgie Yeats; part of 'A Prayer for My Daughter', © 1924 by The Macmillan Company, renewed 1952 by Bertha Georgie Yeats; 'Memory' and 'The Wild Swans at Coole', © 1919 by The Macmillan Company, renewed 1947 by Bertha Georgie Yeats; part of 'In Memory of Eva Gore-Booth and Con Markiewicz', © 1933 by The Macmillan Company, renewed 1961 by Bertha Georgie Yeats; 'The Municipal Gallery Revisited', © 1940 by Georgie Yeats, renewed 1968 by Bertha Georgie Yeats, Michael Butler Yeats and Anne Yeats; Methuen & Co. Ltd. (Associated Book Publishers Ltd.) for extracts from *Confessions of St. Augustine* trans. by C. Bigg; Arnoldo Mondadori Editore and Penguin Books Ltd. for 'Non Gridate Più' by Giuseppe Ungaretti and Arnoldo Mondadori Editore for 'A Roma, a letto . . .' by Giuseppe Ungaretti; Thomas Nelson & Sons Ltd.: from Homer's *The Odyssey* trans. by W. H. D. Rouse; Mr. Nigel Nicolson for an extract from *The Land* by V. Sackville-West; Peter Owen Ltd. and Grosset & Dunlap, Inc., N.Y.: from *A Death in the Family* by James Agee. © 1957 by the James Agee Trust; Oxford University Press, London and Columbia University Press, N.Y.: from *The Pillow Book of Sei Shonagon* trans. and ed. by Ivan Morris; Oxford University Press, London: from *Poems of Gerard Manley Hopkins*, 4th edn.; Oxford University Press, London and N.Y.: from *William Blake: Complete Writings* ed. G. Keynes and from *Keats' Letters* ed. Maurice Buxton Forman, 3rd edn. 1947; Mr. Allen Tate, Oxford University Press, London and The Swallow Press, Chicago: from *The Swimmers and Other Selected Poems* by Allen Tate. © 1970 by The Swallow Press; Penguin Books Ltd.: from Pascal's *Pensées* trans. by A. J. Krailsheimer; Penguin Books Ltd.: from Homer's *The Iliad* trans. by E. V. Rieu, © E. V. Rieu 1966; Penguin Books Ltd. and New Directions Publishing Corporation: from *Lorca* trans. by J. L. Gili, © 1960, J. L. Gili; A. D. Peters & Co. for 'A Maltese Dog' from *Halfway House* trans. by Edmund Blunden; Laurence Pollinger Ltd., the Estate of the late Mrs. Frieda Lawrence, William Heinemann Ltd., and The Viking Press, Inc.: from *The Complete Poems of D. H. Lawrence*, ed. by Vivian da Sola Pinto and F. Warren Roberts. © 1964, 1971 by Angelo Ravagli and C. M. Weekley, Executors of the Estate of Frieda Lawrence Ravagli; Présence Africaine, Paris: from 'Prière d'un petit enfant nègre', from Guy Tirolien's *Balles d'Or* (1961): Putnam & Co. Ltd., London, and Random House, Inc., N.Y.: from *Out of Africa* by Isak Dinesen. © 1937 and renewed 1965 by Rungstedlundfonden; Mrs. Nicolete Gray and The Society of Authors on behalf of the Laurence Binyon Estate: from Dante's *Purgatorio* and *Paradiso* trans. by Laurence Binyon; The Literary Trustees of Walter de la Mare and The Society of Authors as their representative: from *The Complete Poems of Walter de la*

Mare 1969; Thames & Hudson Ltd. and Alfred Knopf, Inc. for 'Drinking the Sun of Corinth' by Odysseus Elytis trans. by Edmund Keeley and Philip Sherrard from *Six Poets of Modern Greece*. © 1960 by Edmund Keeley and Philip Sherrard; Verlag Klaus Wagenbach, West Berlin, for 'Gezieltes Spielzeug' from *und Vietnam und* by Erich Fried; the Estate of Maurice Baring and A. P. Watt & Son: from *Have You Anything To Declare?* ed. by Maurice Baring; Thomas Yoseloff Ltd. for extracts from *Terpsichore and other Poems* publ. by The Golden Cockerell Press 1921. (Alcman's 'The Halcyons' and 'Night' trans. by H. T. Wade-Gery); Mr. Cyril Connolly, Deborah Rogers Ltd., Hamish Hamilton Ltd. and Harper & Row Publishers, Inc.: from *The Unquiet Grave*. © 1944 by Cyril Connolly; George Allen & Unwin Ltd. and Constable Publishers: from *Chinese Poems* and *170 Chinese Poems* trans. by Arthur Waley; Alfred A. Knopf, Inc.: from *Translations from the Chinese* trans. by Arthur Waley. © 1919, 1941 by Alfred A. Knopf, Inc. and renewed 1947 by Arthur Waley. © in 'Lament of Hsi Chun' with translator's note also renewed in 1969; George Allen & Unwin Ltd. and Barnes & Noble Books: from *Three Ways of Thought in Ancient China* trans. by Arthur Waley; David Higham Associates Ltd., Oxford University Press, London, and The New American Library, Inc., New York: from *Giacomo Leopardi: Selected Prose and Poetry* ed. and trans. by Iris Origo and John Heath-Stubbs. © 1966 by Iris Origo and John Heath-Stubbs. The Italian texts: from the Francesco Flora edition of Leopardi's *Opere* (5 vols.) publ. by Mondadori, Milan; Monsieur Maurice Goudeket, Secker & Warburg Ltd. and Farrar, Straus & Giroux, Inc.: for Iris Origo's translation from *La Naissance du Jour* by Colette; the author's Estate, the Agenzia Letteraria Internazionale, Milan, Constable Publishers Ltd. and Pantheon Books: from *Sketch for a Self-Portrait* by Bernard Berenson; Mr. Conrad Aiken, The Hogarth Press and Oxford University Press, N.Y.: from 'Senlin' in *Collected Poems* (publ. by O.U.P., New York) by Conrad Aiken; David Higham Associates Ltd.: for the poem by Edith Sitwell.

INDEX OF AUTHORS

(Italicized names are those of translators)

INDEX OF AUTHORS

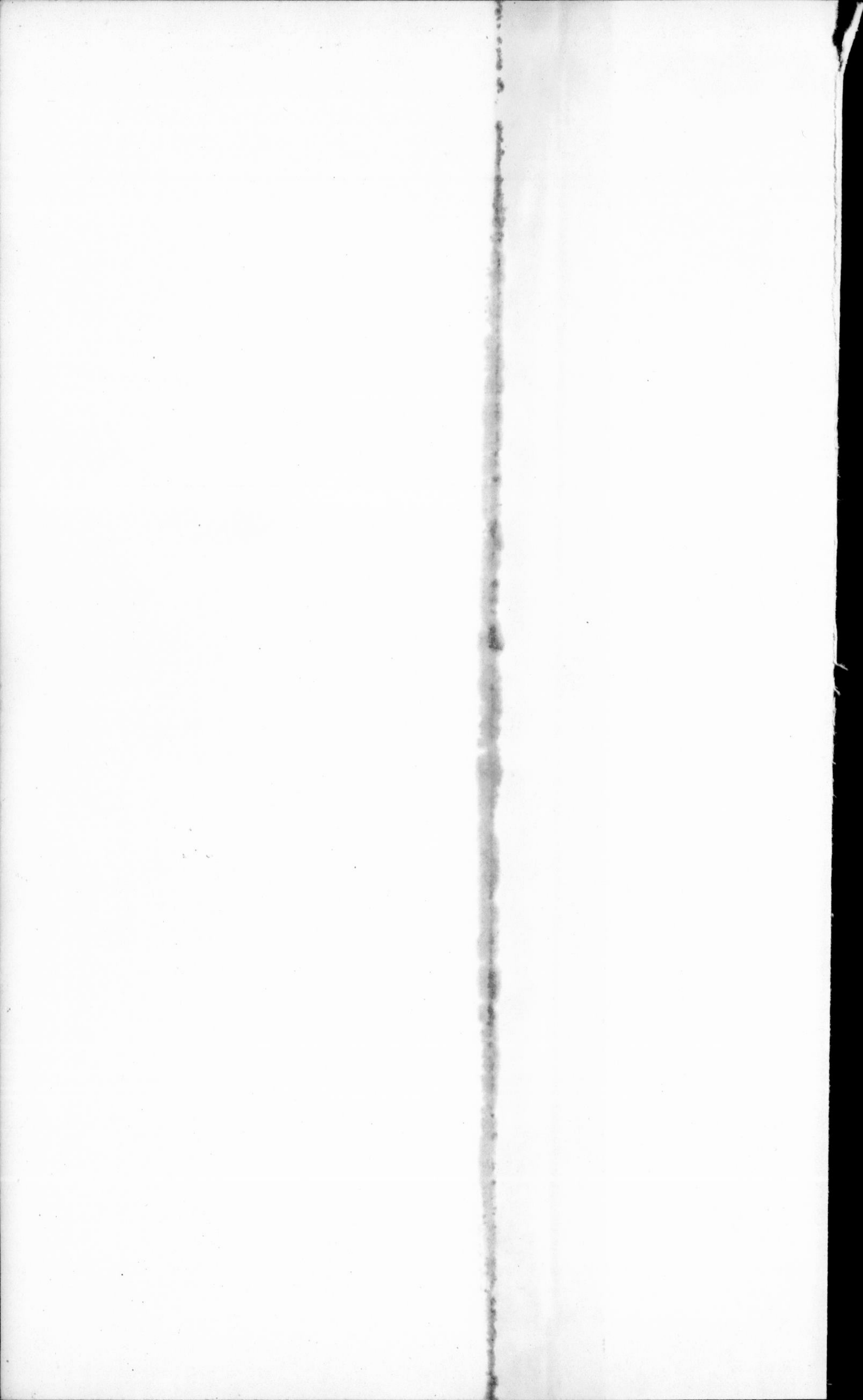